HISTORY, VIOLENCE, AND THE HYPERREAL

Purdue Studies in Romance Literatures

Editorial Board

Patricia Hart, Series Editor
Paul B. Dixon
Benjamin Lawton

Marcia Stephenson
Allen G. Wood

Howard Mancing, Consulting Editor
Floyd Merrell, Consulting Editor
Susan Y. Clawson, Production Editor

Associate Editors

French
Jeanette Beer
Paul Benhamou
Willard Bohn
Gerard J. Brault
Mary Ann Caws
Glyn P. Norton
Allan H. Pasco
Gerald Prince
Roseann Runte
Ursula Tidd

Italian
Fiora A. Bassanese
Peter Carravetta
Franco Masciandaro
Anthony Julian Tamburri

Luso-Brazilian
Fred M. Clark
Marta Peixoto
Ricardo da Silveira Lobo Sternberg

Spanish and Spanish American
Maryellen Bieder
Catherine Connor
Ivy A. Corfis
Frederick A. de Armas
Edward Friedman
Charles Ganelin
David T. Gies
Roberto González Echevarría
David K. Herzberger
Emily Hicks
Djelal Kadir
Amy Kaminsky
Lucille Kerr
Howard Mancing
Floyd Merrell
Alberto Moreiras
Randolph D. Pope
Francisco Ruiz Ramón
Elżbieta Skłodowska
Mario Valdés
Howard Young

 volume 49

HISTORY, VIOLENCE, AND THE HYPERREAL

Representing Culture

in the Contemporary

Spanish Novel

Kathryn Everly

Purdue University Press
West Lafayette, Indiana

Copyright ©2010 by Purdue University. All rights reserved.

∞ The paper used in this book meets the minimum requirements of American National Standard for Information Sciences—Permanence of Paper for Printed Library Materials, ANSI Z39.48-1992.

Printed in the United States of America
Design by Anita Noble

Library of Congress Cataloging-in-Publication Data

Everly, Kathryn, 1967–
 History, violence, and the hyperreal : representing culture in the contemporary Spanish novel / Kathryn Everly.
     p.   cm. — (Purdue studies in Romance literatures ; v. 49)
 Includes bibliographical references and index.
 ISBN 978-1-55753-558-0 (alk. paper)
 1. Spanish fiction—20th century—History and criticism. 2. Literature and history—Spain—History. 3. History in literature. 4. Spain—In literature. I. Title.
  PQ6144.E97 2010
  863'.64093552—dc22

                                                    2009053887

Contents

vii **Preface**
xiii **Acknowledgments**

1 Introduction

27 Part 1
History or Creating the Past

31 Chapter One
Rewriting the Past as Cultural Capital: Sacred Violence in Carme Riera's *Dins el darrer blau*

47 Chapter Two
Reader/Text Solidarity in Decoding the Past in Carme Riera's *La meitat de l'ànima*

63 Chapter Three
Women, Writing, and the Spanish Civil War in *La voz dormida* by Dulce Chacón

85 Chapter Four
The Impossible Invention of History and the Hero in Javier Cercas's *Soldados de Salamina* and *La velocidad de la luz*

111 Part 2
Hyperreality or Creating Culture

115 Chapter Five
Television, Simulacra, and Power in Three Works by Ray Loriga

133 Chapter Six
Textual Violence and the Hyperreal in *De todo lo visible y lo invisible* by Lucía Etxebarria

155 Chapter Seven
(Inter)Textuality in José Ángel Mañas's *Historias del Kronen* and *La pella*

183 Conclusion

Contents

189 **Notes**
199 **Works Cited**
211 **Index**

Preface

The presentation of Spanish social consciousness and national identity in novels of the past twenty years has been varied and at times even contradictory. Ranging from works rooted in the historical to works that defy and challenge traditional narrative and literary language, contemporary novel production in Spain is anything but one-dimensional. Many lively discussions with colleagues and nonacademics about contemporary Spanish literature inspired this study. The task of defining what kind of narrative is coming out of Spain is both frustrating and intriguing. What author or what work best represents twenty-first century Spanish literature? The purpose of this study is not to define and categorize contemporary Spanish novels but rather to further the conversation by pointing to similarities while embracing the apparent differences in style, structure, and language.

Culture is a huge, unwieldy term. Through the lens of various literary and social critics, as well as through the novels that capture contemporary customs, habits, and ideologies, culture takes shape as a concept that connects all social experiences and bridges seemingly disparate sectors of the population. I have chosen to work with culture because it is a living, breathing term that includes all forms of experience and has developed and changed over the years. For example, the creation of the concepts "high" and "low" culture attests to the inclusiveness of the idea that all experience contributes in some way to social consciousness. Culture is also a way to connect and focus the other large ideas in this study: history, violence, and "reality" or the hyperreal. Through a close reading of texts as cultural artifacts, these largely theoretical terms become part of a self-conscious literary production that is decidedly Spanish but defies categorization.

The cultural reproductions in the novels studied here pushed me toward a Structuralist theoretical model based on close textual readings. Nevertheless, the readings are anything but closed off from the notion of history and politics. The balancing act between textual reading and cultural relevance can be tricky; the texts, especially those from the Generation X, can be seen as dated and almost instantly outdated because their immediate cultural relevance makes them time and site specific. The text as

Preface

cultural artifact continues to intrigue me and is the concept that ties all of the various styles and themes together in this book. The idea of the novel as a cultural artifact and document of the times is, of course, nothing new, yet given the revived interest in the Spanish Civil War evident in recent best-selling novels and film, the two-fold nature of the cultural document presents a variety of challenges for the critic. Not only is the historical novel a fictional perspective on History, but also in the cases studied here, it lays bare the mechanisms of historical writing so that the text becomes a document about how history is related from a contemporary point of view. Thus the two-fold nature of the document re-creates an alternative history through fiction while at the same time it inserts a modern value judgment on the nature of historical writing.

The Gen X novels, on the other hand, transform the way in which we document contemporary experience. For the characters in the novels, "reality" is audiovisual, yet the authors reinvent ways to incorporate digital genres into the text. The innovations in language, style, structure, and format heighten the sense of urgency to incorporate the fast-paced technological culture that surrounds us. The notion of hybridity runs through these novels as they draw on various forms of cultural expression to arrive at a narrative that is polyvocal and structurally complex.

The first chapter of this study begins the exploration of how the retelling of history through literature transforms the drive for veracity into an artistic expression of cultural importance. History thus becomes a form of cultural capital in literature and its worth lies in the myriad of narrative possibilities. Carme Riera uncovers multiple discursive possibilities through her narration of the plight of *criptojudíos* on Mallorca during the seventeenth century in *Dins el darrer blau* [*In the Last Blue*] (1994). Her novel is based on documents she examined in Mallorca that describe the events of a particular *auto de fe* that took place in 1691. Through an analysis of the treatment of state-sanctioned and personal violence in the novel, I propose that the text challenges institutional authority, namely, the Catholic Church and the family, but also questions notions of a dominant history and reveals the importance of subaltern groups' histories. The ritualistic nature of the violence portrayed in the novel permits the acts to become part of the cultural legacy and to be tolerated by sanctioned institutions. Through the lens of and feminist critique of René Girard's focus on violence and sacrifice as ritual, I analyze the implications of Riera's historical rereading. Therefore, the novel works to vindicate the victims of the Spanish Inquisition by narrating a version of their side of the story, but perhaps more importantly it shows that the webs of violence used to oppress Jews and women are still in place in contemporary society.

The second chapter examines another work by Riera that exposes the more personal side of rewriting history. In *La meitat de l'ànima* [*The Soul's Other Half*], the search for her mother's true past leads the protagonist on a wild chase that results in a textual play between writer and reader. The role of the reader, as outlined by Umberto Eco, becomes the most important element in the construction of the narrative, and the presence of the reader in the text gives new meaning to textual self-reflexivity.

The third chapter looks again at historical writing and women in Dulce Chacón's *La voz dormida* (2002). Chacón's text follows that of Riera in its aim to tell a side of history that has been forgotten or silenced. The combination of various types of documentation in Chacón's novel, ranging from letters, to official government documents, to oral testimony, creates a multivoiced text that instead of providing a more cohesive picture of certain events of the Spanish Civil War only proves that the perspectives are innumerable. The text challenges traditional norms of historical writing and provides a female perspective on surviving Franco's jails, hiding out in the mountains, and passing covert information for the Republic. However, while Chacón's text does present a feminist perspective of female solidarity, it also blurs the boundaries between "real" documentation leftover from the war and fiction, thus raising a more philosophical question about the nature of history and "truth."

Chapter four shows that Javier Cercas also moves within this same discourse in his 2001 novel *Soldados de Salamina* and in *La velocidad de la luz* from 2005. Cercas takes one step further and presents a version of himself as the narrator/protagonist of the story. The mixing of implied author and narrator leads to a more formal inquiry into the mechanics of the novel. Nevertheless, Cercas uses this narrative trick to propose novelistic

Preface

innovations similar to those of Chacón and Riera. The struggle of the writer/protagonist to write an intriguing version of events surrounding the failed execution of Rafael Sánchez Mazas during the final days of the Spanish Civil War presents a creative tension between fact and fiction. While some critics have read this novel as a sentimental recapitulation of the point of view of the *vencidos*, I propose that the novel's structure demands multiple readings of the text as well as a re-evaluation of the craft of writing and the responsibilities inherent in storytelling. The five historical novels in the first part of this study rely on the double meaning of language that all three authors connect to multiple meanings of history. Also, these three authors embrace the creativity and imagination of Nietzschean historical writing.

The fifth chapter moves from historical fiction to novels rooted in the popular Generation X literary movement. It is interesting to note that a dominant trait of the Gen X movement is detachment, and at times reaching complete evasion, of historical themes. The Civil War is rarely mentioned in Gen X novels, and the transition to democracy is labeled a failed hippie movement. But many of the themes dealing with cultural representations of "truth" and the "real" dominate the novels of the Gen X movement.

Ray Loriga makes the transition from novel to film seem like a logical and natural way to incorporate doubts about language into narrative technique. Loriga's novel *Caídos del cielo* (1995) and the subsequent film version, directed by Loriga, *La pistola de mi hermano* (1997), position the narrative subject within a postmodern framework that jumps between the visual and the verbal with ease. The analysis, in this case, moves fluidly between the novel and the film. Loriga achieves a kind of hyper-reality as defined by Baudrillard in that the novel takes on manipulative narrative techniques employed by television to create an illusory "reality," while the film manipulates image in a way that harkens to a written narrative. The choppy writing of the narrative creates flashes of images, while the film avoids exactly this kind of editing. The film's language does not imitate but rather complements the novel and creates another version of the story, not merely a cinematic interpretation of the novel. Loriga incorporates this vision of crossing genre boundaries and the creation of a virtual reality in his novel *El hombre que inventó*

Manhattan, which posits New York City as an imaginary place dreamed up in the minds of individuals.

Lucía Etxebarria plays with genre and tone in the novels discussed in the sixth chapter. *De todo lo visible y lo invisible* (2001) is a complex text that serves as a playground for author, implied author, and narrator. The use of footnotes throughout the text to reiterate narrative tone or give translations of Basque phrases presents a novelistic space that vacillates between the narrative reality and Etxebarria's reality. Through this implementation of "real" world facts about people and places in a fictional space, the author creates a hyperreal text: a text that contains all of its own referents and is a self-sufficient entity constantly referring to the constructedness of its own identity. Once again the novel as a genre is placed under the microscope, and, in a sense, deconstructed, laying bare the mechanics of authorship. While Cercas shows us the writer's struggle with truth and fiction in narrative, Etxebarria embraces this duality of the text and exploits it in order to be present in her own work yet acknowledge the distance that the book ultimately acquires once it is published and distributed.

In the final chapter, José Ángel Mañas is seen to use structure and style to convey similar themes of intertextuality. The ubiquitous references to North American and British pop culture in *Historias del Kronen* create a form of intertext that goes beyond the incorporation of allusions to known works. Carlos, the protagonist of the novel, imitates fiction in the form of film, books, and lyrics. His "reality" is nothing more than an interpretation of a larger imaginary. The hyperreality in Carlos's case leads to ambivalence and apathy toward any kind of moral consciousness. However, I argue that the epilogue to *Kronen,* which functions in opposition to the main text, opens up the space for judgment of Carlos's actions and primarily of his dependence on fiction for identity. The implicit warning woven throughout the text of *Kronen* points to the ease with which hyperreality can be misinterpreted. The cultural discourse at the center of the novel may seem to point toward saturation of sensationalism resulting in the spiritual numbness of Spanish youth, but through a closer reading of Carlos's relationship with the media and then Roberto's observations in the epilogue, Mañas's novel reveals that the power of commercial language, both visual and verbal, can oftentimes be greater than the consumer. In *La pella*, Mañas shows a shift from the moral apathy of *Kronen* in that class differences come to the forefront in regulating identity. Family and civic responsibility overshadow the hedonistic attitudes of urban youth. As a literary counterpart to *Kronen*, *La pella* incorporates much of the same language and literary style as its predecessor while proposing an alternative outcome to the illegal and dangerous drug dealings. Yet the international markers and consumerist society still dominate the lifestyles of the characters and also dictate certain norms of behavior.

Acknowledgments

I am sincerely grateful to my colleagues in the Department of Languages, Literatures, and Linguistics at Syracuse University and especially those in the Spanish program, who have been flexible and always supportive of my work and family life. I want to thank Gail Bulman, Myrna García Calderón, Alicia Ríos, and Lara Walker for reading sections of this manuscript and giving me their wonderfully constructive feedback. Thanks to Germán Carillo, Jessica Folkart, Mark del Mastro, Catherine Ross, and Sandra Schuum, who are always willing to listen and share ideas on research, coursework, and career. I would like to thank the efficient and excellent staff of Bird Library at Syracuse University for help with locating and retrieving materials. The College of Arts and Sciences and Syracuse University granted me a leave in which I was able to complete a large portion of this book and for which I am truly grateful. I sincerely appreciate the ongoing support for this project shown by Dean George Langford and Associate Dean Gerald Greenberg of the College of Arts and Sciences. A special thanks to the Chairs of my department, Jaklin Kornfilt and more recently Gerlinde Sanford, who have provided funding for conferences and other professional development and have been very supportive in so many ways.

I would also like to thank the people at Purdue University Press and Purdue Studies in Romance Literatures, especially Susan Clawson and Patricia Hart. I am truly grateful for their guidance and thoughtful suggestions. I remain impressed by the great care and respect they showed to me and my work.

None of this would be possible without the constant, unfailing love and support of my husband, Christopher Gascón. The time and energy he puts in to being a scholar, parent, and husband is inspiring. I owe him everything. To Nico and Lucas, who make everyday a delightful adventure, and to my loving parents and extended family, who have influenced me in ways perhaps they will never know, thank you.

And finally I would like to thank the editors of the following publications for their generous permission to reprint earlier versions of the research that appears in this book. Sections of chapters 1, 3, 5 and 6 appeared as the following articles:

Acknowledgments

"Sacred Violence as Social Criticism in Carme Riera's *En el último azul*," *Hispanic Journal* 27.1 (Spring 2006): 91–103. © 2006 *Hispanic Journal*.

"Women, War, and Words in *La voz dormida* by Dulce Chacón," from *Women in the Spanish Novel Today: Essays on the Reflection of Self in the Works of Three Generations,* © 2009 edited by Kyra A. Kietrys and Montserrat Linares, reprinted by permission of McFarland & Company, Inc., Box 611, Jefferson, NC 28640, <http://www.mcfarlandpub.com>, 92–110.

"Textual Violence and the Hyperreal in *De todo lo visible y lo invisible* by Lucía Etxebarria," *Letras Hispanas: Revista de Literatura y Cultura* 4.1 (Spring 2007): 51–61.

"Television and the Power of Image in *Caídos del cielo* and *La pistola de mi hermano* by Ray Loriga," *Generation X Rocks,* ed. Christine Henseler and Randolph Pope. Special Issue of *Hispanic Issues*, Vanderbilt UP, 2007, 170–83.

"Beauty and Death as Simulacra in Ray Loriga's *Caídos del cielo* and *El hombre que inventó Manhattan*," *Novels of the Contemporary Extreme*, ed. Alain-Phillippe Durand and Naomi Mandel (New York: Continuum, 2006), 143–52. Reprinted by kind permission of Continuum International Publishing Group.

Introduction

> The history of the idea of culture is a record of our meanings and our definitions, but these, in turn are only to be understood within the context of our actions.
>
> Raymond Williams
> *Culture and Society*

> Simulation is no longer that of a territory, a referential being or a substance. It is the generation by models of a real without origin or reality: a hyperreal.
>
> Jean Baudrillard
> *Simulacra and Simulations*

The novels produced in Spain in the last twenty years have confounded attempts by critics who sought to neatly categorize them. A noticeable trend in Spanish literary criticism seeks to reconcile the disparate styles, themes, and epistemological approaches found in these novels. Robert Spires points out that this may be symptomatic of the turn of the millennium, which inspired a need to "assign a rubric to the new Spanish fiction" ("Depolarization" 487). Elsewhere he comments on the thematic and stylistic differences between popular, trendy writers of the Generation X group and more historically grounded authors such as Javier Marías and Javier Cercas. Although the writers in these two groups fall into the same generation by age, Spires defines them as "radicalmente distintos" ("Historia" 86). While the Gen X writers focus on the hedonistic lifestyle of urban youth, the other writers he refers to—such as Marías, Cercas, Almudena Grandes, Ignacio Martínez de Pisón, Belén Gopegui, and Juan Manuel de Prada—offer tales of moral responsibility

Introduction

and struggle, a concept apparently lacking in the Gen X novel (87). Spires writes insightfully about the myriad of themes found in contemporary literature and the frustration of critics so accustomed to the neat categorization of writers into generations, such as the Generation of 1898, the Generation or Grupo of 1927, and the Mid-Century Generation. Spires observes: "[g]enerational schemes for classifying literary movements inevitably polarize" ("Depolarization" 507), and this tendency toward strict chronological categorization of texts problematizes the possibility of approaching texts from thematic or stylistic angles.

In the spirit of these observations, this study looks at selected works spanning the years 1994 to 2008 by six writers: Carme Riera, Dulce Chacón, Javier Cercas, Lucía Etxebarria, Ray Loriga, and José Ángel Mañas. While the differences between these authors may seem obvious, there are also significant similarities. These similarities are rooted in the idea of how history is transformed through storytelling into an unstable reality. At the same time, the fascination with what is "real" or authentic redefines textual notions of everyday existence and interpersonal relationships. The historical and the hyperreal depend for meaning on the unstable, shifting base of language.[1] This study explores the similarities between two seemingly disparate forms of the contemporary novel: the historical novel and the Generation X novel. It will analyze how these novels, both structurally and thematically, manipulate history, violence, and hyperreality into different aspects of culture that lead to a distinctly Spanish identity.

Even though the Gen X novels may be considered the more experimental format, the historical novels in this study are anything but traditional forms of narrative. Innovation in narrative style and the restructuring of the novel as a genre are the common links between these two groups of writers. In each work studied here, the author looks to redefine the form and function of the novel, yet this is not to say that these novels are unique in Spanish literary history. The rigorous reworking of novelistic form seen in the Latin American Boom novels, such as Julio Cortázar's *Rayuela*, incorporates similar elements: historical and present-day confusion, multiple narrators, and playfulness with concepts of narrative time and space. In Spain the works of Cervantes, Unamuno, Juan and Luis Goytisolo, among others, set the stage early on for what has been deemed the self-reflexivity of the contemporary novel (Amago 22–25). These Spanish writers sought to bring a philosophy of literature to the page by questioning the value of language and genre. Parallels with these past writers can be drawn to the six authors in this study, but the difference is that these contemporary authors are writing about Spain (not the Latin America of the Boom), as well as employing concepts of culture born of postmodernism and leading to diversity through globalization.[2] The cultural representations may vary but the end result is a re-evaluation of the writer's relationship to the text and to his or her reader. Culture as presented in the novels embraces all aspects of national and regional tradition but also encompasses huge amounts of information instantly accessible via the Internet. With this ease of accessibility, culture as represented in literature, film, television, sporting events, food, and music is offered on a global stage for immediate consumption. The texts produced in this kind of environment challenge the very notion of text. The novels analyzed in this study question the validity and the veracity of the written word. How is narrative style transformed in today's world of instant information and mass communication? These authors employ various narrative techniques that challenge traditional ideas of the novel, of writing, and of storytelling in general.

The novels in this study incorporate representations of culture that challenge the readers' conceptions of "truth" and its relationship to "reality." The first group of novels deals with the effects of history on present-day Spanish identity, and the novel format is used as an experimental stage to question the "truth" of history and to highlight the narrative quality of historical writing. Traditional narrative modes of accuracy and clarity that aim for a concise rendition of events give way to a more open discourse. As David K. Herzberger points out in *Narrating the Past*, "writers of fictions are able to controvert these strategies and assert dissonance through a normative set of principles of their own" (2). The narrative quality of the historical retelling challenges the reader to question concepts of "truth."

Generation X writers use the novel and narrative devices to question the "truth" about reality. Representations of history as fiction and of reality as fiction locate these works in a moment

Introduction

of Spanish narrative production that questions the novel as a genre as well as the verisimilitude of language and writing.

Generation X in Spain

The Spanish literary tide seemed to turn with the onset of the Gen X popularity in the 1990s. The term comes from Douglas Coupland's 1991 novel *Generation X: Tales for an Accelerated Culture,* which suggests a political and moral apathy in North American youth. Gen X in Spain came to mean something very different, as several critics have pointed out. Santiago Fouz-Hernández, Carmen de Urioste, and Toni Dorca all published important articles on the very particular Spanish brand of Gen X literature that takes apathy and transforms it into violence. Urioste defines Spanish Gen X novels as fragmented, first-person narrations that trace urban youth violence to a historical, political, and moral "desencanto" ("Narrativa española" 466). The publication of Ray Loriga's *Lo peor de todo* in 1992 and José Ángel Mañas's *Historias del Kronen* in 1994 shocked the literary world with graphic descriptions of violence and drug use that changed how Spaniards read novels and, perhaps more importantly, how the global market thought about Spanish literature. This rupture from Spanish literary and historical tradition quickly came to define Spanish Gen X literature. It wasn't entirely new; beginning in the 1980s writers such as Rosa Montero, Antonio Muñoz Molina, and Juan José Millás had portrayed Spanish society in a neo-realistic way that gently probes underlying problems of sexism, political corruption, and troubled psychology. These writers move easily between fiction and journalism in their observations of a new democratic Spain trying to shake off the recent past and move forward as a more European nation.[3] The difference was the shocking violence, disregard for Spain's past and present, detailed descriptions of drug use and sex, and alienation from social institutions found in most Gen X novels that presented a new kind of literary voice. Ignacio Echevarría brushed off the young writers as immature and purely market driven in his article "Oiga Usted, joven" from 1999. However, Cristina Moreiras in *Cultura herida* defends the young writers, giving them much more credit than did their initial detractors. She states that the lack of a political agenda or social consciousness presented in the novels in fact creates a space for commentary on political and social issues (191). As Ana María Amar Sánchez notes, "la reorganización o cita de elementos es de por sí una evaluación de ellos" (26); therefore, the reorganization of priorities and the implicit irony of political apathy presented in Gen X novels can be considered critical of mainstream Spanish cultural politics.

The commercial success of the Gen X novels and the promotion of the authors as young, anti-establishment renegades opened the door for comparison between similar trends in the United States and in England, thus catapulting these young artists onto an international stage. The Spanish brand of Gen X literature was quickly disassociated from Coupland's novel (Fouz-Hernández), which left the authors to "define" themselves and their movement. The blatant self-promotion of Lucía Etxebarria in the mass media, for example, especially after her novel *Beatriz y los cuerpos celestes* won the Nadal prize in 1998, completely renegotiated the author's relationship with her public. Etxebarria's use and manipulation of the press, of the Internet, and of her own fame has been the topic of several scholarly articles.[4] Recent accusations of plagiarism serve as a platform for Etxebarria to once again defend herself from what she considers systematic attacks on her writing.[5] She brushed off the charge, pointing out that she was surprised that a newspaper found out about the "offense" before she did (Collera n.pag.). Furthermore several North American critics have defended Etxebarria, declaring that the echoes of poet Antonio Colinas in Etxebarria's poetry collection *Estación de infierno* are "un claro homenaje al autor" ("Tres expertos" n. pag.) and in no way plagiarism. This is an example of how the young authors of the Gen X movement utilize mass media to garner fan support and create a virtual relationship with their readers.

The popularity of Gen X authors and their success with critics in the United States and England may have given the impression that Gen X was the only literary movement happening in Spain at the time. The quick turnaround of several of the novels into successful films added to the movement's visibility. It seems an anachronism to remember that Carme Riera won the National Literary Prize in 1995 for her extensively researched

Introduction

historical novel on a group of condemned Mallorcan *conversos* in *Dins el darrer blau* [*En el ultimo azul* (*In the Final Blue*)].

Riera's novel was the first novel written originally in Catalan to receive the Spanish national prize. These two women, Etxebarria and Riera, writing in Spain at the same time about completely different topics, with distinct styles and literary voices, led me to think about the complexity and richness of contemporary Spanish literary production. The novelistic production that runs the gamut in Spain seems to represent a growing cultural diversity. My aim is not to study the demographics of who reads what and why, but rather to find the connections between the Gen X writers and the more historically oriented writers all producing top-selling books between 1994 and 2008. The differences are apparent but through close readings and textual analyses of the works at hand, several commonalities surface that connect the present literary production in a subtle way while celebrating the great diversity.

What Is Culture?

It becomes somewhat tricky to analyze representations of culture when the term itself is molded and shaped by those who use it. Culture is art; it is popular forms of mass media and entertainment; it is food, clothing, fashion, sports, and music. Culture is also how we use public space: the stadium, the shopping mall, and the apartment complex, to name only a few. The challenge with culture is that it defines the moment in which we live and negotiate our identity with our surroundings and with other individuals, yet at the same time public opinion drives popular culture and is constantly reformulating the construction of cultural identity. In the Spanish novels analyzed in this study, culture is used as an identity marker and as a way to define contemporary Spanish literature in relation to a larger body of literary history. The texts in this study reconsider culture and its function in the Spanish novel through critical representations of history, war, artistic production, television, and institutions such as the Church, family, and media. The turn of the millennium provided writers and critics alike the opportunity to re-evaluate literary production while looking back on Spanish twentieth-century history in an attempt to understand the drastic changes in government, social roles, and national identity that were taking place. Nevertheless, writers look forward to a new age of globalization and instant communication where the local, regional, and national have become expanded and exposed on a world stage. The combination of cultural history and present-day interpretations of reality fuse the writers' contemporary ideologies of the novel and guide the theoretical orientation of the textual analyses.

This study will focus on the construction of cultural identity in Spain and specifically on how contemporary novelists approach ideas of culture through fiction. The chosen authors figure in this study because they all have a profound interest in the question of culture and how it relates to history, memory, and contemporary experience. Another link between all the authors is their trust in literature to in some way represent, interpret, and challenge the readers' notions of culture and experience. Representations of culture that imply a questioning of form and of the very act of writing itself break down the traditional narrative structure of the novel. The authors seem intent on rewriting the novelistic form not only through a postmodern combination of genres and texts but also through an intense deconstruction of historical, political, and artistic traditions. Even though these authors include in their works other forms of cultural production such as letters, official documentation, allusions to film and music, the result is often a critical response to the form of the novel, to the cultural artifact we readers hold in our hands.

The authors in this study explore the phenomenon of the globalization of culture, yet in all of the works Spain remains a central focal point for the narrative voice. Even in Ray Loriga's *El hombre que inventó Manhattan*, where the narrative action takes place in New York City, the reference point and perspective remains with a Spaniard living in the city observing the experience of other immigrants. The literary discourse revolves around contemporary Spanish experience and, therefore, draws on the past and on the specific history that influences the present generation's relationship to national identity. In the historical novels of Carme Riera, Dulce Chacón, and Javier Cercas the past defines the present and perhaps more importantly presents a challenge for the future. The novels in the first section—*Dins el darrer blau* and *La meitat de l'ànima [La mitad del alma (The Soul's Other Half)]* by Riera, *La voz dormida* by Chacón, and *Soldados de Salamina* and *La velocidad de la luz* by Cercas—

Introduction

can be considered apologies for the overlooked and disenfranchised sectors of society that History with a capital H, to use Geraldine Cleary Nichols's term, has forgotten. Nevertheless, the history of Spain with its subaltern voices plays a key role in formulating current notions of Spanish identity, and the novels at hand portray a society finally able to express disquieting "facts" and ghosts of the past. The texts that awaken sleeping voices of Spain's past and present provide a conscientious narrative that takes into account the experience of all citizens, just as the authors display a critical stance toward historical writing in general. This step beyond the specific circumstances in Spain and onto a larger stage of epistemological criticism brings together local concerns about the past and the global discourse on the nature of historical writing.

In the works set in contemporary Spain by Etxebarria, Loriga, and Mañas, the same ideology marks the narrative. *De todo lo visible y lo invisible* by Etxebarria, *Caídos del cielo* and *El hombre que inventó Manhattan* by Loriga, and *Historias del Kronen* and *La pella* by Mañas focus on the experience and struggle of Spanish youth to establish some kind of identity marker for themselves that differentiates them from the past. References to North American and British film, music, and cultural production attest to the international influence on Spanish culture. However, the authors use these allusions to incorporate the globalization of commercial cultural production into the literary works and point a critical finger at the politics of consumerism as an identifying mark for youth worldwide. The global market, represented in the works by television, video, film, music, and internationally known products, remains only a point of departure for the development of the narrative. The authors all find in the narrative form stylistic ways of disrupting the overriding influence of the global market metaphors and turn a critical eye to the novel itself as a form of international cultural representation. Before entering into the analyses of the novels, it is useful to take a look at some key concepts of culture and explore how these ideas connect the literary works under discussion.

The Development of the Idea of Culture

Critics and theorists have grappled with the ideology of culture from a variety of angles and disciplines: the rupture yet

Introduction

interdependence between high and low cultures, the economic implications of class on cultural production and consumption, and the unique social values attributed to artists and writers. The many modifiers we use to talk about culture signal the differing expectations of, for example, pop culture, counter-culture, low culture, and sub-culture. On the other hand, a person who is "cultured" suggests that he or she has enjoyed a privileged exposure to the arts. Of course, no one can escape the defining influence of culture, so in this sense we are all "cultured" beings. Amar Sánchez, in her book *Juegos de seducción y traición,* points to the struggle inherent in the polarization of low and high cultures. Her focus is on Latin American novels, but we see in the Spanish novels as well the struggle between constructed discourses of mass culture, historical truth, and virtual or video culture. These contradictory discourses are fighting to establish themselves as privileged forms of representation (20). Following the leads of Néstor García Canclini and J. Martín-Barbero, Amar situates the political nature of culture in class associations of "low" and "high" or "bad" and "good" taste. Nevertheless, these divisions are illusory and contradictory because cultural discourse constantly fluctuates between mass and elite spheres. "High" culture and mass culture cannot be seen as opposite poles; as Canclini points out, they are constantly changing definitions of discourse that play out on a stage, crossing into hybrids of fluidity that complicate meaning and categorization (Amar 17). From the onset of modernity in Spain to modern day virtual realities on the Internet, cultural discourse has always been a site of tension, struggle, and invention. This study seeks to address how these theories of culture unfold in a contemporary Spanish context; however, the theoretical conceptualization of high and low cultures that reflects a certain ontological and economic perspective sets the stage for more contemporary debates.

Stephanie Sieburth, in her study on Spanish modernity, traces the development of the idea of culture back to pre–Industrial Revolution Europe. In an agrarian sense, the term means to grow and develop, thus implying a process instead of a position within social structure (3). She points to the proliferation of the industrial working class as an important factor in changing the concept of culture from a process (cultivation) to an idea or intellectual status. This tension between the need to spread and

9

yet maintain cultural production began to stratify the newly distinguished economic classes. Citing Samuel Taylor Coleridge, Sieburth describes this development of the idea of culture as a "kind of intellectual perfection, an ultimate standard for valuation" (3). Therefore, culture begins to take on an abstract value that distinguishes groups and individuals. The possession of a knowledge of culture and cultural information becomes tantamount to membership in the upper classes in order to separate their experience from that of the worker. This "cultural capital" relies on an economy of the consumer who will seek out new and exciting forms of cultural production, perhaps originating from a less privileged class but worthy in artistic sensibility.[6]

Sieburth's study revolves around the separation of low and high cultures and how these two spheres dialogue with each other. What she calls "uneven modernity" in Spain can also be read as the beginnings of a specifically Spanish identity that embraces all culture and eradicates the economically imposed distinctions. Sieburth reveals the difficulty in pinpointing the emergence of low or mass culture, since culture originally served to distinguish the upper classes from the lower. But the artistic production, traditions, work habits, entertainment, and living norms of the lower class have always existed and helped to define both "low" and "high" cultural identities. Mass culture does differ from certain forms of upper class artistic performance in that mass culture has a much less restrictive economic accessibility and perhaps a more spontaneous nature. The difference, for example, between going to the opera and attending a typical flamenco *jaleo* resides in the levels of preparation and the premeditated aspect of "high" culture. The opera demands the purchase of tickets, a certain kind of clothing, the anticipation of an event, and the following of a set of social rules, while the spontaneity of a flamenco dance, or any kind of singing and dancing in a bar after a day of work, comes from a sense of unity among the participants and a desire to escape social procedures. The connection between these types of high and low cultural events is their performative nature and the presence of an audience that ensures the realization of the "event" that in turn becomes a form of metaphysical cultural capital. The experience of culture becomes an informed ritual separate from but not entirely independent of a physical thing or space. In this sense the value of cultural experience becomes more important than any physical manifestation of culture. The distinction between low and high culture becomes obsolete when it is the experience that is valued. The participation in this type of ritual places an individual within a certain group that appreciates and values a common artistic expression.

As mentioned earlier, the young novelists of the Gen X movement were initially discarded as untalented pop writers caught up in the marketing and selling of their works. The young aesthetic was considered a form of low culture appealing only to the masses. Critics called their work fleeting, lacking in "arte y de sustancia" (Sanz Villanueva 4), and not well written but extremely marketable (Fortes 27). Nevertheless, this initial harsh dismissal of the Gen X works has given way to a better understanding of their particular artistic approach to language and the novel. The popular culture that the novels represent has become more commonplace in intellectual discourse, and therefore the fusion of the popular and the literary becomes evident. In this way the Gen X movement has surely survived some initial bruising by Spanish academics and critics and does bring together certain notions of high and low culture. The street language, drug-induced monologues, and video culture lend themselves to the creation of a new literary language that represents a different attitude toward the relationship between the individual and society.

Raymond Williams comments at length in *Culture and Society* on the problematic nature of mass culture or what he terms *popular culture*. His observations on the distinctions between "good" and "bad" art may sound outdated to twenty-first century ears, yet his careful scrutiny of the politics of class and cultural production warrant our attention. Williams links the development of the term *culture* not just to industry but also directly to notions of democracy, class, and art that are interconnected and intertwined (xvii). However, beyond the political and economic factors that guide our notions of culture, Williams points to diversity as one of the main components in understanding culture: "The idea of culture describes our common inquiry, but our conclusions are diverse, as our starting points were diverse" (295). The diversity of experience and social positioning can only enhance and nuance ideas of culture

Introduction

and, more specifically, artistic production. While Williams links culture to a social grid of institutions and economic systems, I propose to look at culture in a less stratified and more global sense. The diversity of approaches to culture has multiplied since Williams's study; television studies have elevated a once "low" form of culture to a rigorous academic field, and current cultural studies embrace readings of all kinds of texts, from sporting events to billboards.[7] It seems that Williams did hit the mark with his observation that culture can be seen anthropologically as "a whole way of life" (xvi). The need to incorporate influences outside of the written or visual text, or to consider manifestations as texts themselves, demands reconsideration of the relationship between the producers of culture and the system in which they operate.

The Field of Cultural Production

Pierre Bourdieu, in *The Field of Cultural Production*, comes to insightful and extremely helpful conclusions in his efforts to reconcile the tensions between the subjective and objective theories of artistic production. Bourdieu challenges the notion held during the Romantic Period of the inspired individual writing or painting as a representative of his turbulent times. He also criticizes the Structuralists' theory of the absence of the author in an artistic text. He considers these two extremes inadequate tools for understanding cultural production because they overlook the relationship between the artist and the artistic product (34). Bourdieu's concept of a field of cultural production proves to be especially useful in this study because it allows for various positions of artistic expression within one determined social system. The forces that control artistic production are internal as well as external, according to Bourdieu, and therefore as critics we must take into account the specific position within the system that the artist occupies as well as external factors such as the economy, politics, and history that influence the creation of the text.

For Bourdieu the tension between the various cultural forces that produce art is fundamental to understanding the final product. He explains that first and foremost art is a belief; in other words, art has to be believed to be art. The field or system of cultural production acts in an inverse way to economic production in that the value of the artifact lies not in its usefulness or applicable practicality but rather in the idea of its worth. "There is a specific economy of the literary and artistic field, based on a particular form of belief" (35) and propagated by educational institutions such as universities, museums, and publishing houses. One of the main points of Bourdieu's theory is that the hierarchization of the cultural field acts differently from other fields operating in the social system. The different sectors of society that consume art create levels of artistic acceptability. There are artists who produce mainly for other artists, such as "art for art's sake," and there is a level of artistic consumption that retains a bourgeois attitude of superiority and subsists on rejecting "lower" forms of art. Lastly there exists the mass, or as Sieburth and Williams have described it, the "low" cultural production that is the most market driven and therefore most lucrative form of artistic production. This is not to suggest that mass artistic production is necessarily of lower quality. Shakespeare, Lope de Vega, and Cervantes were considered very popular in their day but have come to represent nowadays a more sophisticated literary taste. These strata of cultural production do not exist independent from each other but create a complex system of cultural understanding in which class and economic standing influence the dissemination of a piece of work.

Despite the appearance of a hierarchy of cultural production, Bourdieu sees the field as in constant fluctuation (similar to Canclini's "hybrids of fluidity"). "High" art such as the often-elusive Vanguard intellectualism of Dalí rapidly becomes mass produced on coffee mugs and calendars. Graffiti painting on the subway walls in Manhattan moves to exclusive galleries in Soho. Marcel Duchamp creates a timeless piece of art simply by placing a urinal in a gallery. The constant ebb and flow of concepts of art and culture depend on the changing positions within the system of individuals. While his theory is akin to that of New Historicism posited by Stephen Greenblatt (Bourdieu, *Field* 19), Bourdieu allows ample space for individual influence in artistic production. His idea of the habitus neatly deals with the problematic individuality of the artist. The habitus is what Randal Johnson calls "a feel for the game" or a "practical sense" (Bourdieu, *Field* 5). It is the combination of

Introduction

experience, upbringing, socialization, language, and nature that places a person within a certain system. The habitus is not considered a personal history but rather the external factors that both consciously and unconsciously shape the intelligence and ultimately the expression of the individual. Combined with several other factors that influence cultural production, the habitus allows the mark of the artist to remain in the literary text or cultural artifact.

Other influences that shape and mold our conceptualization of culture and art are the economics of the time, the supply and demand of the artistic commodity, and the promotion of art and culture as necessary parts of a functioning society. The factor of greatest interest to the present study is that of history. Bourdieu suggests that political, social, and economic history influence both the individual's position within the cultural field and also the circulation of the cultural product. Writers and artists are the result of the meeting of two histories: "the history of the position they occupy and the history of their dispositions" (61). The position and disposition within the field of cultural production come together in a way that allows the artistic product to ultimately express all of the tensions and ambiguities between the system and the individual operating within it. The disposition can be understood as the artist's habitus combined with the actual historical moment in which he or she creates. The position refers to the social elements that influence either directly or indirectly the artistic product such as the political and economic climate as well as the conditions of circulation, publication, and exhibition that promote the art product as such. The importance of applying the idea of position and disposition to the analysis of literary texts is that this strategy allows for a variety of approaches when reading and interpreting cultural texts. This idea dispels the need to categorize cultural production according to one particular time, place, or nationality, for cultural production is seen as the culmination of many factors and influences. Contemporary cultural production in Spain can be considered to be varied and in multiple forms representing multiple positionings within a specific culture. As Bourdieu explains: "writers and artists endowed with different, even opposing dispositions can coexist, for a time at least, in the same positions" (66). The decade that straddles the millennium produced a number of works concerned with the retelling of history and the reconciliation with an often-troubled national history. In the same decade, however, a trend to modernize Spanish literature and move beyond historical specificity allows for another kind of cultural questioning. While one is a questioning of history, the other questions the complicated notions of expectations of the future.

The novels chosen for this study display a concern for the problematic representation of reality. In the first section of this study, the revelatory implications of unearthing forgotten history present an alternate reality in the present that challenges the very concept of history and knowing about the past. In the second section, the novels reveal the problematic relationship between the individual and his or her surroundings in the present and propose a "hyperreality"[8] that is detached from materiality and operates on a virtual plane. The critical re-evaluation of the present relationship between the individual and his or her surroundings links these two literary approaches. In both cases the texts problematize notions of "truth" and "reality" as absolutes, and in both cases the form of the novel becomes an experimental space that is manipulated, molded, and reformed to support in a technical way the philosophical content. The novels are not "experimental" in the sense that they break entirely with traditional narrative modes, but the incorporation of extratextual information and the presence of the implied author play with the reader's expectations and demand a certain kind of attention from the reader that aids in fleshing out the narrative.

Culture and History

Jo Labanyi, in *Constructing Identity in Contemporary Spain,* locates Spanish cultural production in Bourdieu's framework of "taste" that dictates the distinction between "high" and "low" culture. She points out that in Spain certain areas of popular culture such as the romance ballad and flamenco "have been included in the canon because they have been taken up by intellectuals who have consumed them in a non-popular manner" (3). The way a text is read contributes to its legitimacy as a cultural product, yet she goes on to explain that "popular and mass culture by definition cannot be studied as individual texts" (11) because

Introduction

their production and consumption are influenced by habits and modes of the industry. In the Gen X novels the fusion of popular or mass culture, narrative language, and novelistic structure brings together disparate elements of cultural production. The colloquial language, neologisms, and dialogue in Mañas's and Loriga's works constantly challenge and restructure the novel. The incorporation of found documents in the Etxebarria novel (as well as in Chacón's historical novel) creates a tension between what is "real" or considered "official" and the creative imagination of the fictional narrative. The "postmodern cultural hybridity" (Labanyi 9) that governs artistic production and consumption in Spain emerges as a subtext in the novels in this study. All the novels combine elements of fiction and "reality" and ultimately warn us that any sense of the "truth" of either the past or the present is unattainable because it is in constant flux; "truth" is a fiction constantly written and rewritten.

Labanyi situates the search for a distinctive Spanish cultural identity within the larger tradition of cultural studies that emerged in England during the 1950s. However, Spain provides a unique arena for the study of cultural identity in the late twentieth century primarily "because [of] its rapid transition from Francoism to democracy" (Kinder 1). The specific Spanish context is key to understanding the texts produced from within it, considering the unique political and social climate of the transition. Simon During, in his introduction to *The Cultural Studies Reader,* points out the importance of a subjective relation between cultural production and the individual lives of the producer and consumer (1). As cultural studies developed in England during the 1950s and 1960s, key thinkers such as F. R. Leavis, Richard Hoggart, and Raymond Williams addressed the tensions between class and culture that developed into a theory of how "groups with least power practically develop their own readings of, and uses for cultural products—in fun, in resistance, or to articulate their own identity" (During 7). Helen Graham and Labanyi, in their insightful introduction to *Spanish Cultural Studies: An Introduction,* titled "Culture and Modernity: The Case of Spain," relate the British concepts of culture to the specific situations and events of twentieth-century Spain. They point out the importance of culture as a site of power in the class struggle resulting from elitist notions of art and pure aesthetics associated with Spanish Modernism.[9] While this kind of intellectual elitism is not unique to Spain, the way it played out in the Spanish Civil War and resulting dictatorship displayed the extremes of the ideological, political, and cultural clash. The tension within the Republican army came to a head in the Barcelona crisis of 1937 when anarchists and communists fired on each other, displaying the "bifurcated Liberal modernity" (Graham and Labanyi 16) that plagued the Republican government. Franco's reign sought to pacify and control popular aesthetics by selling Spanish folklore to an international market as a distinct national identity and playing up the positive side of difference, which reflected the isolationist political ideology of the first decades of his rule. Franco did not seek to undermine popular culture but rather his regime discouraged "independent critical thought necessary to the development of any form of cultural analysis" (Graham and Labanyi 3). The promotion and preservation of these divisions of high and low culture in Spain and a lack of theoretical analysis on the connections between them have encouraged contemporary critics and artists to explore cultural matters from a historical viewpoint.

Friedrich Nietzsche's understanding of the importance and problems of history as representative of cultural identity in *Uses and Disadvantages of History for Life* can be translated to a Spanish context in order to better understand contemporary interpretations of historical events. For Nietzsche a focus on history and historical events is only useful if it leads to progress in the present. The German philosopher is eager to distinguish original thought or progress (which he calls "life") from simple catalog knowledge of events (65). He suggests that artistic and cultural renditions of history are the most useful because they maintain a certain distance from the search for the "truth" of the events and allow for interpretive renderings of the past. One of the main preoccupations put forth by Nietzsche is that a culture dominated by historical knowledge will stifle progress, and this imbalance between historical knowledge and action will result in what he calls a "historical culture" or a culture without vision, stagnated in the "glories" of the past. However, the literary artifact that captures the interconnectedness of time through renditions of history that project to future readings not only of the historical moment, such as the Spanish Civil War, but also of the historical moment of reading about the Spanish

Introduction

Civil War, allows for critical commentary on the past and on the art of the novel.

Nietzsche's criticism of contemporary culture lies in the complacency of acquiring knowledge about culture or past cultures and not producing a unique cultural product (78). The relationship between art and history demands knowledge of culture but insists on a critical presentation of that very knowledge. "In producing this effect, history is the antithesis of art: and only if history can endure to be transformed into a work of art will it perhaps be able to preserve instincts or even evoke them" (95–96). Therefore, according to Nietzsche, history can only serve contemporary culture well if it is recast as art and open to various interpretations, never rooted in "fact" but allowing creativity to open the doors of analytical possibility. Following this line of thought, recent Spanish novels propose to revisit common knowledge and unearth alternative visions through literary means.

Culture and the Hyperreal

Cultural production in a postmodern world controlled by market values ceases to be representative of society, but rather aims to control and manipulate the artistic values that contribute to cultural ideologies. Eduardo Subirats studies this phenomenon in the Vanguard movement at the beginning of the twentieth century and finds that art becomes less interested in mimesis and more concerned with simulacrum (180–81). He states that the Vanguard movement sought to present "una expresión histórica de la conciencia de las limitaciones o el fracaso del proyecto ilustrado de secularización y racionalización sociales" (180). The spirit of twentieth-century artistic production stems from this consciousness that society is inherently chaotic, but as Baudrillard points out, it also embraces the multitude of possibilities that abstract expression (in art and writing) affords the artist. The Vanguard ideal of actually misrepresenting social reality through the distortion of figures and literary structure in order to suggest marginalized perspectives laid the groundwork for current trends of representation in contemporary works.

Jean Baudrillard argues that contemporary, postmodern society has experienced a shift away from representation to simulation, creating a system that does not refer to anything outside of itself. It seems that he struggles with the concept of reality and has concluded that "reality" in a traditional sense simply does not exist and that what contemporary culture relies on is an artificial sense of differentiation. Everyday experience, or what we would consider "real," is so infused with seductive market strategy and constructed fantasy that we no longer can separate our desires from those produced or manipulated by capitalism. Why do we want what we want or buy what we buy? Is it born of necessity or influenced by advertising, mass media marketing, and subtle commercial suggestion? Baudrillard contends that society has become void of any representation of the real; he claims: "never again will the real have the chance to produce itself" (2). Simulations of reality have subsumed the real, and the simulacra are self-sufficient mechanisms that cease to be recognized as such.

In the chapter on Ray Loriga, I link Baudrillard's theory to the concept of television and, specifically, television news. A newscast is a perfect example of the manipulation of "real" events and the creation of a simulacrum. The news stories are edited (censured) to fit into designated time slots and specific areas of interest and designed to draw viewer interest, not to present accurate information. Loriga criticizes this practice in his novel *Caídos del cielo* when the protagonist finds himself the victim of television's glorification of violence. The "real" story is lost to countless renditions of the event on television and to various versions told in the novel through other characters' perspectives. Loriga delves into questions of cultural representation and fabrication using as a backdrop moral issues that infuse his work with ethical dilemma and problematic social justice. Instead of the lack of moral judgment attributed to the Generation X writers, I find that in their works the blatant confrontation with traditional morality brings to the forefront questions of generational differences and citizenship. Therefore the Generation X has not produced works that avoid or discard moral issues but works that attack such questions head on from a different angle.

Baudrillard's simulacrum of power coincides with the simulacrum of morality presented in several of the Gen X novels. The simulacrum of power that Baudrillard defines as inherent

Introduction

in capitalism and politics perpetuates the idea that it is the appearance of power that influences society and not any tangible manifestations of leadership or usefulness. Much of what Bourdieu talks about as the "production of belief," or the convincing of the public that something is art, has to do with a moral consciousness. The validity of moral questions concerning lifestyle, citizenship, and family comes to the surface in the Gen X novels precisely because the protagonists seek to fill a void left by traditional values. The broken families, unsatisfying relationships, and urban boredom launch the characters into a search for some kind of engaging experience that will bring the importance of moral issues to the forefront of their lives. Therefore the simulacrum of social morality surrounding the young characters in the novels is revealed as exactly that, and the focus falls on release from historically rendered models.

The illusion of present reality and morality found in the Gen X novels plays off of the illusion of historical truth in the other novels studied here. The novelistic genre is historical in that the form necessarily takes into account previous incarnations and revisions. The novelistic form survives on the reliability of simulacrum to define human existence. The written word and artistic expression in general are symbolic: they are a simulacrum of some kind of reality that exists beyond the pages, frame, or reel of the artwork. The novel succeeds at the endeavor of creating a hyperreal artistic space in that the novelistic reality is self-contained within the pages of the book. The author takes time to elaborate detail, to provoke recurring images that will create the illusion of a real world, a narrative reality which the author can meddle in or leave to the narrative voice. All of the novels in this study toy with the awareness of the hyperreality within the novel and present a perspective on the constructedness of the narrative process. The lines between author, implied author, narrator, and protagonist become blurred and crossed in an attempt to rethink the structure and purpose of narration. The illusion of art is exposed in order to examine the illusion of history and of reality in a kind of textual manipulation that often results in violence toward the text, toward historical accuracy, and toward contemporary ideas of morality. The violence emerges both as a theme and as an aberration to printing norms, such as jagged or cascading words and footnotes in the work of Etxebarria. The historical novels deal with political violence and war, while the Gen X novels look to an inner, psychological violence that eventually manifests itself as outward attacks and self-destruction. Violence as a part of cultural production steers the interpretations made by the novels because violent history emerges as a point of contention that demands the attention and justification of a contemporary consciousness. The Gen X writers exploit violent themes in much the same way: the deliberate search for violence allows for temporary identification with and alienation from certain social groups. In both types of novel the theme of violence, either historical or urban, presents a crisis moment in which the individual seeks to identify himself or herself through cultural markers in connection with a larger concept of society.

Culture and Violence

Several studies have broached the topic of violence as intrinsic to human nature and identity from many different angles. Jacqueline Cruz and Barbara Zecchi take issue with the rising problems of inequality in all sectors of society in their collection of essays *La mujer en la España actual ¿Evolución o involución?* The title suggests this preoccupation with the false sense of success women may have about the strides gained toward equality. In their introduction, Cruz and Zecchi closely analyze the troubling rise of domestic abuse statistics in Spain. Lidia Falcón[10] and other Spanish feminists have recently raised the same issue. Other studies have focused on the cultural impact of a fast-paced, postmodern culture where rapid urbanization leads to individual alienation, detachment, and a lashing out toward the mass industry known as society. Much of the success of the Generation X seems to reside in the ability of the authors to appropriate and disseminate images of violence and discontent. Cristina Moreiras explains the double meaning in the politically apathetic texts of the Gen X by noting that this distancing from social polemics actually "pone a trabajar reflexivamente ese agotamiento articulando así una intervención o inscripción política" (191). The absence of social commitment is itself a glaring commentary on the feelings of isolation, resentment, and violence expressed by most of the Gen X protagonists.

Introduction

I use violence throughout this study in an abstract, ideological way. While the terrorist attacks in the United States of September 11, 2001, and in Madrid on March 11, 2004, certainly have shaped how we think and write about culture, I will not depend on these kinds of phenomena to guide my reading of the works. My interest lies more in the psychological repercussions of historical violence and in the literary manifestations of an innate human connection to the cycle of destruction and creativity. More in agreement with the idea of ritual and violence posited by René Girard, I locate violence at the intersection of culture, humanity, and the individual. The novels in question break with tradition in several ways and thus move toward different representations of the relationship between the individual, history, and society. Chacón and Etxebarria manipulate the aesthetic quality of the novel by inserting documentation that confuses the reader. Etxebarria uses footnotes in her novel and plays with the visual composition of lines on the page to render a sense of freedom with the novel's structure. She also challenges traditional notions of the reader/author relationship and inserts the author's comments and opinions into the text via footnotes. Chacón also deconstructs this relationship, yet in a different way. In her novel, *La voz dormida*, she freely uses letters and official documents to adorn the narrative, creating confusion between "real" documentation and fiction. She also changes how we read by using different fonts and layout to emphasize different versions of history. Both authors achieve a complete upheaval of the novel as a particular version of the "truth." For these writers, the truth can never be understood, and "reality" is made up of multiple perspectives of history and of writing.

Loriga and Mañas are known for their own unique perspectives on the "reality" of urban youth. The "dirty realism" they present is skewed, steeped as it is in the fantasy of visual arts, drugs, and music (Gullón v). They both use violence as a tool to shock readers, to criticize the apathy of young people, and to condemn the system that ignores its youth. Nevertheless, violence in the works of Mañas and Loriga is highly stylized and serves a narrative and thematic purpose to criticize hierarchical power because law is the enemy, and justice, in a traditional sense, seldom prevails. Walter Benjamin questions the role of violence in society in terms of law and justice in his essay

"Critique of Violence." Benjamin explains the role of the serial killer who attains heroic status simply because he can operate outside of the law, giving his actions legitimacy in the eyes of the public. The fact that law seeks to deprive the individual of a natural tendency to violence "arouses even in defeat the sympathy of the mass against law" (281). This notion of the renegade who defies authority in his use of violence is fundamental to the protagonists in Mañas's *Historias del Kronen* and in Loriga's *Caídos del cielo*. The young men are both defiant and psychologically antisocial, and their use of violence to challenge an overbearing, hypocritical system makes them unlikely heroes.

Nevertheless, Benjamin's critique of violence does not pose a literary connection but clearly identifies with class struggle and political inequality. How, then, can we define a specific type of literary violence? How can we translate the history of violence into textual interpretation? In this study two novels deal with the appropriation of silenced voices in two of Spain's most violent time periods: the Inquisition and the Civil War. But how does violence itself become artistic? The novelistic violence conveys a sense of urgency and the prohibited that at once entices and repulses the reader. The text forms a buffer between the reader and the "reality" of violence implied in the narrative. This formal distancing allows for intellectual grappling with the themes presented in the narrative. In a vein similar to Ortega's "deshumanización," the representations of violence in literary venues require detachment and consequent reflection on the part of the reader.

The novel as a literary form creates this kind of philosophical arena more readily than other art forms. The art of narrative in the novel creates a dialogue between the implied narrator and reader as suggested by Mikhail Bakhtin in *The Dialogic Imagination* and by Wayne Booth in *The Rhetoric of Fiction*. This symbiotic relationship between implied author and reader that Bakhtin defends as an artistic "system" of various registers and "languages" (262) develops over the course of the narrative and through actions and reactions that demand the constant reevaluation of the text by the reader. The reader becomes somewhat of an "obstacle " for the author, and simultaneously is an important element in creating the perspective and opinion of the text (Booth 90). This interaction between implied author and reader that for Bakhtin amounts to a question of style becomes a matter of rhetoric, construction, and negotiation for Booth. Nevertheless, both theorists maintain that the narrative space of the novel allows for a more intimate artistic experience, from the tactile feel of the novel in one's hands to the time and energy dedicated to the material. This crucial relationship between reader and writer determines how we analyze violence in the text. The violence represented in the novels in this study varies from historical renderings of the Spanish Civil War to the burning of Jews during the Inquisition to the psychological violence brought on by gender inequality and alienation in a post-modern world. In some of the texts, violence becomes another aesthetic that we assimilate within the writerly style; while in others it shocks us into a realization about human nature and the nature of writing itself. Violence appears in many shapes and forms in these novels: as suicide, murder, sexual violence, psychological violence, and textual violence. Specifically, the textual violence that can be considered a postmodern break with the long, character-driven, chronological structure of nineteenth-century novels combines genres, discourse, and language in search of new forms of expression. Bakhtin's categories of "stylistic unities" are expanded from voices and registers to breaks in syntax, neologisms, and implied silences that come together to create a chaotic, yet cohesive style. José Ángel Mañas looks to English and American counterparts to incorporate a sense of global disquiet and latent violence that connects contemporary youth. The troubling aspect of Mañas's characters is that they do not draw their violent tendencies from national strife or political disillusion, but rather it comes across as a universal condition of the generation gap, and while youth in Spain find themselves in an identity vacuum, at least they can take comfort from knowing that on an international level, they are not alone.

In other cases, the mixing of registers and tones creates a text that calls attention to itself by breaking with traditional narrative practices and visual expectations of the book. Etxebarria, like Cercas, plays with the writerly mode by incorporating her own voice into the narrative and inserting information that would suggest the protagonist truly "exists" in our world: the protagonist has her own e-mail address, for example. Chacón uses different typefaces, and Mañas inserts ellipses in parentheses to suggest other voices within a character's rambling monologue. These are all examples of textual violence; these uncommon narrative techniques allow the author to break with traditional narrative form and structure not only to manipulate content through visual metaphor but also to break the visual flow of the novel. The text does not read from left to right in some cases. The change of font changes tone and therefore meaning. The presence of the implied author in the text creates another dimension that is added to the narrative structure. All of these elements lead us ultimately to the reader and the role of the reader in the text. The novels require an active reader ready to take on the sometimes confusing, disconnected, and fractured narrative.

Commonalities amid Diversity

Through the growing discourse of culture as capital as expressed by Bourdieu, literature has become a hot commodity in terms of its representational value. The value of a literary project has come to reside in its ability to challenge traditional cultural norms as well as traditional notions of genre. Art is said to reflect the times in which it was created, but these novelists reject the very idea of an era. The historical novels in question here do not represent History but rather a turn-of-the-millennium preoccupation with historical methodologies. The Gen X novels do not represent current reality or try to paint a "cuadro de costumbres" of what life is like in Spain for youth of the twentieth and twenty-first centuries. The six authors presented here defy literary notions in general. The novel has become somewhat of an anti-novel as it probes and tests its own limits and boundaries. The idea of a generation of writers comes under fire not only because several of the writers studied here published their thematically disparate works in the same years—Riera and Mañas both in 1994—but because the members of the Gen X movement themselves reject the restrictions that a literary label places on them.[11]

The work cut out for the critic then is to draw parallels between the cultural climate in which the works were produced and between the texts themselves. In doing so, we can gain an appreciation for the varied and provocative literature coming

Introduction

out of contemporary Spain. The publication of *Soldados de Salamina* and *La voz dormida* in 2001 and 2002, respectively, marks a shift in the recuperation of Spain's painful past and presents two texts that reinterpret history at the same time as they reinterpret the novel. The current tendencies in the novel in Spain bridge the gap between taboo and sacred subjects, bringing all cultural issues to the forefront of a diverse literary production. History, reality, storytelling, and imagination combine in one literary vision that plays with all of these ideas and obligates the reader to take an active part in the creation of art. The link between culture and text is the reader, and the role of the reader has never been so important. Umberto Eco's "model reader," imagined by the author for the accurate interpretation of the text, anticipates a contemporary reader molded by culture who shares (or rejects) the cultural positioning of the author and who is culturally "literate" in the areas of mass media, film, technology, and television.[12] In this way the novels at hand invite yet challenge the reader to reconsider certain aspects of culture and of literature itself.

As testaments to the abundance and vitality of current Spanish letters, these novels are representative of the various modes of cultural capital circulating in contemporary Spain. The search for reconciliation with the past and present has given way to an exercise in decoding traditional literary mores. These novels delve into questions burning in the Spanish cultural consciousness, such as historical legacy, cultural inheritance, and prospects for the future. The themes are local, yet they transcend regional circumstance to address much more universal questions of humanity and experience. In this way the representations of culture in contemporary Spanish literature have something to say to us all and illuminate the ways in which we read, think, and live.

Part 1

History or Creating the Past

The first part of this study focuses on the controversial nature of the historical novel. Trained historians defend the need to unearth facts that establish concrete truths about past events, while writers and critics in the literary field play precociously with the existence of absolute truth and give precedence to the imaginary as a perfectly legitimate way to understand the world in which we live. The novels in this first section, by Carme Riera, Dulce Chacón, and Javier Cercas, consciously confront the notion of historical truth, yet it is important to note that the writers do not set out to correct historical misconceptions. Rather, the historical revelations in the novels provide insight into alternate or marginalized views of History in a way that suggests the existence of unlimited versions of histories, known and silenced, that make up our contemporary sense of the historical.

Throughout the study I identify a dominant conceptual History by using the capital H to denote an approach to the past that accepts writing and language as authoritative and accurate. This History is opposed to a more imaginative, literary approach to the past that addresses the need to narrate and create stories that contribute to a whole understanding of history. While I do not intend to challenge my colleagues in History departments about the nature of recording the past, I do propose that a literary vision of history can be inclusive and revealing without becoming reductive. Instead of locating the novels in this study within their particular historical time frame, such as the Inquisition or the Spanish Civil War, I focus on the contemporary experimentation with language and form that perhaps tells the reader more about the current state of the novel than about the conditions of the past.

Part 1

The authors in question have done the historical research. Riera spent months on the island of Mallorca going through archives and reading the existing *autos de fe* in order to re-create a literary version of seventeenth-century *converso* reality. Chacón privileges documents, letters, and diaries of many women jailed during the early years of the Franco regime in order to find the literary voice that tells a version of desperate post-war Spanish society. Cercas turns to past literary sources to underscore the writer's importance as a witness who documents the times: the poetry of Rafael Sánchez Mazas, a journalistic piece on Antonio Machado's war experience, and meetings with the writer Roberto Bolaño are examples of how the literary infuses the historical with inspired, creative language. Perhaps a writer's relationship to the past reflects his or her relationship to the present: language connects the individual to experience, and words are a tool that shapes our perception of "reality."

However, "reality" poses a unique problem, because it is precisely experience that evades language and definition. As we will see in Part 2 of this study, "reality" in the Gen X novel ceases to serve as a cultural referent for human experience, and the virtual or created experience becomes the dominant mode of interpersonal relations. Culture is the bridge between the two seemingly disparate modes of experience that history and the virtual represent. The cultural embraces all forms of experience and instead of suggesting boundaries on what may be considered "real," it authorizes the blending and mixing of social interactions that bring together different elements of a vastly multifaceted network.

Hayden White, in *Tropics of Discourse,* proposes a re-evaluation of the nature of historical conceptualization. His concern lies with the very nature of history as an academic discipline and its hybrid nature: a "semi-science" and "a kind of art" (27). It seems that the dual nature of history as a scientific study of the past that must embrace narrative suffers more from the rigorous divisions within the academy than from its own schizophrenia. Only in recognizing the ends as humanistic, as mediating "human perception," can we fully appreciate the complexity of historical discourse. Nevertheless, White turns to metahistory as a way to understand the production of historical data, "the structure of a peculiarly *historical* consciousness," and "the possible *forms* of historical representation" (81). White's observations about form and consciousness can be applied to the historical novels in this study. These novels consider an event or personal experience that represents a larger historical event and incorporate this information into a novelistic form that questions what is "true" and "real."

We can look at the historical events portrayed in the novels that follow as incomplete in some sense, given that the novels present an alternative viewpoint or, in some cases, an underrepresented and previously silenced perspective. The historical importance of the Inquisition, the Spanish Civil War, and the Vietnam War cannot be disputed, but the importance of these events as cultural phenomena that shape and influence the contemporary social identity of the nation and of the individual goes beyond the repercussions of the events themselves. In the same vein, David K. Herzberger, in his discussion on White, comments: "historical and fictional narratives share the configurational element of temporality. Both fiction and history are symbolic discourses to the extent that they mediate human perception of the workings of life" (7). The novels that represent certain marginalized aspects of historical discourse produce an engaging form of metahistory that begs us to rethink the very nature of the past in relation to the present and the historical in relation to the imaginary.

Chapter One

Rewriting the Past as Cultural Capital

Sacred Violence in Carme Riera's
Dins el darrer blau

> Religious, ethnic, or national minorities are never actually reproached for their difference, but for not being as different as expected, and in the end for not differing at all.
>
> René Girard
> *Violence and the Sacred*

The tension between History and violence seems to plant the seeds of resentment and prejudice. The act of forgetting violent events as a form of self-preservation can be attributed to a national consciousness as well as to individuals. Carme Riera's award-winning novel *Dins el darrer blau* [*In the Last Blue*] begs forgiveness in its deliberate presentation of the lives, persecution, and deaths of Mallorcan Jews. Riera considers History a desperate, destructive tool that chips away at the victims' version of events and in doing so destroys any possibility of a comprehensive historical picture. Riera dedicated several years to extensive research on her native island of Mallorca in order to unearth the existing "facts" about a group of *conversos* who were condemned to die for trying to escape from the island in 1687. The novel is a reworking of the information from the point of view of the *conversos*. The commingling of historical "fact" and fictional renderings of actual people make this work an example of hybrid historical narrative that allows the author great liberty with issues of historical accuracy. The fact that the *conversos'* account is not documented and that there only exists a version written by a priest leads Riera through a labyrinth of experimentation with characters and events.

Riera cites her sources clearly in the final note of the novel and adds that her novel does not have, "encara que pugui semblar-ho, cap intenció polèmica" (432) ["even though it may seem so, any political agenda"].[1] The polemics that, in my opinion, are clearly presented in the novel do not dispute past actions or motivation but rather question notions of historical justice. She claims that the purpose of the novel is to vindicate the Mallorcan Jews by finally giving their side of the story a place, a physical space on the shelves of time, but she also writes to condemn common notions of what history is and how it functions within our society. The debilitating kind of history that Nietzsche describes impedes progress with a historical culture that relies on dates and events as representatives of the past instead of using interpretive texts that question events, figures, and outcomes.[2] The polemics in Riera's novel lie not only in her unflinching ability to interpret the violent history of the Inquisition and the lack of authoritative material available to scholars representing the victims' side but also in her creation of characters that live and breathe within the novelistic reality and come to represent human beings instead of just numbers and data. Maryellen Bieder connects the seduction of the reader common in Riera's works to the notion of cultural capital when she claims: "she [Riera] interweaves the question of national identity into her play of gender and language" ("Cultural" 53). It is this stagnant idea of national identity based in historical "fact" that Riera challenges in her works and specifically in *Dins el darrer blau*.

    The risk inherent in the representation of the past lies in the unearthing of the humanity or in some cases the inhumanity of history, yet understanding these elements of society is exactly what allows a civilization to progress and develop. The polemics of the novel concern not so much how certain elements of the past are represented or omitted but rather how these representations shape contemporary notions of history and culture.

    Not surprisingly Riera unveils several levels of violence in the novel that serve to criticize historical decisions and actions but also present violence as a hierarchical marker that distinguishes between classes and genders. Women's issues have always been at the forefront of Riera's novels and short stories.[3] Many of her works investigate the problematic formulation of female identity when the subject is forced to conform to patriarchal norms (Camí-Vela 14). *Dins el darrer blau* seems at first glance to eschew issues of women's identity in favor of a larger historical project. Nevertheless, this novel can be read as a condemnation of the violence against the disempowered that upholds social structures. Riera differentiates between masculine and feminine sacrifice in her novel and concludes that the two serve a different social purpose. The sacrifice of men upholds economic and religious structures, while the sacrifice of women maintains gender inequality. Riera also challenges biblically sanctioned ideas of violence and sacrifice. Read through the lens of sacred violence posited by René Girard, *Dins el darrer blau* becomes a stage for ritual sacrifice, a patriarchal rite that ultimately threatens both men and women. Riera not only lays bare the precarious process of historicizing events but also challenges the very notions of ritual and sacrifice that nurture violence as a controlling social force. Riera goes beyond the particulars of seventeenth-century Mallorca and achieves a more global vision of violence by addressing gender issues within socially acceptable forms of violence that support existing patriarchal structures.[4]

Dins el darrer blau appears to be a literary attempt to identify with and revindicate the victim. The literary project that seeks to provide a different and perhaps more accurate version of history offers a perspective not often found in traditional historical documents. The sacrifice of the Jews because of their religious practices, family relationships, eating habits, and daily customs comes to represent the larger sacrifice of those oppressed and marginalized sectors of society. The parallel that Riera draws between religious and gender oppression leaves the women characters in a double bind: they are oppressed as Jews and as women. This hierarchy and order is maintained though the various physical, emotional, and psychological sacrifices described in the novel.

The sacrifice that Girard deems fundamental to upholding social order is particularized in the novel to the religious rites of the Catholic Church. The routine reprimand, confiscation of property, and burning of the Jews, all in the name of God, function as a method to channel the violence that exists within the institution of religion itself. The marginalized group becomes the scapegoat, easily sacrificed to maintain order. However, the deterioration of the Catholic Church presented in the novel, seen in the quarreling between priests and in the dismissal of

Chapter One

the Viceroy of Mallorca for his questioning of the Church's motives, spills over into Judaism as well. Most of the condemned Jews choose to renounce their faith in order to avoid being burned alive, and they all face certain death in any case. Gabriel Valls, who chooses to defend his faith until the end, echoes the desperation of Christ with his plea to God: "Per què m'has desemparat, Adonai? (214) ["Why have you forsaken me, Lord?"]. In his attempt to understand the monolithic religious structure, the character reveals the inadequacy of institutionalized religion to comfort the individual or to harmonize conflict. Riera criticizes the corrupt nature of certain individuals within the Catholic Church and monarchy. Her observations on the decadent morality of certain powerful leaders within the Church create a bridge between seventeenth-century Spain and the twenty-first century. Her criticism of institutionalized religion in the novel, just as her criticism of violence and gender inequality, plays out during the Inquisition but reflects on issues in contemporary society as well.

Furthermore, religion is portrayed in the novel as exclusionary and ultimately abusive toward women. Girard's constant allusions to the Bible that illustrate his analysis point to the very violent nature at the heart of religion. He defines nature and death as sacred, as that which is increasingly mysterious despite efforts to dominate and control it. Therefore: "violence is the heart and secret soul of the sacred" (31). It is this secret soul of violence that Riera exposes as detrimental to the well-being of society. Centuries-old actions still have glaring repercussions, and the cycle of violence continues precisely because of the occult nature of the power behind institutional violence. Women suffer more from institutional violence because the constructs of society are intrinsically patriarchal.

The patriarchal constructs that sanction violence against women are also so entrenched in cultural coding and behavior that they seem insurmountable. Celia Amorós dismantles the concept of virility and shows it to be strictly a social construct that defines women as nondesirable. She claims: "el conjunto de los varones como género-sexo no está nunca constituído, sino que *se constituye* mediante un sistema de prácticas, siendo la de autodesignación la que desempeña a su vez el papel de *articularlas*" (2; italics in original). Therefore the articulation of certain behaviors serves to propel the notion of an identity. Amorós continues: "la virilidad no existe sino en tanto que *idea-fantasma regulador* del comportamiento de los varones" (3). She points out that masculine identity is not intrinsic to the individual, but rather the acting out feeds the fantasy of male dominance. In several episodes from the novel, the masculine acting out of virility at the expense of women's subjectivity shows the need for the power play to establish hierarchical gender modes. In one case, with the prostitute Beatriu Mas, this hierarchy is inverted and thus revealed as a construct and as not intrinsic to gender. While Riera seems very aware of the notion of socially programmed behavior, Girard seems unaware of the connection between the masculine struggle for power that leads to violence and the displacement of the female.[5]

Girard explains the existence of violence as a way in which societies maintain order. The disruptive threat usually arrives in the form of an outsider, someone who can easily be targeted in acts of ritual violence. However, Girard takes this one step further in suggesting that more commonly a surrogate victim appears and can be "substituted for all the potential victims, for all the enemy brothers that each member is striving to banish from the community" (79). Therefore, a lone representative or surrogate dies in a symbolic act that embodies the expurgation from the society of his or her kind. In Riera's novel, Gabriel Valls and Isabel Tarongí are both burned at the stake, representing Jews and Jewish women, respectively. Girard points out that this cycle of symbolic violence found in the sacrificial ritual is essentially what upholds social order and, I would add, patriarchy. In all manifestations of violence, from *autos de fe* to domestic violence, Girard's words ring true: "Men cannot confront the naked truth of their own violence without the risk of abandoning themselves to it entirely. They have never had a very clear idea of this violence, and it is possible that the survival of all human societies of the past was dependent on this fundamental lack of understanding" (82). Clearly, Riera challenges this lack of understanding in her representation of the violence suffered by the Jews in Mallorca and by women in general. Although Girard overlooks important gender issues, his theories can be extended to explain how a ritual form of conscious and subconscious violence upholds patriarchy. Nevertheless, the reaction from various feminist critics to Girard's theories does prove insightful and useful for reconstructing a more comprehensive view of woman as sacrificial victim.

Several critics take issue with Girard's omission of the female desiring subject in his construction of a cultural system based solely on male rivalries. Ruth El Saffar comments that Girard's theoretical model is based on fear and paranoia and that it "blocks out certain areas of human experience, places where there might be occasion for optimism, for reconciliation, for growth" (6). She sees these omitted areas as distinctly feminine. Toril Moi takes issue with Girard's reading of Freud that disregards the direct (unmediated) desire of the pre-Oedipal stage between child and mother. Sarah Kofman criticizes Girard's interpretation of Freud's narcissistic, self-sufficient woman, who, according to Girard, cannot incite male desire, for she is "actually the metaphysical transfiguration of the rival-model" (Girard, qtd. in Kofman 41). What these feminist critics argue is that Girard strips woman of agency and desire, for her actions and impulses are not her own but rather only validated by the dueling desires of men. On the other hand, Susan Nowak comes to Girard's defense, stating that his revelations on the relationship between myth, ritual, and victimization are tools that theorists can use to further a feminist agenda (21). Nevertheless, it seems that the idea of difference is fundamental to those who attack Girard for his "blindness" toward the feminine and to those who defend his critique of violence.

Girard sees differentiation as key to understanding the roles and positions that maintain a balance in society. When two elements appear to be identical, as in the case of twins, for example, the boundaries of identity are rocked and violence ensues (57). Thus, difference becomes desirable for its capacity to separate, alienate, and structure social interactions and discourse. Nowak asserts that there is a celebration of differences at all levels that should "take place without violence and victimage" (27). Critics of Girard argue that his brand of difference serves to subordinate and marginalize the Other as the only means of sustaining a productive society. The problem of difference lies at the heart of Riera's novel. How are these differences determined and by whom? She explores how each microcosm of society exerts its power according to the differences embedded in its cultural code. It seems that Girard can only theorize the positive forces of difference in the negotiation of space and power primarily because he does not take into account the position of the Other. Nor does he explore the compounded nature of difference and oppression that women historically have experienced.

Most analyses of Riera's novel center on the author's intent to reinvent a historical discourse that voices the experience of marginalized Mallorcan Jews and do not focus on the role of women in the novel. History and literature join in defiance of a monolithic interpretation and categorical silencing of the victims (Coll-Tellechea, Nichols, Pérez, Rodríguez, Tsuchiya). Neus Carbonell raises a most important and neglected point regarding the discourse of the novel. She cites the difficulty in rendering a true or at least impartial narrative portrait of the Other by a mainstream voice. In assuming a voice for the voiceless, the text willingly propagates an authoritarian stance that "speaks" for the oppressed. "If the Other is represented by the Self, the logic of silence that is being denounced is also being reproduced" (222). The critic raises the problem of the representation of Jews by a Catholic woman who intends to position herself *in relation* to the other, for she can never fully occupy that position (224; italics in original). Throughout the novel, the Jews are represented as the marginalized group in order to recreate with historical accuracy their existence but the "position of the Jew-as-Other" (226) seems almost inevitable even in an attempt to vindicate the underground society.

By pointing out the problematic subject position of the author, Carbonell taps into the fundamental importance of the novel: Riera's version is only another version of historical events. Truth is a myth propagated by institutions that claim superiority, such as the Church or monarchy, but writing and language are always at the mercy of a particular vision. Riera does not claim to reveal the truth behind the suffering of the Mallorcan Jews; she states, "el meu llibre no és d'història, sinó de ficció" (430) ["my book is not historical, but fiction"]. If her point is to uncover the fictional nature of traditional historical discourse then inevitably her own work, and historical writing in general, can only be considered fiction. By adopting a more tolerant view of the Other, Riera succeeds in redefining the subject position, "suavizando nuestra angustia ante la realidad de la diferencia (y del antagonismo) y afirmando la naturalidad de nuestra situación de recepción" (Beverley 7). Difference defines the subject/object relationship and, as Girard suggests, maintains the hierarchy regulating violence (49).

In Riera's novel the subject/object relationship becomes threatened when social boundaries are crossed. Girard claims that when the difference becomes vague or the terms become equal, the system is thrown into chaos and the lack of demarcation causes violence (65).[6] In the novel, the threat of economic domination by the Jewish merchant class is transformed into a religious threat. Because the success of the merchant class cannot be easily identified as different from the economic success of the church or monarchy, another identity marker must be sought out. Thus, religion plays a decisive role in differentiating groups of people. The Jewish religion bears no actual threat to the domination of Catholicism, but rather the unstable economic hierarchy requires the elimination of the emerging Jewish merchant class in order to redistribute the power of that class to the monarchy that funnels money to the church. While Girard's theory of sacrificial violence reveals much about the structure of society and institutions, he does not address the complicated nature of power struggles nor does he address issues of the implicit gender hierarchy embedded in every aspect of society. Riera takes on these issues, pitting violence against power and gender in order to elevate the historical novel to a timeless cultural criticism of institutions.

Riera's novel proposes a compounding of Girard's theory in that she defines two groups victimized as scapegoats. The first group, Jews, becomes the scapegoat in order to maintain religious order. The other group, more diverse and therefore more difficult to identify, is women. "Woman" as a group confuses identity issues because every woman also belongs to a specific religious, ethnic, or economic group as well. Therefore, the ability to bond together to form any meaningful resistance requires a radical break with the other dominant, patriarchal classification. "Woman" as a category is itself a patriarchal social construct that necessarily fits into a certain role that problematizes female identity and possible camaradería. María Pilar Rodríguez has observed that in Riera's novel, "la caracterización de las figuras femeninas se propone un escenario más amable y más cercano al entendimiento entre los seres humanos" ("Exclusión" 256). While the men are separated in jail to avoid conspiracy, the women are incarcerated together, suggesting that the jailers highly doubt the ability of the women to organize. This assumption proves to be false as the women, led by the prostitute Beatriu Mas, orchestrate the romantic liaison between Rafel Onofre Valls and his fiancée, Maria. From the outset, the resourcefulness of Beatriu overshadows the desperate conditions of the *Casa Negra*. The prostitute, accustomed to living with many women in a small space, makes the best of it and eventually convinces the jailer to loan her a comb and a mirror. The acquisition of these basic beauty implements allows the women to maintain a small amount of dignity by introducing some normalcy into their desperate situation. Riera suggests that female solidarity can be seen as the only positive result of the incarceration of the Jews, and this complicity shines as the only glimmer of hope within a disastrous context.

Riera explores the consequences of feminine sacrifice in the novel through the figure of the prostitute and in relation to the family. The women who are all marginalized within a particular social structure are symbolically sacrificed in order to maintain the patriarchal hierarchy. The prostitute is a woman who works in the public sphere and is self-sufficient yet marginalized by the sexual nature of her profession. The sisters, wives, and mothers function within the family structure as caregivers and lack power over their own lives and destinies. The inclusion of the feminine in the novel is deliberate and highly symbolic in terms of revealing the inequalities suffered by women at the hands of the Inquisitors and men in general.

Nevertheless, in order to unveil the social construct of power relations, Riera masterfully inverts the established sexual and economic hierarchy of prostitution in the central female character of the novel, Beatriu. Beatriu willingly hides Rafel Onofre Valls from the police after the failed attempt to leave the island. Rafel's father urges him to hide in the forbidden space of the brothel, which ironically becomes a refuge and sanctuary for the young Jew. Even though Beatriu functions within the society as an object desired by all men, she operates within the context of the novel as an independent agent, conspiring to save Rafel and arranging the reunion between Rafel and his fiancée

Chapter One

in the jail. Beatriu's function in the text can be seen as giving voice to the "object" in the love triangle of the rival men and female. Known as the most skilled prostitute in the city, she is desired by all men, yet her active gaze and organizational abilities give the Object in the triangle a voice, and the power of language incites action.

Beatriu clearly enjoys Rafel sexually in the brothel, and her desire is evident as she quickly waives his fee and distinguishes him from her other clients: "aquell al.lot, alt i cepat li paregué un ésser miraculós, una mena d'àngel" (222) ["that boy, tall and strong, seemed like a miracle to her, some kind of angel"]. As she admires his body while he sleeps, searching for an identifying mark "que li fes comprendre de cop el seu origen" (223) ["that would instantly reveal his origin"] she finds nothing "més que bellesa" (223) ["other than beauty"]. Therefore, her desire remains unmediated, since she is intrigued by the male object, unaware of its relation to others and ignorant of how he is perceived by other desiring subjects. The fact that his identity is a mystery serves to further the distance between Rafel and the Girardian triangle of desire.[7] Beatriu is unaware of his social, economic, and marital status, thus rendering his desirability purely physical. As a prostitute, she can never be considered a serious rival and compete with other women to realize her desire, but rather she simply appreciates his presence and beauty. Riera inverts the accepted hierarchy as the prostitute becomes the desiring subject, objectifying the male client, who in this instance is in a vulnerable position fleeing from the authorities, and she holds his fate in her hands.

The inversion of the "male gaze" involves not only sexual politics but economics as well. She waives his fee for her services but in exchange he is indebted to her for providing a hideout and a disguise for his escape. The female prostitute, normally at the mercy of men for economic survival and subservient to their sexual whims, now becomes the power broker. Riera describes extensively the way Beatriu gazes at Rafel's body: "Seguí contemplant-lo adormit, molta estona ... el mirà, primer a bocins, a poc a poc i de prim compte i tot seguit" (223) ["She continued admiring him for a long time as he slept ... she looked at him, first at each part, slowly, and then at his entire body all at once"]. This focus on the gaze, on the role of the subject to contemplate, define, and possess the object, places Beatriu in a position of power as she assumes sexual and moral superiority over "aquell al.lot" (222) ["that boy"]. She has exercised her will over him and, by not accepting money, she has established an emotional form of indebtedness. Thus through the language of the gaze, Riera deconstructs the sexual/gender hierarchy.

However, in contrast to Beatriu's triumphant plotting and the inversion of the gender power structure, the other women in the novel, the mothers, sisters, and wives, fall victim to harsh physical and mental abuse. Rafel Tarongí coerces his sister Isabel to leave her children behind and flee the island. She cries and trembles as the group heads toward the port to embark on what will be a failed escape. She releases her grip on her brother's arm and takes a few steps back, but "en Rafel no la deixa" (185) ["Rafael stops her"]. She has no choice but to continue on; her will is determined by Rafel, even though "[a] ca seva deixa dos infants, el que més estima" (185) ["at home she leaves two children that she loves more than anything"]. Isabel's lack of determination to stay with her children results from her inferior status within the family hierarchy. She is powerless to defy the wishes of her brother, who acts on her behalf.

Rafel's concern for his sister and her family becomes blurred and tainted by his condescending remarks. He tries to comfort her: "No et vull amb aquests ulls vermells i sa cara botargada. Estàs lletja, tu que passes per ser s'al.lota més preciosa des carrer ..." (186) ["I don't want to see you with those red eyes and that puffy face. You look ugly, you, the most beautiful girl in the neighborhood ..."]. Rafel's patronizing, avuncular tone dismisses any feelings or intellectual capacity that Isabel might exercise and trivializes her plight by focusing on her appearance. Her duty is to remain beautiful in the face of deserting her children and risking never seeing them again. The emphasis on the physical reduces Isabel to a contemplated object and the points of suspension that end Rafel's statement suggest that his comments lack a response. Riera invites the reader to imagine the response, and by using the points of suspension instead of a period to mark the end of the thought, the author introduces ambiguity and openness. There is no finality in what Rafel says; his reduction of his sister's feelings to her looks remains

Chapter One

to be judged by Isabel and by the reader. While Isabel, in this instance, does not suffer from physical violence, the emotional abuse and disregard for her desire to stay with her children manifests the powerlessness of women in the family social structure. The violence is against her self-esteem and capacity as a human being to determine her own fate. Riera points out that even in the hero's corner, even in the close-knit families of the *conversos*, the gross inequality between the sexes limits women's freedom and decision-making ability.

Isabel's beauty is not gratuitous in the novel. In fact, it is important that Isabel is labeled as the "most beautiful" woman, for she is the only woman to be burned alive. Her devotion to her religion and the implausible reality of leaving her children behind make her the emblematic sacrificial victim for women Jews, while her beauty makes her the perfect female sacrifice. Beauty figuratively is torched and burned in the most painful and ugly way, revealing the superficiality of the physical body. This is significant in that Riera chooses to end her novel with the burning of Gabriel Valls and Isabel Tarongí, the leader of the Jewish community and the epitome of feminine beauty. Riera has created in Isabel a physically beautiful character devoted to her faith, torn between her children and loyalty to her brother. The burning of Isabel is doubly symbolic and the sacrifice twofold: her death embodies the sacrifice that will maintain both religious and gender order.

Sara de les Olors falls victim to the same kind of persuasive techniques as Isabel. "Si acompanyà son pare a l'embarc fou per imposició d'aquest" (314) ["She only went with her father to the dock because he ordered her to do so"]. Sara is a visionary who patiently awaits a visit from the Virgin Mary while incarcerated. She represents the mystical side of religion, the side not associated with an ideology but rather a spontaneous somewhat schizophrenic yearning for redemption. Ironically, Sara confesses her devout Catholicism, but she is ultimately killed for accompanying her father. Her case is an example of the injustice and oppression of women within the family because Sara cannot speak for herself, and her allegiance to the Virgin Mary and Catholicism that would absolve her falls on deaf ears as she is immediately and inevitably linked to the patriarch. Her father speaks for her and acts for her, unfortunately to her detriment.

The inability of women to function independently of male influence paralyzes all of the female *criptojudías*; they are presented in the novel as the coerced, voiceless property of the men. Sara de les Olors ends up hanged "per visionària i endimoniada" (402) ["for being a visionary and possessed by the devil"]. Through these details, Riera sets up a double sacrificial rite for the women: they are sacrificed as Jews but also, and more so, as women. Sara is punished for her atypical relationship to Catholicism manifested in unconventional behavior.

The physical abuse of Maria Pomar reveals her disturbing relationship to Judaism and serves as a parallel to Sara's unconventional relationship to Catholicism. The Inquisitors put her squarely in the role of the surrogate victim, the one representative of her kind that will adequately pay for the "crimes" of her people. They ask her "Res heu fet? … Res, vols dir? Des de matar el Bon Jesús fins a voler fugir de Mallorca!" (311) ["You've done nothing? … You mean to say nothing? From killing Jesus Christ to trying to flee Mallorca!"]. Maria replies, "Jo no hi era quan l'enclavaren" (311) ["I wasn't there when they nailed him to the cross"]. Her answer emphasizes her innocence and disbelief in the violence that she must suffer in the name of her religion. She realizes here that the violence is indeed symbolic and does not result from a specific act she committed. The description of her dislocated arms and bruised body becomes more horrific when one of the priests comes to give her confession. She cannot respond "perquè Maria delirava" (312) ["because Maria was delirious"]. Beyond the physical abuse suffered at the hands of ecclesiastical men, the moral abuse of the failed confession reveals the multiple layers of violence in this scene, for both the physical body and the spiritual self are completely disregarded, denigrated, and then discarded.

Perhaps the most important scene in the novel in terms of the abuse of women as surrogate victims is the scene with the two Moorish slaves, Aixa and Laila. Lisa Vollendorf explains how this episode leads to the Viceroy's fall from grace and that "such representations of the individuals who occupied positions of power in early modern Majorca point to the process inherent in reconciling the past with the present" (160). The scene presents the Viceroy in a negative light and exposes his fear and weakness in the face of a "threatening" other. Riera creates an

Chapter One

alternative historical reality that strips the Viceroy of his historically sanctioned power and reveals another side to the class and gender hierarchy. Aixa and Laila represent what Girard calls the intruder or foreign presence that disturbs the status quo. These women are slaves in service to the Viceroy, yet they posses the power to control him sexually. Again, Riera redefines the role of the prostitute, just as she has done with the character Beatriu. The prostitute's power of seduction and her ability to gauge and provide pleasure for men is seen as a positive, empowering force. However, when this power becomes too apparent, violence intervenes to reestablish the patriarchal hierarchy. When the Viceroy cannot perform sexually despite the "esforços discilplinats" (277) ["disciplined efforts"] of the two prostitutes, he turns to violence. In a bizarre and frightening scene, he loses his mind, barks like a dog, and physically attacks the two girls, disfiguring one's breast and the other's clitoris. This scene becomes more disturbing when we discover that after the troubling events the Viceroy arranges for the kidnapping of the two girls, fearing they will talk and reveal his alarming behavior. Through his thought process we see him absolve himself of all responsibility for harming Aixa and Laila. As Viceroy and as a Christian, he considers himself absolutely just in his actions and comforts himself by thinking "On s'ha vist mai creure en la paraula de dues miserables esclaves mores ...?" (279) ["Where had he ever seen anyone believe the word of two miserable Moorish slave girls?"]. This violent act places Aixa and Laila in the dual position of foreigner and female, both scapegoats, both representing a threat to the Viceroy's idea of power and authority, so that the violence becomes a stylized ritual that purges his wrath against these two specific groups.

Riera's novel explores the complicated nature of ritual violence and the sacrifice of the Jews that maintains religious order in seventeenth-century Spain. However, she also incorporates carefully constructed female characters who in their roles as sacrificial victims attest to the complicated dynamic of gender order and patriarchy that operates in contemporary society as well. By challenging preconceived notions of the prostitute, of beauty, and of power, Riera uses sacred or ritual violence as a way to criticize religious, economic, and familial social structures. In this way *Dins el darrer blau* works on two distinct levels: one being the vindication of the *criptojudíos* of Mallorca and the other, a much more universal level, the undermining of institutions of power that sanction abuse against women in order to maintain gender inequality.

By creating a literary bridge between the past and present through her representations of history and culture, Riera manages to not only critique the past but also to point to the repercussions of history in the present. The narrative force of the novel advances the discourse of violence and injustice that contemporary society would rather leave behind in the seventeenth century. But by wielding the word and unveiling certain perspectives, Riera insists that the implications of the past can be readily seen in the present. The power structures of institutions that regulate gender hierarchies are as alive today as they were during the Inquisition. Using the Catholic Church as an example, Riera points to all kinds of social structures that repress women and other marginalized groups. Consecrated institutions such as family, marriage, and the monarchy fall under the critical microscope of historical revision, for these structures representative of culture also need to be revisited and reevaluated in the Nietzschean spirit. Only when cultural representations of family, for example, are presented from various viewpoints can the full history of the family structure be understood. This mainly comes from incorporating a woman's view into the generation of historical writings. As Hélène Cixous suggests, women must write themselves into history.

The relationship between violence, history, and redemption that incorporates questions of religion and gender in the novel represents the use of history as a way to express contemporary social concerns. In this sense history as cultural capital has a certain value and in revisiting the past with the present in mind the author can highlight and manipulate historical instances to draw connections to present circumstances. As in the novels by Chacón and Cercas, the past itself ceases to be important but rather its implications in the present make it a timely topic. The novels do not present corrected versions of history nor do they dispute what History has told us, but they bring to the present versions previously ignored, pushed aside, or simply forgotten. The postmodern tendency to decentralize and destabilize the speaking subject provides ample space in which to experiment with narrative voices. History is culture when it becomes a discourse circulated and promoted not as fact but as a narrative, which allows for interpretation. The interpretation of the Inquisition founded on Jewish perspectives and again from a female perspective presents history with a different cultural value. That is not to say that history becomes fantasy but rather the narrative qualities pointed out by Hayden White lend an element of invention that must permit the presence of other voices. What Riera and the other historical authors show is that delineations of historical narrative can be expanded to include feminine or feminist readings of history and that the distance between the present and the past is, at times, an arbitrary fabrication.

Dins el darrer blau is a cultural artifact in that the text repeatedly undergoes renewed analysis, just like any well-circulated work of literature. The boundaries disappear between history and fiction, the past and the present, as the novel comes to represent a contemporary reading of events of long ago. The compression of space and time may not seem evident at first as Riera makes every attempt to re-create language and customs of a bygone era, yet an analysis of the work reveals the timeless relationship between the written word and the culture it promotes. The literary becomes historical because it represents the culture of the seventeenth century as well as the interpretation of that culture by a twentieth-century audience. Vollendorf explains: "The novel powerfully argues that the alliance between writing and history must be found in a collective belief in the power of the written word to impact people's understanding of themselves as individuals and as members of communities" (164). Riera crosses the boundaries of history and fiction, thus proving them surmountable, and her work stands as a representation of the timeless cultural concerns of contemporary society.

Chapter Two

Reader/Text Solidarity in Decoding the Past in Carme Riera's *La meitat de l'ànima*

> We long to communicate, to establish contact with our readers, as if we were touching them with words so as to awaken or caress them.
>
> Carme Riera
> "An Ambition without Limits," *Moveable Margins*

Carme Riera's interest in vindicating the oppressed sectors of society through historical rewriting is clearly evident in her 1994 novel *Dins el darrer blau*. Nevertheless, throughout her literary career, the Mallorcan author has effectively evaded categorization and refused to be labeled as any one kind of contemporary writer. She deftly handles feminist narrative, the historical novel, the detective genre, and the epistolary novel, among others. Her novel *La meitat de l'ànima* [*The Soul's Other Half*] (2004) also deals with themes of history and vindication yet from a personal instead of national perspective. In this novel, the protagonist sets out on a literary search to find out the "truth" about her mother and consequently about her own identity. The linear concept of personal history becomes clouded through information presented in found documents. Riera steps beyond the idea of official and unofficial history in this novel as she proposes that even the most intimate and personal of all experiences may be invented through the power of language and writing. If we are to gain knowledge about ourselves by looking back at history and making space for the forgotten voices, then we must do the same in our personal histories as well.

With *La meitat de l'ànima*, Riera joins the ranks of authors writing in a self-conscious narrative mode that has come to define one of the current trends of literary production in Spain.

Chapter Two

Cercas and Chacón revisit the Spanish Civil War through narrative journeys that unearth hidden voices from the past while pursuing very specific contemporary agendas, as we will explore in subsequent chapters.[1] Cercas breaks down the distance between past and present by writing himself into the narrative as the main character trying to give voice to past injustices. Chacón inserts women's experience into the wartime picture, and her vision brings feminist implications to the forefront of historical writing and to larger notions of history and historical documentation. However, Riera steps back from Spain's particular history in order to articulate a much more intimate space in the text, a kind of textual self-consciousness. Riera highlights the constructedness of personal history that reflects the speculative nature of truth and of the past. Maryellen Bieder sees this revision of history as moving beyond the matter of national identity to embrace a more universal reassessment of the individual's relationship with culture: "much of Riera's fiction puts into play the constructedness not only of Catalan nationality but of language, gender and culture" ("Cultural" 55). However, by mingling the narrator's personal history with that of post–Spanish Civil War espionage, Riera seamlessly combines the national with the personal to create a mystery that ultimately goes unsolved yet reveals the importance of voicing, uncovering, and legitimizing unofficial histories. Her textual self-consciousness emerges in a pact of complicity with the reader as the narrator addresses the reader directly, begging for help and insight into her problems. She expects the reader to respond in the only way possible, by reading. Simply by telling the story, the truth will be revealed, and by implicitly inviting the reader into the textual space as another character in the novel, Riera creates her own model reader.

In a short essay that appears in the 1996 collection *Moveable Margins*, Riera writes: "I believe, as Umberto Eco assures us, it is the reader who truly completes the literary work with his or her active participation. In order that the heap of words that constitute a book have meaning, it is necessary that the reader confer meaning, something only he or she can do" (30–31). Nine years after writing this statement, Riera gives us a literary creation that embraces and celebrates the challenge of reading in *La meitat de l'ànima*. The "heap of words" that is the novel only derives meaning from a reader's perspective and, in this particular case, Riera relies on the idea of a model or ideal reader to finish the tale. Nevertheless, I argue that the backbone of this text is not the revelation of "truth" but rather the negotiation between text and reader that creates a unique solidarity, focusing on the role of the reader. As Eco has stated, the model reader and open text revolutionize the narrative and the way in which the reader approaches the text. I will explore the various ways in which Riera creates a pact between the reader and the text that privileges the discourse and minimizes the importance of truth and historical accuracy.

The narrative of *La meitat de l'ànima* centers on the mysterious life and death of the narrator's mother, Cecília Balaguer. The fact that our narrator is also a writer is important because it allows the reader to depend on and trust the skill of the narrator to tell the story. A writer is familiar with creating a convincing story with characters, plot, and resolution. The opening of the novel reads much like a mystery or detective novel as it plants certain questions of an unknown woman's identity firmly in the text and in the reader's mind. A mysterious woman is about to get off the train when the narrator jumps in and interrupts her own description of the scene: "Ignor si l'andana és buida o plena, i encara que la circumstància té interès—tant de bo hi hagués molta gent—me deman si paga la pena prendre el detall en consideració" (9) ["I don't know if the platform is full of people or empty and even though it is an interesting case—it would be great if there were a lot of people—I ask myself if it is worth it to consider such details"].[2] Thus, the reader is immediately confronted with the writer's inability to know the past. The text prepares us for the ambiguity of recalling past events and the powerlessness of words to reconstruct what is not known.

The narrative then jumps back in time to set up the circumstances that drive the narrator to investigate her past and take us along as complicit readers. Our narrator explains that she was busily attending to her duties at the annual Sant Jordi festival in Barcelona, signing copies of her books for interested readers. Suddenly a stranger hands her a folder and a business card. In the midst of the hustle and bustle of the crowd, our narrator throws away the business card, thinking this stranger has handed her a manuscript to read. Days later she sees the folder and looks at it only to discover that it contains a number of incriminating letters written by her own mother. She frantically tries to locate the stranger, cursing herself for so flippantly throwing away his card, and thus the action begins. Our narrator embarks on a search for the mysterious letter-bearer and, more importantly, to uncover the mystery of her mother's strange death in France, her love affair with noted writer Albert Camus, and her ties with the foreign opposition to Fascist Spain. The story pulls us into the narrator's childhood and into the exciting, exotic world of her mother's post–Civil War existence.

What we realize at the end of the novel is that none of the facts have checked out. We don't know anything more about the narrator's mother's death than we learned from the initial communication in the letters. We still don't know the identity of the mysterious man at the book fair who left the letters in the first place. However, what we do know is that "truth" is a perception and that there are multiple versions of history and of our own past. Melissa Stewart has pointed out the importance of the text as artifact in that "[t]he author/protagonist's attempt to restore her sense of self though this creation reminds us of the power of literary creation, which in this case seems to offer a path to certainties unavailable in either historical documents or contemporary reality" (236). One certainty presented in the text is the valuable role of the reader in the construction of the narrative. The value of the literary work lies in its ability to render multiple versions of the past and to present a critical view of "historical documentation or contemporary reality." In this sense the ambiguity surrounding the narrator's identity and her mother's past is the only certainty presented, as well as the catalyst for breaking down the narrator/reader barrier.

Our narrator pleads with us, the reader, to help her figure out the mystery surrounding her mother's death and possible involvement in espionage, yet the telling of her own journey to find out the truth of her mother's past leads her to understand the instability of language and the seduction of the written word. Before entering into a textual analysis of the novel, I will explore the theoretical approach that may help in understanding the relationship between the text and the reader through the ideas of an "open text" and the "model reader" set forth by Umberto Eco in *The Role of the Reader*.

Eco considers the text to be a kind of road map for the reader in that it does not dictate or tell a story, but rather it suggests meaning to the reader on both a conscious and subconscious level. Eco understands narrative as a dialogue between language and reader in terms of open and closed texts. The closed text is one that overtly guides the reader, leaving signals and putting up signposts that lead to a single conclusion (8). This is not to say that a closed text may not have multiple interpretations, but Eco insists that these are levels of reading. He gives the comic *Superman* as an example of a closed text, but in this highly symbolic mode we certainly can appreciate levels of interpretation. Such levels might include the superficial, action level; the allegorical interpretation of good and evil; and perhaps even a religious level that posits Superman as the only son of a man from Krypton sent down to earth to show humanity how to live an exemplary life helping others. In any case, the text does not allow for ambiguity, confusion, or mistrust of the narrative voice.

The open text, on the other hand, invites the reader in to find his or her own way. Eco gives *Finnegan's Wake* and *Ulysses*, both by James Joyce, as examples (9). In these cases the narrative requires the reader's active participation to engage in the text and find even the most basic level of signification. The reader must approach the text with some kind of literary knowledge in order to decipher allusions, symbols, and metaphor. This text is open in that it does not guide the reader through the language of the story but rather it insists on giving precedence to the way in which the story evolves, or, in other words, the discourse.[3] The structure and language become center stage, and the facts become secondary to the form. Another important idea presented by Eco that helps to better understand Riera's literary seduction of the model reader is *fabula*. Eco unpacks the act of reading by differentiating utterances and meaning, and he defines *fabula* as made up of the expectations and hypotheses the reader makes throughout the text. As the word suggests, it is a level of interpretation of the story where the reader explores certain possibilities and outcomes suggested in the text. This kind of extratextual reading or speculation on the part of the reader forms the core of the story in Riera's novel. However, Eco emphasizes that these are not random musings but rather educated guesses "elicited by discursive structures and foreseen by the whole textual strategy as indispensable components of the construction of the *fabula*" (32).

As the reader moves through the text, she imagines outcomes and possible ways that the story will develop given the information presented in the text. Bieder points out that Riera uses language to confuse or seduce the reader into (mis)understandings and (mis)readings, but that language is, at the same time, a "collaboration between author and reader" ("Paradox" 173). In this revisionary approach to writing and language seen also in *Dins el darrer blau*, the "text loses its authoritative dimension as a recorder of certain hidden or lost realities and instead becomes an idea, a process full of contradiction and friction" (Everly 163). However, this is not to suggest that the text is unclear or confusing in any way. The reader has just enough information to make educated guesses and invent possible narrative paths. In fact, the open text must adhere to a tightly organized structure that anticipates the model reader's tangential thoughts and then carefully reins her in without losing the thread of a cohesive story.

Given the dynamic interplay between text and reader, the open text relies less on facts to relate the story than on the structural elements to highlight the act of reading. Perhaps one of the best examples of this contrast is Julio Cortázar's *Rayuela*, which can be considered as both a closed and open text. If the reader chooses to read the first part of the novel in a linear way, then the story is about Horacio and his search for La Maga, or a love story about loss and isolation. However, if the reader chooses to "hopscotch" and after every chapter go to the indicated chapter in the second part of the book that includes extratextual information not intrinsic to the story but fundamental to the idea of the novel, then the text becomes open. It invites the reader to make the connections between seemingly unrelated topics. The reader must work harder to fill in the gaps and thus create meaning out of the "heap of words." Cortázar's novel is exemplary in that he was able to highlight the reader's participation physically with the actual turning of pages and jumping from the front to the back of the book. Theoretically this is the work of the model reader in Riera's novel as well. With the twists and turns of the plot, the reader must jump back and forth within the textual reality in order to piece together meaning.

The facts and data presented in Riera's text ironically do not provide the necessary information that will lead to concrete conclusions, but the reader must understand the larger implications of what is being told: namely, that history, identity, and writing are bound up in a literary exercise of self-realization. Therefore, in Riera's novel as in other open texts, it is not necessarily the plot elements that reveal the meaning but rather the work of the model reader constructing the larger picture.[4]

In *La meitat de l'ànima*, as in many of Riera's works, the letter is central in the formation of the discourse that invites the reader to speculate about the outcome of present and past events. The epistle is a document that overtly addresses a certain recipient while implicitly addressing the model reader. The use of the epistle in the novel is nothing new but in this case it not only functions to set up a conversation in which the reader must actively imagine the second part of the dialogue but also delineates a separation of time and space through documented experience. The letters the narrator receives from her mother through a mysterious stranger question the role of the epistle in that the eventual receptor is not the originally intended one. Thus the letter in this novel documents the mother's past experience and personal history, which conflict with the preconceived present reality of the narrator. The focus then shifts from the dialogue between writer and receptor to that of present and past. Therefore, the facts are not the important element of the letters, but the unreliability of history and discourse comes to the forefront as facts unveil only more doubts and confusion about the narrator and her mother's "true" identities.

The letter imagines and expects a response yet gives only one point of view. Riera exploits this imagined reader of letters and investigates what happens when the dialogue is cut off, when the communication achieves other ends than the one intended. In Riera's novel the letter is a document of the past; it is proof of some event or action that took place, but the relationship to the present remains unclear. We discover that it is not really the outcome of the events described that is important but the bridge between generations created by the maternal voice in the letter

Chapter Two

and the contemporary reading by her daughter. Thus, the text of the letter represents a connection between mother and daughter, past and present, regardless of what it says.

The letter presents only one perspective but includes in its form a receptor and anticipated reaction; therefore, the use of the epistolary mode in Riera's work anticipates Eco's ideas of the model reader. In Eco's words the model reader is "supposedly able to deal interpretatively with the expressions in the same way as the author deals generatively with them" (7). So, if the author constructs a narrative in anticipation of an analytical reaction from a reader who will understand the discourse employed, then we may be able to conclude that the author is indeed his or her own model reader. The construct of the author figure in the text, as in Cercas's *Soldados de Salamina*, exposes this intersection between author and model reader. Samuel Amago writes about the presence of the author and textual self-consciousness as he links this tendency to a postmodern aesthetic of metafiction. Yet he is careful to explain that the self-conscious "examination of narrative in fiction does not spell out the demise of the form"; that is to say, that the contemporary novel in Spain offers a "constructive alternative to the pessimistic worldviews articulated by the more negative critics of cultural postmodernism" (14). In addition, this self-consciousness that breaks down the barriers between implied author and reader can be considered a structural tool that not only demands that the reader take part in the creative process but also acknowledges the slippage between traditionally delineated concepts of author and reader. The presence of the author in any text seems to create a bridge between the implied author or the authorial voice in the text and the model reader: it makes us feel as if the author were talking directly to us, inviting us in, letting us know that the text was written specifically for us. The play between author and implied author is seductive in that it creates an intimate space for the reader: the presence of the author in the text as implied author suggests an ongoing consciousness on behalf of the author, a suggestion that is completely fantastic, for once the text is packaged, promoted, sold, and consumed, it exists outside the author's influence.

Riera neatly inverts the self-reflexivity of the text and turns it outward. She does not mention herself specifically in the text but instead addresses the reader directly. She acknowledges her model reader and asks for help with the mysterious case of her mother's death. We readers are accomplices from the very beginning in the creation of the text and in the re-creation of the past events it tries to decipher. Our narrator explicitly describes to us the process of decoding the text when she says, "no abandoni aquestes planes abans d'acabar-les, que arribi fins al final, no fos cas que vostè fos o tu fossis la persona que em pot conduir fins al que cerc, o la que em pot oferir la pista necessària per arribar-hi" (17) ["please do not abandon these pages before you finish them, get to the end just in case you are the person who can lead me to what I am looking for, or maybe offer me the necessary clue to find him"]. Here our narrator has acknowledged the familiarity between text and reader and changes her address to the informal "tu" form. She even gives us a way to contact her: "A l'editorial, l'adreça i el telèfon de la qual figuren vora els títols de crèdit d'aquest llibre, li diran, et diran, on pot trobar-me. Gràcies per endavant per l'ajut" (17). ["At the publisher, the address and telephone are next to the copyright information in the book, they will tell you where you can find me. Thank you in advance for your help"]. Should we readers call up Editorial Proa, ask for Riera, and tell her that we figured out who the character is in the novel? Obviously the offer to contact her is ironic, but this moment of our reality intruding into the pages of the novel links the narrative to the experience of the reader. We model readers understand her reasons for inviting us to call her up at the publisher's: we, narrator and reader, are a team in the textual experience.

The irony of the textual collaboration between reader and writer is indeed the fact that the text is already written. Riera nods in this direction when she alludes to the fictionality of the work by stating the opposite. "Els deman perdó per endavant. Però emprar noms ficticis, amagar fets o donar dades falses no tendria cap sentit" (16) ["I ask for your forgiveness in advance. But to use fictional names, hide facts or give false information would not make any sense"]. Despite our narrator assuring us that any intent to invent information or characters would not be logical, she does just that in the creation of the novel. In fact, the names are all fictitious, all of the facts are invented, and the story is completely made up. Riera insists on the verisimilitude of her story to give us a sense of the instability of language and the blurred lines between history and fiction. She claims to write a personal history of her mother and her search for the "truth" about her past. The mixing of the historical and the fictional is a literary tradition or trope that ultimately leads us to reconsider the very nature of history itself. Historical writing and, in fact, all writing, be it historical, political, or fiction, is the invention of one mind and one perspective, so inevitably something must be left out. By claiming ironically that nothing is left out of a fictional creation about the narrator's past, and that offering invented facts "no tendria cap sentit" when invention is really the only component of a fictional narrative, Riera implies that all writing is subjective and the "truth" can be as fantastic as fiction.

Nevertheless, the narrator never abandons the importance of the written word and, in this case, of the novel form itself. She admits that she is publishing this book as a last resort. Since she has been unable to find out the truth surrounding her mother's death in France, she turns to her public, to her readers, for help. In an explicit nod toward Eco's notion of the model reader, we are summoned by the narrator to read and help her decipher the codes that will help her to understand the past. She explains: "si el que estic escrivint finalment es publica ... voldrà dir que ja només depenc dels lectors per acabar de completar aquesta història, i en conseqüència que no em puc permetre el luxe de perdre'n cap" (22) ["if what I am writing is finally published that would mean that I have come to depend solely on my readers to complete the story, and consequently I cannot permit myself the luxury to lose even one"]. Once again, Riera confirms that there is always more than one version of the story and in her narrator's desperate attempt to know the truth, she is determined not to lose even one reader, even one interpretation of the text. This co-dependency established by the narrative voice between the reader and the text is typical of postmodern novelistic style but what is unique to Riera's brand is the solidarity implied against a larger evil. The loss of the past looms large in the novel as a threat to individual identity. If our narrator does not find out about her mother's last days, then her own sense of connection to the past is threatened. The reader must help the narrator understand who she is. This kind of inversion of the traditional reader/writer relationship points to a reconsideration of the novel genre. In a traditional Structuralist context, the reader is given signals and signposts that direct the reading and the interpretation. Even in Joyce's open texts the reader is free to wander about and engage in the language and malleable structure that the author has strategically put in place. But in Riera's highly philosophical inquiry into the nature of the model reader, the reader takes on extratextual importance as well. The reader is asked to pursue the narrative beyond the text in our hands. Once we have all of the information, we are to help the narrator piece together the puzzle, which we see at the end of the text is left completely unsolved.

At the end of the novel our narrator once again turns to the model reader, pleading for help, and says:

> No sé si també suposava que jo intentaria demanar-li a vostè l'ajut dels seus records, dels seus punts de vista per acabar de completar la història de Cecília Balaguer i la de mi mateixa, ni fins a quin punt aquestes planes només poden adquirir un sentit definitiu comptant amb la seva col.laboració. D'ella depenc, li ho puc, t'ho puc ben assegurar. (234)

> [I don't know if I assumed that I would have to ask for the help of your memories and your points of view to finish Cecília Balaguer's story, and my story as well, not even up to what point these pages would make sense only with your collaboration. Now I am counting on it, I can assure you of that.]

We also realize the parallel between Cecília and the narrator, as the text points out that both stories are unfinished and that our collaboration is necessary to complete them. In this final statement of purpose, the text confirms that the narrator cannot finish the novel herself and that the story is a point of departure for the less concrete reality of the relationship between reader and text. In any case, at the conclusion of the novel the reader is accepted into the text as an integral part of it, and the reading of the story becomes secondary to the discourse of how it is told and how the reader must play a part in that telling.

Another interesting aspect of the novel is the relationship posited between memory and identity. Through her investigation into the past, the narrator comes to realize that she does not know the identity of her biological father. Her mother had an affair in France with a man who may actually be her father, and with this doubt, all of the narrator's memories of her family come crashing down around her, leaving her in a deep depression. The trauma that the narrator experiences when she is stripped of her identity suggests the fragile nature of self, which is a postmodern notion of the fractured subject. Just as Julia Kristeva proposes the idea of a subject in process or more ominously "on trial," the narrator of Riera's novel finds herself undergoing a kind of psychotherapy instigated by the ideological "loss" of her mother and father.[5] The narrator retreats inward, avoiding social contact, and confesses at one point that she feels as if she is going crazy. Her decision to seek help from her ex-husband and go to a therapist proves fruitful in that she finds the means to recover from her broken sense of identity. Through sessions with la doctora Sender, the narrator comes to terms with her fears of her unknown and questionable origins. However, it is not necessarily the therapy that brings her to a higher level of self-knowledge but as she explains: "Les paraules em donaven vida, em servien de suport. Eren les crosses amb les quals aprenia altre cop a caminar perquè, fins i tot això, ho feia amb dificultat" (130) ["Words gave me life; they became a support system. They were the crutches that taught me to walk again albeit with great difficulty"]. The narrator refers here to her session with the therapist, but the narrative can be interpreted as metatextual. The outcome of this search into the past is the novel we hold in our hands, thus the words that "give life" refer to the text itself. The work of documenting the story and creating a textual relationship between writer and reader becomes the medicine that allows the subject to move on and survive the loss of a supposed stable identity.

The narrator claims during a conversation with her sister-in-law, Diana, that memory is necessary to identity. The positioning of Diana's past experience next to that of the narrator's brings to the forefront of the narrative several philosophical approaches to memory. Diana explains that forgetting is at times the only way to renew and reinvent the present. She shares her personal experience with the narrator in telling a horrible story about the torture and death of her parents at the hands of intruders in their home in Buenos Aires. Diana becomes emotional after telling the story, and the narrator apologizes for making her "reviure" ["relive"] the experience (169). The connection between words and reality becomes clear in this episode as Diana explains that to forget is to not articulate past events, and the narrator confirms this by recognizing the power of words to re-create events in the present. Therefore, memory does not reside in the past, as Diana seems to imply, but rather in the present and in the power of words to reconstruct not only images but emotions as well.

The narrator takes the opposite stance: she embraces the past and relies on memory to complete her sense of present identity. She claims: "Per a mi la memòria és imprescindible, sense memòria som morts. La memòria és l'ànima de les persones i tal vegada és per això que jo seguesc cercant la meitat de la meva ànima" (168) ["For me memory is fundamental. Without memory we are dead. Memory is a person's soul and perhaps that is why I continue to search for half of my soul"]. This analysis of memory and the past suggests that through verbalizing or writing the experiences of the past in the present, a sense of self takes shape. Therefore, it is not the past nor the memory per se that creates identity but the reiteration of the past in the present. In this sense the narrator is successful in her quest to find out who she is and to understand her mother's past, for even though the story is left open-ended, the discourse provides testimony to the importance of telling the story. The language that captures the past in the present provides a kind of virtual document that legitimizes the past. However, present reiterations of the past do not clarify or reveal a "truth" but concretize the importance of the writerly project to provide some version of past events. For Riera's narrator, the uncertainty and confusion about her past lead her to write a version of her personal history that serves as a catalyst for an intense re-evaluation of her current sense of identity. The "soul's other half" of the novel's title and to which the narrator alludes in her conversation with Diana can be considered the text itself. It is not the facts about her mother or the revealing of her true origins that will complete the narrator's identity but the words that "give life." The enigmatic relationship established between narrator and reader through the language of the text completes the character's identity and relies on the presence of the implied model reader to complement

Chapter Two

the opening up of the textual space demanded by the narrator's voice.

Stewart comments on the interplay between fact and fiction in "regard to the veracity of the text" (238) when the narrator claims it would be much easier to write if the "characters" were indeed mere creations of her imagination. The narrator claims: "Si Cecília Balaguer no fos la meva mare, si fos només la mare de la narradora d'aquest relat, si aquesta i jo no coincidíssim, també fora de l'àmbit d'aquestes planes, puc garantir-li que l'hauria fet més heroica" (222) ["If Cecília Balaguer were not my mother, if she were only the mother of this story's narrator, if she and I never coincided outside of these pages, I can guarantee you I would have made her more heroic"]. The impact of this statement lies in its absolute irony as an implicit homage to the power of literature. The implied author negates her role as creator of fiction, but given the context of the novel, we are forced to "play along" with the narrator's insistence that what she is telling us is "true." We must accept the terms of the narrative contract, and it falls to the model reader to fully understand the implications of the implied author's denying her authorship: that is the space and range of the literary work, to move beyond storytelling and into a reconstruction of narrative relationships between implied author, narrator, and reader.[6]

La meitat de l'ànima is a novel representative of the current trend in Spanish narrative of the self-reflexive text in which the author assumes a voice through an implied author, plays with the reader/writer relationship, and openly struggles with how the text should or should not be interpreted. Riera is unique, however, in that she does not focus on the role of the author in the text but rather on the role of the reader, and she proposes that the reader is the most important part of textual self-reflexivity. Following the ideas of Eco and the model reader, Riera actively constructs her ideal reader through metatextual discourse. The implied author directly addresses the reader, giving him or her the illusion of control in the text. The reader must find that solidarity with the text that allows for a flexibility of interpretation and the restructuring of past events. The end result is that the truth about the past events is all quite secondary to the act of reading and of engaging with the construction of the story.

Riera claims in the short essay "An Ambition without Limits" that while Eco has pointed out that "man is a fabulating animal," it is really "women who have best developed that faculty as compensation for the monotony of their existence, lacking any perspective other than that of the oppressive domestic world" (36–37). Once again Riera recognizes the importance of Eco's understanding of the reader, but she seems to suggest that if women are more adept at inventing a good story, then perhaps her model reader is a woman as well. However, Riera's comments that women may perhaps be better storytellers than men stem from her observations of socially constructed roles that separate men and women into private and public spheres of activity and have nothing to do with biological aptitudes. If Eco recognizes the crucial role of the reader in creating and sustaining literature, then Riera has effectively reconstructed the co-dependence of the implied author and model reader in her novel *La meitat de l'ànima*. Her obvious awareness of and interest in narratology is foregrounded in a novel that challenges traditional notions of reader and writer, as do all of the works in this study. Riera's novel stands apart in that not only is the relationship between reader and writer questioned but also cast as the main character in the novel. The story never comes to an end. We do not have answers at the end of the final chapter but we do find ourselves as readers completely involved in the process of the storytelling and beyond the page we remain responsible for finding the answers to the mystery. As the novel ends, the focus moves from the mysterious circumstances surrounding Cecília's death to the future investigation carried out by the reader. The model reader becomes the protagonist of the novel, thus completing the inversion of author, implied author, narrator, and reader.

This geometric construction of narrative and deconstruction of reading leads to a bigger question about the veracity of the written word. As we have seen in the alternate version(s) of History and history explored in Riera's novel *Dins el darrer blau*, the historical fabric of personal experience is cut and reshaped in *La meitat de l'ànima*. In both cases, the mode of presentation of past events eclipses the importance of the events themselves. Riera succeeds in luring the reader into the creation of the story

Chapter Two

while probing and testing the nature of narrative. Chacón and Cercas seem to experiment in much the same way with the narrative form. They also bring historicity to the foreground in a problematic way, questioning the nature of language and expression through the unconventional presence of the author in the text. In the following chapters the analyses of novels by Chacón and Cercas reveal different ways of representing history and reality in the novel: through the incorporation of historical documents juxtaposed with fiction and the unmediated presence of the author in the text that challenges ideas of authorship and ownership of the text.

Chapter Three

Women, Writing, and the Spanish Civil War in *La voz dormida* by Dulce Chacón

> Woman un-thinks the unifying, regulating history that homogenizes and channels forces, herding contradictions into a single battlefield. In woman, personal history blends together with the history of all women, as well as national and World history. As a militant, she is an integral part of all liberations.
>
> Hélène Cixous
"The Laugh of the Medusa"

Just as Carme Riera crosses narrative boundaries with her 1994 vindication of Mallorcan *criptojudíos* in *Dins el darrer blau* studied in Chapter 1, Dulce Chacón's *La voz dormida* (2002) reveals the unique experience of women during and after the Spanish Civil War. Chacón also subverts the narrative norm as does Riera in *La meitat de l'ànima,* but Chacón does it by artfully combining historical documents with narrative. Once again the relationship between the implied author and reader is reevaluated and revised. While Chacón does not explore extratextual narrative technique the way Riera does, her work brings new meanings to historical writing and reading history. Chacón's work is a novelistic eulogy to the unsung female heroes of the Spanish Civil War and at the same time it serves as a hybrid testimony of Spain's national memory. The novel relies on multiple layers of language as a means of cultural representation and expression, and the words that women use to reflect upon their wartime experience cross all types of boundaries. Their personal experience becomes public in the form of letters and official documents regarding their situations during the war. These expressions of experience become representational:

they are glaring evidence of the gaps that exist in the attempt to record history. The narrative discourse necessarily omits some events and perspectives in order to privilege others, revealing the transparent nature of language. In the novel, women's words are compared to and contrasted with the patriarchal, dominant discourse, resulting in the commingling of two distinct versions of the same event. José F. Colmeiro talks about the "hybridization of memories" in the novel that confronts the "combined legacies of patriarchal and Francoist discourses" (193). Through the echoes of various voices, the absolutism of history and the veracity of documentation come into question. The historical picture does not become clearer, but the details of disparate versions reveal that the "truth" of the events can never be known.

Nietzsche criticizes the kind of history that I consider here as "masculine," that is, recorded acts and dates that become "monumentalized." The events from the past that are constantly brought to mind in the present become aggrandized and mythologized and eventually overshadow less prominent voices. The circulation of the knowledge about specific events such as the bombing of Guernica in 1937 or the siege of Barcelona in 1939 nurtures a cultural value that exists independent from the event itself. The contemporary gaze, with its value judgment of the past that is selective by nature, tends to threaten other versions of these events and of history in general. The tendency to package history and understand it through isolated events leads to a situation in which "the past itself suffers *harm*: whole segments of it are forgotten, despised, and flow away in an uninterrupted colourless flood" (Nietzsche 71; italics in original).

Chacón's novel unearths the forgotten contributions of women during the war and the horrific treatment of women in Franco's jails. This untold story reveals the brutal and shameful legacy of the national conflict. Therefore the "masculine" mode of history that tends to monumentalize certain events is eclipsed in the novel through a distinctly female language that relies on hybridity and testimony.

The feminine discourse of history is difficult to describe because doing so now is an ideological attempt to fill in the blanks of an already recorded history of events. Nevertheless, through an evaluation of how language is used in the narrative, the possibilities of a feminist revision of history become clearer. The fictionalization of history in the form of a novel allows for greater creative insight and speculation concerning the "truth" of events and outcomes. This brand of historical criticism provides an opportunity for a variety of previously ignored or oppressed voices to be heard. The plurality of voices springs from differing sources such as oral testimony, private letters, and diary entries, all forms of writing that are considered feminine because they pertain primarily to the private sphere of the domestic space. Once these sources are incorporated into a historical discourse, the veracity of the past takes on different angles. Nietzsche warns "[s]uch a historiography would, however, be altogether contrary to the analytical and inartistic tendencies of our time, which would indeed declare it false" (96). Chacón's text integrates both types of historical information in order to avoid such criticism. The textual originality stems from comparisons of the same events in different types of documentation. Through this juxtaposition of official, masculine, state-sanctioned language with that of the more intimate letters and diaries of women, the text succeeds in transcending the notion of a complete, coherent history altogether.

The novel uses language in a two-fold way: it inserts women's experience into the official discourse of history and denounces the practice at the same time. Words can only represent a limited view of past events, or a version of history. But what the novel insists is that these multiple versions are endless and must be taken into account in order to move toward a more encompassing comprehension of the past. Despite the dismal setting, pending firing squads, and debilitating isolation of the Ventas prison in Madrid where much of the novel transpires, the power and necessity of female solidarity prove triumphant.[1] Chacón skillfully juxtaposes locations in the novel to highlight the sense of imprisonment even outside the Ventas walls. Women hiding out in the mountains with other militia also feel the very real constraints of political oppression as even the concept of freedom has been stained by war and is bound to a rifle. Yet, as Hélène Cixous has observed, the shared raw emotion provoked by war binds women together in a unique, historical way. Chacón's novel celebrates the role women play in the many versions of history, in the historical development of women's liberation, and in Spanish political and literary history.

As Cixous points out, woman "is an integral part of all liberations" (253). Her version of events is also an integral part of a larger sense of history. Women's suffering in the novel becomes a metaphor for the suffering of the nation and of all Spaniards. Unlike other novelistic accounts of women's experience of the Spanish Civil War—such as Mercè Rodoreda's *La plaça del Diamant*, for example—*La voz dormida* does not try to tell the other side of history, or the *her*story of war, but rather places women directly in the midst of the political and social activity of the time. Women not only bond together, but also bond with men for personal and political survival and to nurture a very weak and dying liberal Spain. Using imprisonment and death as a gender equalizer, Chacón weaves a complex tale of how women help each other overcome physical and emotional distress and support the Republican ideology even while in prison and isolated from loved ones.

Imprisonment, depression, starvation, and death did not discriminate between the sexes in the aftermath of the war. The text manages to bridge the personal and the political stylistically in the novel through different forms of the written word. One objective of this novel is to record history and not allow these women to fade into oblivion; therefore, the written documents include diaries, journals, letters, and dialogue that are complemented by official, state-issued documents, often typeset in a font resembling an "old-fashioned" typewriter. The inclusion of both personal and official documentation suggests a more complete picture of Spanish Civil War history.

History, in this novel, places the private, intimate letters and journals, a typically female form of expression, next to more traditional official documents. Chacón breaks the barrier between these traditionally masculine and feminine forms of writing by showing that the same content can be expressed in different forms. The language, style, and structure of the documents are very different, yet the information regarding prisoners' sentences, long-awaited prison releases, and political manifestations is the same. Virginia Trueba Mira describes the use of a typewriter font as "tipografía de época, como un modo de certificar la verdad de lo expresado" (314). The official-looking documents following dramatic scenes echo and confirm the personal histories in the novel establishing a symbiotic relationship between "masculine" and "feminine" language. While the government documents confirm the reality of the narrated events, the letters and personal testimonies correct and elucidate the stiff prose of official state records.

The novel combines both types of discourse: the officially historical and the historically personal. The novel as pure artifact defies genre because it uses narrative, poetry, and history as a means of creating a unique literary voice. *La voz dormida* is perhaps Chacón's most accomplished work and is a powerful testament to her dedication to unearthing the truth about women's wartime experience.[2] The four years she spent researching the novel and interviewing survivors of Franco's jails stand as evidence of her interest in how the individual lives of the women portrayed in the novel fit into and resist traditional historical accounts (Prat 9). In order to fully appreciate the importance of the novel in terms of historical significance, I will briefly consider the social and political changes women experienced during the Second Republic and Civil War.[3]

Women and Civil War in Spain

The highly visible role of women in the Second Republic and in the Spanish Civil War brought women's issues to the forefront of both private- and public-sphere politics. Women who held positions in the Parliament argued for and against female suffrage while women emerged from their homes to take on tasks at the front lines, in factories, and in civic life that were previously left to men. During the Second Republic divorce was legalized, feminist organizations flourished, and women won the right to vote (Mangini 24). "The Republican scenario was to prepare women—both visible women, who were serving in the public sector, and invisible women, who had previously never ventured out of their private domain—for the challenge of the civil war, turning them into public citizens of new dimensions and new identities" (24–25). However, critics have pointed out the dichotomies produced by this coming together of human and women's rights issues. "This debate involved a division between those who felt that women should postpone their demands until the war was won and those who believed the revolution to be meaningless as long as social inequality between the sexes continued to exist" (Asunción 293). Spanish feminism's political affiliations are clear from its inception and seem to be one of the problems stifling a full-fledged feminist movement in Spain. Women, both young and old, involved in politics and social change refuse to be called feminist because they consider the term hierarchical and anti-male (Ackelsberg 2). Some women were loyal primarily to a political party and only secondarily to the fight for women's rights. "[M]any anarchists treated the issue of women's subordination as, at best, secondary to the emancipation of workers, a problem that would be resolved 'on the morrow of the revolution'" (Ackelsberg 17). So while the Communist, Socialist, Marxist, and Stalinist parties held differing views on the economic future of Spain, women too were divided along party lines.

Granting women the right to vote proved to be arguably the most divisive legislation during the Second Republic. Margarita Nelken, an outspoken defender of women's rights, lobbied against female suffrage, claiming that women were not yet equal enough to vote. Spanish women, according to Nelken, were "silent, submissive, and essentially antifeminist" (Martínez-Gutiérrez 280) and were determined to uphold the convictions of their husbands and priests. Victoria Kent and Clara Campoamor, both lawyers and members of the Republican parliament, went head to head over the issue. Kent warned that women's lack of true autonomy would negatively affect their vote, while Campoamor demanded the equal right for women. The law was passed and women won the vote in Spain in 1931. The subsequent election proved Kent and Nelkin correct: the conservative party easily won the election.

Republican women were not the only ones in the public eye. Danièle Bussy Genevois points out the increased activity of right-wing supporters as well. She notes that women came out of their homes to rally against female suffrage, divorce laws, and abortion rights. Even if women were encouraged by men to organize, later they took the reigns of control themselves. Monarchist Rosa Urraca Pastor held fifty rallies in four months against the Republican government and, like all monarchists, condemned not only female but universal suffrage (Bussy Genevois 184). The Woman's Falange was founded not in 1939 after the Civil War when Franco gained full control, but in 1934, two years before the outbreak of war (Bussy Genevois 189). Thus, women with varying opinions and political interests made their voices heard during the years leading up to the conflict. Nevertheless, not only was all legislation repealed under Franco, but also women's voices were silenced and pushed back into the home.[4]

The changes for women during the tumultuous years before the war included a move to the public sphere and a public persona representing different aspects of political life in Spain. The involvement of women from all walks of political life cannot be underestimated, especially given the abrupt and brutal shift brought on by the Franco regime. Women had a voice and were given public space in which to argue, rally, and create a particular niche in the social fabric. For Chacón this is the sleeping voice that once was vibrant and loud and that needs to be restored and given its legitimate historical place.

Writing Women into History

The political nature of Spanish feminism is at the forefront of Chacón's novel, albeit at times in the form of disillusion with the freedoms promised by the Republic. The complex weave of the personal and the political forms the basis for the novel. Through intimate diary entries, testimonies, and official documents, Chacón presents a totalizing vision of the war and its devastating consequences. She insists on the power of female camaraderie as a motivating force behind the survival of both men and women during the long post-war years. In an effort to record this history, language with its tenuous relationship with the truth becomes crucial. Chacón makes very clear in her novel that language is a tool and meaning is slippery; nevertheless, it is the tool for writing women into history.

The difficulty of incorporating women's experience into official history using language becomes apparent when Hélène Cixous questions women's writing and talks "about *what it will do*" (245; italics in original), that is, what ends it will achieve. She struggles with the idea of history as a monolithic ideology that excludes women, yet she insists that women bring themselves to understand "their meaning in history" (245). This conflict of interests guides the notion of history in Chacón's novel

Chapter Three

as well. Woman must be included in the recounting of past events and taken into consideration in the study of cultural development, but how can she emerge from behind the shadow of male-centered discourse? How can she avoid always falling into the category of second in command, of the dedicated spouse or partner always working in support of phallic progress? Cixous's answer is to write. Her purpose is "to break up, to destroy, and to foresee the unforeseeable, to project" (245). *La voz dormida* is a text with that same ambition that combines historical fiction and pure fiction in an effort to retell a past that has to be reconsidered from a female viewpoint in order to move toward a notion of equality. The fusing of literary and non-literary language produces a unique experience for the reader; we are faced with several levels of reality within the novel. On one plane, the novel is a re-creation, a fictional account of real people and events based on years of research and interviews with women who experienced first-hand the circumstances in the Ventas prison. Secondly, Chacón intersperses official-looking documents that proclaim in a detached, emotionless way the events that unfold in the novel. The two versions of history collide, thus creating a fuller, more detailed picture of that particular time in Spain and of historical writing in general.

Understanding women's place in historical events becomes tantamount to understanding the reality of postwar Spain. Chacón indeed does break up traditional modes of storytelling and historical writing in order to project an inclusive version of history that places women at the forefront of politics and war. She is not relegated to the home front but, as one of the characters in the novel, Elvira, she participates in the action: "la niña se ha puesto los mismos cojones que el hermano" (Chacón 285). The following examples of parallel representations of events through traditionally feminine modes of writing and then through traditionally masculine modes of official discourse show the nature of Chacón's project to vindicate the experience of women and place them beside the men who fought and suffered as well.

The novel describes the historic assassination of thirteen young women in the Ventas jail. Las Trece Rosas were marched out of the chapel, across the patio, and loaded onto vans to be taken to their deaths. The text describes the scene as witnessed by another character who peers though a window of the prison: "Salieron de la capilla de dos en dos, sin humillar la cabeza ... Algunas cantaban, Julita Conesa siempre cantaba" (198). A letter written by Julia Conesa on August 5, 1939, appears after this narrative account in the novel. It is the last in a series of letters the young woman wrote to her mother and in it she says: "Besos a todas, que ni tú ni mis compañeras lloréis. Que mi nombre no se borre en la historia" (199). The relationship between the larger concept of an ongoing history that will remember Julia and the intimate form of the epistle, addressed not to her comrades but to her mother, clearly integrates the personal and the political. The layering of female and generational perspectives in the letter creates a matrilineal connection between the words and the events. Julia relies on her mother to tell her story, confident that the female voice is strong enough to maintain a place for it in the cacophony of history. This mingling of the real and fiction becomes even more acute when we realize that the letter is in fact a document that exists. Julia Conesa, a political prisoner in Ventas prison, wrote the letter, word for word as it appears in Chacón's novel, and was executed along with the other twelve women of the Trece Rosas. The letter is reproduced in Fernanda Romeu Alfaro's study in a facsimile of the original, which was written in pencil on worn paper (285). Chacón does not reveal to her reader that this letter is a document she found, but she does thank Romeu in the acknowledgements "porque hizo posible que yo tuviera en mi casa las cartas originales de Julita Conesa" (386). The handwritten words of the "real" letter reprinted in Romeo's study cross the textual boundaries and infuse Chacón's episode with a humanity that forces the reader to see the person behind the words. In the reprinting of the letter, which first appeared alone in Romeo's book in its original form and then in a dramatic context in Chacón's novel, Julia's wishes are fulfilled. Her name has not been erased from history but moves through an intertextual discourse that draws from historical document, fact, and fiction.

Most of the characters in the novel are based on real people, and Chacón gratefully acknowledges them in the epilogue to her book. Through her tireless efforts and research she has produced a novel that documents women's reality. Chacón was not the first person to do so; however, she did bring attention to the plethora of literature about Spanish women's condition through her writerly skill and established fame as a published author. Many other books exist that tell the story of women in the Ventas jail.[5] The testimonies and narratives create an intertextual flow of characters and events so that the reader becomes familiar with the plight of the Trece Rosas and the unflinching camaraderie that held these women together. At times it is difficult to read the horrific descriptions of children dying in the prison, of hunger, and of torture. One particularly graphic account published in Paris in 1967 by Mercedes Núñez recounts torture methods used in the Ventas jail. She describes how the authorities tortured older women, beat pregnant women so they would miscarry, and used genital mutilation to humiliate prisoners (39–40). The stark, journalistic narrative of Núñez's personal account haunts the imagination in its effort to reconstruct the horrors of the Ventas prison.

The authors of these testimonies and novels are, in most cases, women with minimal education and minimal experience in the craft of narrative. Dolores Media's novel, for example, is heavy with political jargon and names of regiments and generals. Sara Berenguer admits in her introduction, "Mi léxico será restringido y, a bien seguro, carente de estilo. Sólo fui a la escuela hasta los doce años" (11). Therefore, Chacón takes this body of information with these vibrant, brave women at the front and writes a dramatic history that incorporates their words and experiences in a stylistically accomplished historical novel.[6]

As a counterpoint to the incorporation of Julia Conesa's letter in the novel, Chacón describes the execution of another prisoner, Hortensia Rodríguez García, whose name "no consta en el registro de fusilados del día seis de marzo de mil novecientos cuarenta y uno. Pero cuentan que aquella madrugada, Hortensia miró de frente al piquete, como todos. —¡Viva la República!" (220). Without the proof of a real letter written by the victim, in this case, Chacón creates a moment around one of the main characters, thus giving all of the "undocumented" women a voice. Hortensia is jailed while pregnant with her daughter and spends her pregnancy knowing that she will be killed once the child is born. Chacón opens the novel with the declaration "La mujer que iba a morir se llamaba Hortensia," (13) immediately naming and thus identifying the character. With this bold affirmation, Chacón metaphorically names all of the women that died in the prisons and in battle, for we know that it was not just one woman but many who suffered and died during and after the war.

Photography also serves as a universalizing form of language in that one woman becomes representative of many. The narrative describes a popular photo of a *miliciana* that has been published elsewhere and serves as the cover of the Alfaguara 2002 edition of *La voz dormida*.[7] A young, smiling militia woman gazes straight into the camera as she holds a laughing baby. Chacón reinvents this woman's identity as Hortensia holding someone else's baby. The woman's dangling earrings that seem a bit out of place considering her military garb and rifle become a focal point in Chacón's narrative. Mateo, Hortensia's husband, gave her the earrings as a gift and she wore them all the time as the photo proves; even when dressed in her uniform, rifle slung across her back, she has them on. As Hortensia prepares for the delivery of her child she prepares a packet of things for the authorities to give to her sister, Paquita, who will take care of the baby. In this bundle she has hidden some things for the baby: her notebooks full of writings and the earrings (220). The appropriation of certain details from the photograph for narrative purposes is yet another example of how the novel crosses genre boundaries. The photograph tells a story of women in the militia, and Chacón furthers her literary agenda by naming the woman and giving her a multidimensional personality. The image evokes its own narrative, suggesting the bittersweet success of this woman as she clearly plans to participate actively in the Republican cause but must, of course, leave her child behind. The triumphant moment captured in the photo, for both the woman and child are smiling broadly, incites a conflict of reason and emotion. The photograph promises that the woman and child were "real" and not invented but the drama surrounding the mother/child bond is purely speculative. The discourse of war becomes the discourse of women at war, and the photograph becomes less a document than a narrative tool for creating a certain historical moment. Just as Julia's letter brings a touch of reality to the novel, the interpretation of the photograph lends historicity to a fictional rendering of the events.

Chapter Three

Another document that Hortensia hides in the packet for her daughter is her sentencing. The document appears in the novel juxtaposed with the dramatic moment of her death. She cries "¡Viva la República!" and after she is shot "dicen, y es cierto, que una mujer se acercó a los caídos y se arrodilló junto a Hortensia ... Y le cerró los ojos. Y le lavó la cara" (220). The narrative device of creating and propagating an oral testimony of the event by using "dicen, y es cierto" gives the episode a legendary tone. This implies that many people have talked about the execution for "they" have told and retold the events. More importantly, our narrator assures us that the testimony of the witnesses is true, "es cierto." The legitimacy of an oral tradition confirms the truth of un-documented events. We need not rely on official documents to relate past realities. Nevertheless, the official document sentencing Hortensia to death immediately follows this scene. The jarringly different font from a typewriter notifies the reader that the information is official, outside of the women's narrative reality, yet historical. The change of font suggests not only a different tone but also a different time and space. The typewritten document and official language are a stark contrast to Hortensia's valiant and poignant narrative death. For example, the parallel moment of Hortensia's death in the official document reads: "condenamos a la procesada, como autora del delito de ADHESIÓN A LA REBELIÓN, con las agravantes de trascendencia y peligrosidad, a la pena de MUERTE y accesorias legales correspondientes, para caso de indulto, debiendo ser ejecutada la procesada por FUSILAMIENTO" (222). The lack of emotion, the capitalized words that seem to jump off the page in a shout, and the convoluted sentence structure provide a completely opposite rendering of Hortensia's death. In this way, the novel presents two different versions of the same event. The linguistic and stylistic contrasts force the reader to piece together a new reality and question the role of official documentation, testimony, and oral tradition. In this case, the death sentence document confirms the facts while the personal observations and word-of-mouth testimony give Hortensia's death a unique, individual, and human element.

Another document in the novel that joins the human with the political officially declares the formation of the militant political party hiding out in the mountains. Through the use of official language and structure, the unofficial and outlawed become legitimate in the eyes of the writers. Chacón takes us out of the prison and into the public, masculine sphere of action. We follow the character Elvira as she manages to escape from the Ventas prison and joins her brother and other militia members in the Cerro Umbría. This movement symbolizes a permeation of boundaries, for Elvira moves from the enclosed all-female space of the prison to the male-dominated, active space of the war. Susan Sontag has observed that war, in general, is a masculine phenomenon. Quoting Virginia Woolf's *Three Guineas,* she points out that men are responsible for warfare and that as Woolf describes, men find "some glory, some necessity, some satisfaction in fighting" (3). While Sontag seems to agree in part to the masculinity of war, she poses this question in order to reevaluate the need to gender social phenomena. Elvira has to prove to the men in the novel that women do have a place in the mountains and on the front lines. The link between the women in the Ventas prison and the few women hiding out in the mountains is their dedication to the cause, but despite their conviction, women still have to fight to define their place during and after the war.

While it is Elvira who literally escapes prison, Hortensia's presence, through her absence, dominates the narrative in the mountains. Hortensia's husband, Mateo, seeks Elvira's company just to hear her talk about his wife.[8] The dramatic link between the tragic events in the prison and the constant fear of death in the mountains brings a commonality to men and women's experience during and after the war. Mateo "no le gustaba que las mujeres estuvieran en el monte" (260), but he tolerates Elvira because she helped deliver Hortensia's baby. The emotional connection he feels to Elvira as one of the last people to be with Hortensia emphasizes the difficulty of family separation and loss during wartime. Even though Mateo does not trust women in combat and only is impressed when a woman can "manejar las armas como un hombre" (260), the tenderness with which he remembers Hortensia (Tensi, he calls her) adds an emotional nuance to the novel. Men are killed on the front lines, while women are killed in the jails, and both suffer the consequences of loss. Chacón breaks through the gender barriers by attributing the emotion of memory and loss to an outwardly stoic male.

Chapter Three

Mateo talks to Elvira at length about Hortensia and eventually has to leave her presence "para ocultar el llanto" (294).

In contrast to the emotional suffering of both men and women, the declaration of political intent seems to justify the sacrifices of those loyal to the Republic. The creation of the "Agrupación Guerrillera de Cerro Umbría" appears as a separate, typewritten document in the novel declaring that all present "bajo la dirección estratégia de la Junta Suprema de Unión Nacional Española, que dota al pueblo español de una dirección nacional de combate antifranquista por la salvación de España" (289). The terse language rings of authority in its detached declaration of intent. The contrast with Mateo's emotional outpouring is notable and creates a unique sense of fluidity between feminine and masculine forms of communication. The pain and isolation Mateo feels upon losing his wife is channeled into his political convictions.

Following the document declaring the unification of the guerillas, Chacón writes "La Agrupación la componían sesenta y dos guerrilleros. Uno de ellos era Elvira" (289). She then jumps into a conversation between Elvira and her brother: "¿Cómo estás, chiqueta? —Yo estoy bien, no toso ni siquiera cuando corro" (289). The jump from the official to the easy, family chatter brings the reader back to the narrative present. Words such as "chiqueta" and the preoccupation with Elvira's health give the reader insight into the close sibling relationship. The result of this sequence both in content and in structure is a mixing of two distinct types of discourse. The document juxtaposed with the conversation jolts the reader out of a particular comfort zone where we know what to expect and who is speaking. In this case the male writers of the document—Mateo, Jaime, and El Tordo—also exhibit more traditionally female nurturing characteristics. And on a narrative level the jump from the formal tone of the declaration to the conversation breaks with conventional modes of storytelling. Just as Hortensia's death sentence becomes more brutal when read in the detached tone of the state, the failure of the rebels in Cerro Umbría to defeat fascism becomes more devastating given their record of stated determination.

After officially declaring their position as an organized group, the rebel hideout is ambushed by the Guardia Civil.

Mateo is at the river away from the camp and when he sees himself surrounded by the enemy he fires his pistol in a final act of solidarity to warn the others. His act saves lives yet he is another casualty in the ongoing Civil War conflict. Six men and one woman are killed in the mountains, and the police photographs of the cadavers are displayed in the shop windows of a nearby town. The grotesque display attracts viewers who are questioned by the suspicious police, for any association with the rebels is grounds for arrest. Sontag analyzes the power of war photographs that "turn an event or a person into something that can be possessed" (81). In this case, the authorities appropriate death in order to display their persistence and to discourage further subversive activity. The male and female cadavers are symbolic to the extent that they are nameless and represent the equalizing nature of death. They also represent hope in that they affirm that some rebels escaped and are still active in the mountains. The photographs convey the impossibility of separating the personal from the political because they represent a selected moment deemed important by the photographer.

As Sontag points out, every photo frames the action or subject, thus leaving something out. Reme, a woman released from prison, takes a train to the town in order to check whether the woman in the photo is her friend Elvira. She breathes a sigh of relief and repeats, "No es Elvira, No es Elvira," while her husband lifts his eyes in horror as he recognizes his friend's daughter (306). The photographs' ability to reconstruct the events of the ambush leads to a more universal interpretation of how the images construct memory. Just as Chacón chose to narrate the story of the young woman in the photograph on the cover of her novel, Sontag points out that these photographs can only selectively represent history: "collective memory is not remembering but stipulating that a certain image or event is important while another is not" (86). What is framed in the picture necessarily excludes some information, and therefore photography is as representational as writing. The image evokes a mental narrative and the viewer must reconstruct events that led up to the photographed moment. In this way writing and photography elicit a response from the reader/viewer. The gaps in the written text between official language and narrative prose require the reader to make the connections between official and

Chapter Three

personal history. The image framed by the edges of the photograph works in much the same way, as the viewer must create a situation that leads to a comprehensive interpretation of the image. In this way both written and visual narrative represent only a partial history and reveal that language and photography confirm through their limits that we will never know what really happened and that truth does not exist. In the case of the photos of the dead rebels in the novel, truth ceases to be an issue. Identity, family, and voice all fall into oblivion, because the purpose of the photos is to officially comment on the progress of Franco's government to suppress the outlaws. By reminding us of the scare tactics used by the police and of the manipulation of the image for official purposes, the photos emphasize the importance of the larger project that is the novel that gives voice to previously silenced history.[9]

In opposition to the public display of cadavers, clandestine notes and personal letters also play a role in the novel and emphasize the importance of communication. The photographs displayed in the store window exemplify the official government's attitude toward the struggling Republican forces, while the innovation and cunning of the Republicans prove their will to survive. Pepita, Hortensia's sister, plays a key role in moving secret correspondence between liberal sectors. She has contacts both inside and outside of the prison and is able to gather information from a number of sources. For example, she deliberately goes to the Ventas prison on a visiting day not to see her sister or other inmates but to question her boyfriend's grandfather. She knows he will be there visiting a family member and thus seizes the opportunity to quietly ask if he has any information. Although they both seek information about Jaime, neither knows his whereabouts.

Despite the fruitless outcome, Pepita's refusal to sit and wait for information about Jaime leads her to action. Before she decides to go to the jail looking for Jaime's grandfather, she expresses disillusion and resentment at the ideals of a political party that is falling apart:

> Y yo aquí, esperando meses y meses porque el dichoso Partido le viene diciendo a usted que me tengo que estar quietecita y que tenga paciencia. Pues ya se me ha acabado la paciencia. Y mire lo que le digo, señora Celia, no crea usted

> todo lo que le dice el Partido, que si fuera verdad que los aliados van a entrar pronto para echar a Franco, no estarían todos tan escondidos. (234)

Pepita counters the official party line that has encouraged the defeated forces to wait for help with a cry for action. Her impatience forces the reality of the Spanish condition to light. We readers know that the Allied forces will not come to the aid of Spain even when Hitler is defeated. Speaking out of fear and rage, Pepita laments her own situation but also the situation of all Spaniards: "Estamos más muertos que vivos. Estamos todos muertos. Y solos. Estamos solos" (234). She equates loneliness with death symbolizing the interior death of love and sentiment the wartime separation produces. The uncertainty surrounding Jaime's location and survival push Pepita to the limits of political solidarity. Thus, for Pepita the personal and the political clash in an effort to understand the sacrifice and death required by political idealism. While Mateo fights to hide his emotions, Pepita finds the strength to finally let hers out. Her diatribe against the party that has taken Jaime from her stands as a testament to the voice of those left behind. She represents the voice of frustration and disappointment of the women forced into silence by their own political party to protect the men in hiding. This imposed inaction leads Pepita to action and she determinedly goes to the Ventas prison in search of information about Jaime.

Earlier in the novel Pepita serves as a messenger for the Republican Party, delivering clandestine messages that would implicate her and lead to her execution. This kind of risk and living in constant fear lead Pepita to denounce the Party and speak out against the sacrifices that she and her family have made in the name of political solidarity. Nevertheless, the events surrounding Pepita's clandestine communications provoke an ironic twist in the role of documents in the novel. When Jaime first disappears, Pepita receives a letter from him postmarked Toulouse, France where he is in exile. She delights and savors the letter, reading it several times. Unfortunately, the authorities show up at her door a few days later and take her in for questioning. Before the questioning begins, however, Pepita faints. She cannot be of any help to the police, so instead they make fun of her weakness, using sexual innuendoes, but she is eventually

Chapter Three

released. In this case, the invention of a new identity saves both Jaime, formerly Paulino, and Pepita. He wrote the letter using his "new" name, Jaime Alcántara, and describes their dates and relationship in a code that only Pepita can understand. In this sense, when personal letters become public, the false identity saves the author and alters the meaning of the document. The movement from a private literary space, represented by the letter, to a public space of humiliation and reprimand alters the value of the correspondence and shows how fragile and dangerous language can be.

While the letter from Jaime could have seriously implicated Pepita, her previous experience as a messenger for the party placed her in more serious danger. She becomes involved somewhat innocently when she promises Paulino/Jaime that she will take a message to a mutual friend, Doctor Fernando. She must ask the doctor to help Felipe, who has been badly wounded in the mountains and needs medical assistance. Pepita dutifully goes to Don Fernando's house to relay the message, and the doctor's astonished reaction and tentative response frighten her. She seeks some form of assurance when she tells the doctor outright what Jaime had promised: "… también me lo ha dicho, señorito, que usted no va a denunciarme" (93). Pepita is overcome with anxiety and emotion when she arrives home at the pension and sees her landlady, Doña Celia. "[L]e cuesta respirar. Descubrirá que le cuesta mantenerse en pie y mirarla de frente" (85). The rush of adrenaline and inability to think straight or even focus seem to threaten Pepita's capacity to go through with her assignment. Of course in this instance the message is not physically documented, but the fear of capture and torture loom large. Even though there is no physical evidence to implicate the players, the knowledge itself is dangerous. Don Fernando does not report Pepita, and he does help the rebels on the run, saving Felipe's life.

A comparison of the episodes involving Pepita's and Jaime's correspondence shows once again that the mingling of personal and political revolves around documents. The letter provides a personal insight into their relationship yet avoids implicating them both by using a false name. Documentation, in this sense, reveals the danger of recorded history instead of the necessity to restore lost voices. The letter represents the fabrication of reality manifested in documents, for even personal letters at times must lie in order to preserve life. In contrast to Julia Conesa's heartfelt, revealing letters or the blue notebook Hortensia leaves to her daughter, the letter from Jaime stands as a testament to the troublesome connection between personal correspondence and political affiliation. Pepita's verbal message for the doctor goes one step further to demonstrate the necessity to avoid documentation at all costs. The messenger becomes the document, at once valuable and vulnerable if caught by opposing forces. While a letter may be encrypted and undecipherable, a person can be persuaded to speak. Looking back to some of the horrific descriptions of torture in the women's memoirs mentioned earlier, one has to wonder how many political prisoners have been tortured to death with their secrets intact.

Jaime Alcántara's prison release papers are another example of how an official document fails to represent the human side of events. Jaime spent seventeen years in a Burgos jail, and Pepita loyally traveled from Madrid on the one annual visiting day. When it finally becomes clear, in 1963, that certain political prisoners will be released, Pepita begins to make arrangements for the wedding. She hears the news in the BOE (Boletín Oficial del Estado) that the government will grant amnesty to certain prisoners and she begins planning their future together. After the civil marriage ceremony in Madrid, the couple walks "por la calle Atocha" (374). The specificity of Calle Atocha in Madrid highlights the changes and progress of Madrid from thirty years earlier, when bombing and gunfire swept the city. The novel ends on this note of hope and renewal, drawing the city into the scene as another character that has survived the tragedy of war. The simple ending reads like a poem: "Pepita mira a Jaime. Y Jaime no deja de mirarla. Llueve. Fue larga, aquella tormenta de verano" (374).

On the following page of the novel, the word "Instrucciones" appears in a different font, indicating an abrupt change in tone. What follows is detailed information on Jaime's conditional liberty that instruct him to go directly to the address he gave the police and that he must stay there "hasta que se le conceda la libertad definitiva si observa buena conducta" (375). At this point in the narrative, the official jargon sounds trite and patronizing given the years Jaime has suffered in jail. To create

Chapter Three

categories and levels of liberty for a man leaving jail for the first time in so many years demonstrates the controlling state force and lack of humanity. Jaime's spiritual and emotional freedom can best be expressed through the few words and poetic form of the narrative previously cited that describes how he and Pepita walk through the streets of Madrid. The official papers confirm his release and state openly the control the government will exercise on his life, but they cannot match the impact of the small, intimate moment shared with Pepita. Perhaps the final lines of the document have the greatest impact: "Burgos, a veinte de julio de mil novecientos sesenta y tres" (376). The passage of time recorded in the instructions letter is almost unbelievable. Not only does it record the lost years of Jaime's (and Pepita's) life but also it solidifies the fact that in the 1960s Spanish authorities still adhered to Fascist doctrine and upheld decades-old prejudices against political opposition. As Chacón has noted: "el horror debió haber acabado al finalizar la guerra y no fue así" (Velázquez 3). Chacón chooses to end the novel with this information in order to underline the lack of social and political development during Franco's reign.

Nevertheless, the novel ends on a positive note with Jaime's release and marriage to Pepita. After the devastation, death, and loss that drive most of the previous narrative, this quiet moment at the end of the novel brings a sense of peace and closure. Chacón includes a short paragraph at the end of the narrative and before the acknowledgments that firmly grounds the story in reality. She separately thanks Pepita for her contributions to the story and adds that Jaime died in 1976 in Córdoba. She explains that the authorities would visit their house every year on May 1 to assure that Jaime had no intentions of participating in an annual political demonstration. They arrived ironically on the day after Jaime's death, and Pepita led them to his body and told them that now they could take him away (281). This poignant moment provides an example of peaceful death in contrast to the torture and suffering in prison but also serves an important structural purpose in the novel. By bringing the characters out of the fictional reality and placing them squarely in this biographical anecdote, the author once again decidedly crosses the genre boundaries of fiction and fact. This short epilogue that stands outside of the fictional space but relates intimately to it attests to the nebulous nature of historical writing in general. We have been reading a fictional account of real people's lives mixed in with created characters and invented situations. Chacón proves that the real, the remembered, and the speculative all contribute to forming a complete story, a whole picture of how things were.

In the longer list of acknowledgements that appears at the end of the book, Chacón reveals her sources. She thanks the many people she interviewed and mentions the women who have authored testimonies and studies of the war and specifically of the Ventas jail. This tribute to other texts and other voices augments a truly intertextual and cross-disciplinary project. For Chacón, her voice is not the only or official representation of the female experience during those difficult decades in Spain. She purposefully includes the voices and testimonies of many other women and she explains: "Lo que he buscado es la memoria colectiva, sobre todo de las mujeres, pero también de los hombres, que perdieron la guerra y que fueron represaliadas" (Crespo n.pag.). In this way, her work is not creative fiction but a unique hybrid of testimony, documentation, and extrapolation that encourages other voices, all voices, to play a part and be heard in Spain's collective memory.

Language in *La voz dormida* pushes issues of personal and collective memory to the forefront of the narrative discourse. Julia Conesa's letter, Hortensia's death sentence, Jaime's documented "libertad vigilada," all represent specific events told in multiple versions highlighting the impossibility of ever knowing the "truth" of those days during and after the Spanish Civil War. Instead of separating language into "fact" and "fiction," Chacón has mixed private and state discourses in one historical novel that points toward the fusion of individual and collective memory. The stark contrast between the individual, narrative recollections and the state-issued documents referring to the same events suggests that personal and national memory can be in conflict and, perhaps more importantly, that all versions of past events must be taken into account in order to understand what constitutes our notion of history. Photography as a selective art omits information that lies beyond the camera frame just as language implies another silence. By weaving together the personal and the state-sanctioned language, the novel points to

Chapter Three

that which is left out. The contrast in language suggests confusion and error and this becomes an integral part of the novel's purpose, which is to unearth the silences, the omissions, and the constructedness of history. The feminine voice of the novel contributes to our understanding of the Spanish Civil War and of historical language in general. Through words and writing about the traditionally masculine space of war, Dulce Chacón succeeds in creating a novelistic project that challenges notions of history and memory. She has woken the sleeping voice of women's experience during and after the war but also of absolute notions of history and documentation.

Chapter Four

The Impossible Invention of History and the Hero in Javier Cercas's *Soldados de Salamina* and *La velocidad de la luz*

> Escribir consiste, entre otras cosas, en fabricarse una identidad, un rostro que al mismo tiempo es y no es el nuestro, igual que una máscara.
>
> Javier Cercas
> *Relatos reales*

In the prologue to *Relatos reales*, a collection of essays written for Barcelona's edition of *El País*, Javier Cercas comments on the idea of his preferred genre, the "relato real." Following the literary footsteps of great Spanish writers, Cercas reinvents the idea of genre in his attempt to fuse historical facts and fiction. Not unlike Unamuno and the "nívola" or Cervantes's literary experimentation with genre in *Don Quijote*, Cercas investigates and exploits the tension between reality, truth, and literary invention and insists that every story is somehow tied to reality but that the idea of a "true" story is inconceivable because inevitably it contains some amount of invention. He claims: "es imposible transcribir verbalmente la realidad sin traicionarla" (*Relatos* 16). What does it mean for a writer to betray reality or history? Or is it perhaps the unreliable tool of language that makes it impossible to remain faithful to fact? In the previous chapters we have seen how Carme Riera and Dulce Chacón rewrite historical versions of truth in order to include a marginalized, forgotten voice. These specific literary projects incorporate alternative versions of history in an attempt to present a more complete understanding of the past and of how we relate to the past in the present while pointing to the narrative quality of historical discourse in general.

Cercas also proposes an innovative approach to retelling historical events. In his novel *Soldados de Salamina* (2001), he abandons notions of historicity, clearly favoring the fictionalization of character, plot, and even author. In *La velocidad de la luz* (2005), Cercas steps back from Spanish history and turns his focus to North American history and the Vietnam War, yet maintains in the narrative the problematic relationship that exists between contemporary notions of history and the "truth."[1] While *Velocidad* is less about events from the war, the narrator struggles with similar literary demons such as the definition of a hero and the necessity to record events that breathe life into the past. In this chapter, I explore Cercas's presence in the novels as the implied author aware of his role as creator of the story and of history. This analysis will bring us back to Nietzsche and argue that the narrative "I" of the text and ultimately the text itself is a manifestation of the progress brought on by historical forgetfulness.

Nietzsche's concept of the function of history in social progress relies on a balance of remembering and forgetting that allows societies to learn from the past and at the same time move forward and progress as civilizations that avoid repeating past errors.[2] The tendency to demonize or aggrandize past heroics leads to "monumentalizing" the past and thus leaves the present and future unattended. Progress and advancement of any kind become truncated and eventually stagnant when society becomes obsessed with glorifying past achievements and grieving past failures. The ability and necessity to forget and consequently to move away from monumentalizing the past lead to a healthy critique of historical events. A detached mode of thinking that allows an analysis of the past calls forth an active questioning not only of events but also of historical discourses that link the past to the present. Nietzsche writes: *"there is a degree of sleeplessness, of rumination, of the historical sense, which is harmful and ultimately fatal to the living thing, whether this living thing be a man or a people or a culture"* (62; italics in original). He observes that to live is to forget, and to appreciate the present and look toward the future requires a letting go of the importance of the veracity of past events. War presents an especially controversial issue because there is inevitably divisiveness in perspective—winners and losers—but never a clear-cut, historically sanctioned right and wrong.

Nevertheless, for Nietzsche as well as for Cercas, any moralizing about the unfolding of past events or in the relating of these events stands in the way of productivity. As David Richter points out, "memory mediates the stories and histories in *Soldados de Salamina* and foregrounds the ambiguity between the fictive and the historical" (286). In a similar way the sudden suicide of Rodney Faulk's character in *La velocidad* suggests a disconnect between appearances and "reality" in that the event emphasizes the inability to enter the mind, thoughts, and memories of someone else. The impossibility of truly understanding another's experience runs parallel to the impossibility of ever truly knowing the past. The ambiguity drives the narrative as the reader becomes an accomplice in sleuthing and piecing together incidental information.

In a step beyond Riera's seemingly autobiographical narrative, *La meitat de l'ànima*, in which the author invents a suspiciously familiar version of herself as narrator in an attempt to establish empathy with the reader, Cercas uses his own name in *Soldados de Salamina*, revealing the importance of the writer in the pages of the text. The narrator Cercas becomes the alter ego or mask of identity for the writer of the novel. However, this move to consolidate identities of real author with the implied author and narrator only serves to augment the ambiguity of the narration. Readers enter willingly into the fabrication of reality inherent in the literary text and are aware that the author remains outside of the text and the fictional world the novel traditionally provides. The mixing of fact and fiction in a novelistic account bridges the gap between "reality" and literature and presents a shift in the focus of the writing. Not only does the narrative voice become stained with the implied author's presence but also the plot tends to fall to the sidelines and the unraveling of the writing process takes precedence. Alexis Grohmann describes this tendency in Spanish letters as narrative that develops from diversions or tangents instead of from traditional plot elements (298). The structure of the novel or how the novel is pieced together from various perspectives, diversions, and versions leads to a different understanding of storytelling. Instead of excluding elements for the sake of clarity, multiple perspectives and versions are introduced into a

Chapter Four

sometimes-chaotic rendition that ultimately sacrifices accuracy for inclusiveness. This is precisely what Chacón achieves in *La voz dormida* as studied in the previous chapter and what Cercas exploits even further in his novel.

Cercas does not shy away from the past but instead brings the art of forgetting to the forefront of his text. His contemporaries of the Generation X literary movement scarcely mention politics let alone the Spanish Civil War, and this form of forgetting or ignoring clearly paves the way for alternative literary discourses to emerge such as those apparent in their novels: sexuality, gender identity, addiction, and identity crisis.[3] Cercas, on the other hand, embraces the act of forgetting in a stylistic and structural way that highlights the ability of the novel to effectively generate multiple versions of history and "reality." Cercas takes a concrete event of the Spanish Civil War—the killing of Fascist soldiers at the hands of a Republican army firing squad on January 30, 1939, at Santa Maria del Collell—and creates a mystery surrounding what really happened.

Ana Luengo and Antonio Gómez take issue with Cercas's rewriting the past and softening the brutal violence of the Spanish Civil War by pointing out the obvious political implications of glossing over painful collective memory. The result is "un proceso idealizador que recrea un pasado mítico" (Gómez 126). These and other critics have written about the novel's interest in resurrecting a hero: Sánchez Mazas or Miralles. Gómez explains at length Sánchez Mazas's position within the Falange as a "fetiche" and "un nuevo héroe para el nuevo estado" (116). Others posit Miralles as the hero (Yushimito) or the invention of a more ideological mythology of heroism (Spires). Robert Spires writes, "De hecho, es justamente lo inventado lo que presta valor transcendente a la obra, lo que convierte un caso un tanto melodramático e inusitado en una contemplación existencial sobre la vida humana" ("Historia" 80). José V. Saval looks at the structure of the novel and the many parallels between characters and themes that Cercas incorporates in the novel: "el autor se valdrá de una estructura realmente innovadora y de una serie de paralelismos y simetrías que formarán el complejo andamiaje de la acción" (63). Samuel Amago also sees the novel as a self-reflexive exercise that proposes a historical truth that can be accessed "through the dynamic processes of writing history in the present" (149). All of these critics recognize the constructedness of history and character in the novel that in a sense disregards the larger historical context in favor of melodrama.

In my opinion, *Soldados de Salamina* proposes an alternative reading of the Civil War in that it does not reconstruct events from the war but rather deconstructs how we, contemporary readers, interpret and think about the events and outcomes of war. The narrator and main character is Javier Cercas, a writer struggling with his ability to narrate as he questions his own talent and contribution to the profession. In order for the writer to regain his sense of craft, he delves into the past, thinking that history may serve as a more stable ground for invention. The novel takes us on a journey through the eyes of a writer trying to regain his narrative voice, and the Spanish Civil War provides the historical event that allows him to write again. Therefore, I argue, that the novel is not really about what happened during those moments at Santa Maria del Collell in 1939, nor is it about the benevolence of a Republican soldier or about the fate of poet Sánchez Mazas, but it is a metanarrative on the art of writing. The novel becomes a playground for historical observation, interpretation, and revelation. In the end, the mystery remains unsolved, but we have the novel in our hands that explains the journey of a writer into the past and proposes that the fictionalization of history leads to deeper understanding of our own time and of ourselves.

Booth affirms that when we read first-person narration in a novel, "we are conscious of an experiencing mind whose views of the experience will come between us and the event" (152). The testimonial value of the "I" in fiction sends a predetermined signal of personal investment through the narrator. The story is first and foremost worth telling, and the narrator feels a sense of privilege to tell it. Nevertheless, the author himself is distanced from the implied author, or the persona created to tell the story through the first-person narrator, in terms of his moral, intellectual, and temporal situation. Even though our narrator of *Soldados de Salamina* is Javier Cercas, it is not the author Javier Cercas, but rather a construction of the author that lends veracity to the story. In Cercas's case the writer has a distinct relationship to other characters in the novel, for he is both a literary subject and object. The novel is about the writing process,

Chapter Four

and our narrator retraces his steps guiding us to the grand finale that is the production of a work of literature. As with all first-person narrators, the reliability of only one point of view poses a dilemma for the reader. Can we trust this one perspective? Is our narrator sufficiently prepared to give us an accurate account, and what has he chosen to exclude?

The reliable commentary lies not in the veracity of events in the text but rather in the ability of the writer to invent an intriguing story. In the opening sentence we collide with the narrator's attitude and unreliability when he claims, "yo habiá abandonado mi carrera de escritor. Miento" (17). Of course he never abandoned his writing career or we would not be reading his novel, and the frank admission of his lie attests to the power of the narrator to mold and form the tone of the text. We readers suspect from the outset that we are dealing with an unreliable narrator who is conscientious about his duty to tell a good story. He goes on to explain that he cannot abandon a career that never really took off but then gives the publication date of his first novel. The narration plays games with the reader, pulling us in and at the same time convincing us that our narrator/writer cannot be trusted. However, the false humility creates a sympathetic reader and capitalizes on the manipulations of the literary trope.

In a later scene Cercas meets a local historian, Miquel Aguirre, who is also intrigued by the events of 1939. Our narrator's lack of writerly confidence takes the form of a subtle joke that seems to go unnoticed by his lunch companion. Aguirre has contacted Cercas after reading his piece in the newspaper on the anniversary of Antonio Machado's death in which he mentions Sánchez Mazas's escape from the firing squad in Collell. The two agree to meet for lunch to discuss the episode, and during the meal Aguirre mentions that he recognized Cercas from the picture on the back of the dust jacket of his first novel, which he had read some time ago. Cercas replies "¿Ah, fuiste tú?" implying that only one person, Aguirre, had read his first novel. The self-deprecating jab does little to impress Aguirre, who replies "no entiendo," and our narrator quickly changes the subject. This short scene may seem just a moment of levity or an insight into the insecure nature of the writer, but given the tone of the narrative and the unreliability of the first-person narrator, this short exchange reveals the uncertainty the writer feels toward his own work and the hostile relationship he has with his own writing. Thus, once again we readers are faced with unfamiliar territory, as our writer/narrator seems to undercut his own abilities to produce a valuable work. The end result of this short exchange is to once again highlight the struggle our narrator confronts as he tries to tell a story encased in history. The facts are never clear, and his role as the storyteller becomes nebulous as he searches for the story he wants to tell as opposed to the "truth" that he thinks exists.

Cercas's text, much like Chacón's, incorporates diary pages and samples of extratextual material in order to give the novel a documentary value. To a much lesser extent, Cercas reaches out to a historical presence, hoping to rectify common misunderstandings and give voice to the forgotten and silenced. Chacón achieves this by distancing herself from the narrative and highlighting the autobiographies and letters of women who suffered in Franco's jails. Cercas as narrator, on the other hand, steps in and tries to interpret these texts for us, showing us how the writer tries to understand cryptic messages from the past. The two documents that I will look at in the following section are the article that attracts the attention of Miguel Aguirre written by our fictional Cercas about the death of Antonio Machado and the facsimile of a diary page reproduced on page 58 of the Tusquets edition of *Soldados de Salamina*. As the reader gains a more complete understanding of the use of and creation of documents within the larger text, the role of the writer becomes clearer and the progress toward historical "truth" is revealed. I will analyze the third and final section of the novel that leaves our narrator's questions about those events in Collell unanswered, but gives us insight into the creation of history and the impossibility of achieving truth. Nevertheless, in the spirit of Nietzschean progress, the cultural implications of the questioning of historical events and the problematic recording of history do in fact result in a better understanding of our own circumstances and regardless of what "really" happened, speculation on what may have happened allows us to move on and let go.

Cercas uses documentation in the novel to reiterate the importance of the written word. Writing is used as a tool against forgetting even when the memory produced is less than accurate.

Chapter Four

Progress, in Cercas's terms, is not so much an appreciation of the past as a foraging of its contents that mixes up binary terms like good/bad, Nationalist/Republican, or winners/losers. As David Richter points out, "*Soldados de Salamina* disintegrates the Aristotelian distinction between fiction and history in favor of the mediation of memory, a sort of factual subjectivity that is based in a third space: what *may have* happened" (287; italics in original). Once this area of speculation becomes central to historical discourse, as it does in the other novels studied in the first part of this book, then monolithic ideas about the past and present are discarded for a more inclusive discourse. History, in this sense, provides the foundation for concepts of present national identity, and only when the historical discourse becomes less exclusionary will the cultural sense of identity open up to allow for a more diversified notion of what "nation" means.

In the short article that appears in the novel, supposedly written by our narrator on the anniversary of Antonio Machado's death, the scene is set for what will develop throughout the rest of the narrative. The piece is titled "Un secreto esencial" and refers to the mystery and ambiguity that belies historical truth. The narrator advises us that this piece "es esencial para esta historia" and so it appears "reproduced" in the main text. This article serves several purposes within the structure of the novel: first it functions as a "found document" or a piece that supposedly exists outside of the narrative reality because it was published first elsewhere. Also the article affirms the author's success as a writer and his ability to publish in a well-known periodical, thus contradicting his aforementioned lack of confidence, or perhaps it indicates the unsteady and volatile nature of the profession. In any case, the Machado article is not really about Antonio Machado, just as the novel in our hands is not really about Sánchez Mazas and his execution.

The article mentions Machado's flight from Spain to France in 1938 accompanied by his mother and then digresses to a more philosophical contemplation about the randomness of political affiliation. The article compares Antonio to his brother, Manuel, who supported the Fascists, and suggests: "[e]s razonable suponer que, de haber estado en Madrid, Manuel hubiera sido fiel a la República" (25). The author of the article also suggests that perhaps Antonio would have abandoned his leftist ideas had he settled in Burgos, a zone that supported the rebellion against the Republican government. The narrator then transitions to the events of Rafael Sánchez Mazas's failed execution that forces him to hide out in the woods for several days. However, right after the few prisoners escape from the firing squad and we follow Sánchez Mazas as he is hiding, cowering in the bushes, a young Republican soldier sees him. Instead of handing him over to his superiors, he shouts that no one is around, thus granting Sánchez Mazas his freedom and his life. The seemingly random nature of the Machado brothers' political affiliations is echoed in this larger-than-life moment in which all faith in humanity is placed in the hands of one young soldier. Political affiliation aside, the compassion of the soldier as he looks Sánchez Mazas squarely in the eyes proves that underneath the uniforms and badges that show allegiance to an ideology, we are all simply human. In the article the narrator suggests that perhaps if we can speculate about how Manuel Machado felt about his brother who died in exile then we can speculate about this fleeting moment and split-second decision between a Fascist and a Republican and understand the essential secret of humanity.

Although Cercas's article about Machado may smack of sentimentality, the role this text plays in the structure of the novel adds to the intriguing nature of the narrative. This short piece lays the groundwork for our narrator's complete submersion into the world of those woods in 1939. The possibility that through historical investigation the writer may uncover a small part of history that in essence is more literary than "real" drives the narrative on. Instead of upholding the notion of two sides at war driven to kill each other at any cost and given that Sánchez Mazas was a very important figure in the Fascist party and the Republican soldier probably knew who he was, the act of peace in a time of war seems completely idealistic and unconventional. It is precisely this rendering of history, this uncommon occurrence that lights the spark in the writer's mind and pushes him on to find out if this really did happen and if that same Republican soldier is still living to verify the facts. Therefore, the historical information is much less important than the possibility of a good story.

The fact that the piece was published and circulated to the public is essential to the novel as well, for it is one response he receives about the article that spurs him on in his search for

Chapter Four

answers. The historian already mentioned, Miquel Aguirre, writes to Cercas, telling him about some of the people that helped Sánchez Mazas while he was hiding out in the woods and about another text recounting the same event. It is the interest of a historian that leads our narrator to consider writing a book about Sánchez Mazas. The marriage of history, represented by Aguirre, and literature, represented by Cercas, creates a document that appears as the second chapter of the novel and combines the mystery and suspense of fiction with the names and places of traditional historical writing.

Another key found in the article on Machado that alludes to the larger literary project that is the novel lies in the expressed distinction of histories. When the narrator has finished telling about Antonio's escape from Spain and his untimely death in France, he describes how the other Machado brother went to Collioure, the small village where Antonio and his mother had died, to pay his respects. The narrator continues: "Pero la historia—por lo menos la historia que hoy quiero contar—tampoco acaba aquí" (25), and he goes on to tell the story of Collell and Sánchez Mazas. This transition from Machado's depressing end and the emphasis on the divisive results the war had on his family leads to the speculative scene between Sánchez Mazas and the Republican soldier that at once suggests a solidarity between enemies and a closing of the large political chasm between countrymen and brothers. The narrator suggests that perhaps the story of Sánchez Mazas and the young soldier who saved his life gives hope to salvage some form of humanity from the Civil War that tore apart families and brothers like the Machados. This reconsideration of national history fits neatly with Nietzsche's ideas of leaving specific details behind for the good of mankind and heading toward a progress that allows for speculation and fabrication in the understanding of historical events. The newspaper article that guarantees a certain emotional distance from the subject because of the journalistic quality of the writing fits into the novel as a found document that affirms the facts and veracity of the event but allows the narrator to extrapolate on the theme and include a more personal, thoughtful approach to the relationship between past events. By incorporating a "document," the newspaper article, in the body

History and the Hero

of a fiction novel, the levels of reality multiply within the text. Even if the document is invented, the appearance of material that supposedly exists outside of the narrative reality creates a playful confusion about what is real and what is not. And, of course, this is the basis of the entire novel, the search for "truth" that ultimately turns out to be futile.

Another example of a found document that links the past to the present is found on page 58 of the Tusquets edition of *Soldados de Salamina,* where a facsimile of a diary page appears within the narrative text. Curiously there is no mention of the authenticity of this diary page, but it represents the importance of a found document that provides crucial information in the text of the novel. The presence of this page reprinted in the novel stands as undeniable evidence that the story is "true." Jordi Gracia explains: "la novela reproduce la fotografía de una página del diario de Sánchez Mazas para añadir exactitud documental a un relato que, sin embargo, no deja de tener su origen en la transmisión oral de padre a hijo y a un grupo amplio de amigos que se lo oyeron contar" (248). Gracia sees the inherent orality of the book as one of its primary focuses, as opposed to any historical aspects of the war or of Sánchez Mazas's biography. Therefore, the photograph of the diary page seems to appear as an official document giving historical credence to the events related in the story, but when considered in the context of the whole novelistic project, the diary page becomes more of a testament to the many ways in which history is recorded. The facts are sparse and do not contribute new information to the text, but the form reveals a man's need to write down and document his experience for fear of being lost and never found and never heard, much as do the letters reproduced in Chacón's *La voz dormida*.

The page is from Sánchez Mazas's diary, which he kept while hiding in the woods after escaping the firing squad in Collell. The diary entry appears on the page of the novel as a photographic reproduction, and the shaky handwriting scrawled across the page suggests someone writing under stress. The narrator comments on the difficulty he has deciphering the handwriting but reprints the information for the reader. On the page preceding the facsimile of the letter, we read its contents:

Chapter Four

> ... instalado casa bosque—Comida—dormir pajar— Paso soldados.
> 3– Casa bosque—Conversación viejo—No se atreve a tenerme en casa—Bosque—Fabricación refugio.
> 4. Caída de Gerona— Conversación junta al fuego con los fugitivos— El viejo me trata mejor que la señora.
> 5– Día de espera— Continúo refugio— Cañones.
> 6– Encuentro en el bosque con los tres muchachos— Noche— Vigilancia [*palabra ilegible*] al refugio— Voladura de puentes— Los rojos se van.
> 7– Encuentro de mañana con los tres muchachos— almuerzo medianamente de la cocina de los amigos. (57)

The diary ends here but the names of the friends appear at the end. What is notable about this diary entry is the lack of detail and reflection characteristic of personal writing. Instead this diary entry records only the bare minimum of essential details, simply marking the survival of the writer another day in the woods. The stiff, jilted prose suggests a man struggling with survival and jotting down the days to simply mark their passing. As the diary entries end, the three boys he met on the sixth day have become "los amigos," affirming that he has found trustworthy company and consequentially his need to record the days ceases. In this sense, the diary does not serve as a way to express Sánchez Mazas's perspective on the events but simply indicates that by writing down words on a page, his experience is bearable. By recording what very little happened, he confirms that he is still alive. Therefore it is not what is written down in the diary but rather the fact that a document exists at all that proves he made it through another day in hiding. This small example within the novel reflects the larger literary project as well, for even if the historical novel we read does not prove or disprove any accepted facts about the war, it does offer perspective on the events and suggests that the recording of any perspective, as long as it is recorded, is a valuable tool to understanding contemporary repercussions of historical events. Just as Sánchez Mazas had to write down something about his survival in the woods to justify his existence, the novel that does not answer every question about the chance meeting in the woods between a Fascist and a Republican justifies the realm of possibility, the area of what *may have* happened (Richter 287).

History and the Hero

After reading this disjointed description of Sánchez Mazas's days in the woods, we turn the page and are confronted with the facsimile version of this very same diary page. The jolt into "reality" forces the reader to accept the historical quality of the information because the diary written in Sánchez Mazas's own hand attests to the veracity of that moment in the woods. Just as in Chacón's novel *La voz dormida,* the intermingling of fictional narrative and "fact" provided by a facsimile reproduction of an authentic piece of material is a literal mixing of the two genres. This literal transgression in the novel prompts another philosophical inquiry into the nature of the novel itself as well as into the documentation of events through personal diary entries. Sandwiched between a complex narrative structure that plays with the exact kind of trust the reader places on historical "fact" and documentation, the reproduction of the diary page becomes transformed into a somewhat problematic entity. The reader stops in her tracks and asks, "Did Cercas the author create this fake diary page just to trick us into believing his story? Is this really Sánchez Mazas's handwriting?" However, the novelistic implications of including outside material that corresponds to a fictional setting provides insight into the renovation of the novel as genre that Cercas proposes.

Cercas's narrator unearths the facts about a certain historical event and continuously runs into contradictions, roadblocks, and uncertainty. The narrator's quest to write the story of a hero that doesn't exist parallels the author's struggle with the novelistic form. The narrator writes a version of history that is the second chapter of the book but, as he declares later, "el labor no era malo, sino insuficiente, … le falta una pieza" (144). The missing piece, he decides, is the identity of the Republican soldier that let Sánchez Mazas go free. He needs to identify the hero in order to give the traditional novelistic form a more definite conclusion. His efforts to locate this man constitute the third part of the novel, but the search for the hero is only a backdrop for the writer's quest to complete the perfect novel. Just as the hero does not exist, the perfect novel does not exist either. The narrative leads us to question history, and through the inclusion of the diary page, we question the recording of history and how these personal documents augment or confuse more "official" versions. But more so, the narrative turns on itself and

Chapter Four

poses the question of the form and function of narrative: can a novel really be a historical novel? Can history be anything other than just another story? It seems that the narrative journey of the novel leads us to an unsatisfying conclusion about the events in Collell but offers tremendous insight into the nature of writing and thinking about the past. Ana Luengo writes about the link between the past and present in the novel: "la perspectiva de un soldado republicano capaz de perdonar a un fascista [es] lo que se espera precisamente de una novela comprometida en el año 2001" (252). Her analysis of the novel questions the need to see a positive side of the war, and she suggests that this is perhaps a way to soften the reality and ease very real political tensions (251). Nevertheless, in this way, the novel elevates history from a study of facts to an intellectual exercise on our reception and interpretation of them, thus leading to progress, or a development of how we consider the repercussions of the past on our present-day situation.

    The third part of Cercas's novel, titled "Cita en Stockton," joins together the historical background of the first two parts of the novel with the invention of a living hero. Our narrator Cercas feels compelled to find the Republican soldier that let Sánchez Mazas live and recognize his courage and humanity in the face of war. Cercas conducts a series of interviews with the Colombian writer Roberto Bolaño, who tells him of a man he knew from his days working at a camping site in Castelledefells.[4] This man had served in Lister's troop during the war, the same troop stationed at Collell at the time of Sánchez Mazas's failed execution. Cercas embarks on a desperate search to find this unknown hero, this man named Miralles, and after relentless searching and several setbacks he does find Miralles living in a retirement home in Dijon, France. But, as the text points out repeatedly in this third part, the search for a historical truth inevitably gives way to speculation, and perhaps the most valuable understanding of the past lies in its invention. Thus, the function of the historical fiction writer is to record perspectives that provide room for interpretation. Through Bolaño's comments, Cercas's encounter with Miralles, and finally the narrator/writer's own assessment of his literary project, we gain access to the progress or life that Nietzsche suggests is inherent in a fictionalization of history.

History and the Hero

The title of the third part of *Soldados de Salamina* refers to the film *Fat City,* in which two boxers promise each other to reunite in the town of Stockton. After seeing the film while at the campsite, Bolaño shared a running joke with Miralles that echoed the sentiment from the film: whenever they parted ways, they would shout "see you in Stockton!" While this anecdote shows the friendship that developed between Bolaño and Miralles, it also suggests the importance of imaginary spaces in which the characters define themselves in the text. Stockton appears in the film as a place of encounter; this imaginary locale that promises a future for the characters in the film serves as a mythological meeting space for the characters in the novel. Thus the concept "Stockton" is doubly mythified in the novel, once in the film itself and another in Bolaño and Miralles's idealization of a future meeting place that of course only exists in the realm of cinematic fantasy.

As the characters project their hopes to a future meeting in another time and space, the text points to the meeting of Cercas and Miralles as the culmination of not only the novel at hand but also of all the history that has come before. The narrative pushes forward and hinges on the possibility of finding the hero and eventually publishing the book that Cercas has envisioned. He has spent so much time and effort unearthing the facts about Sánchez Mazas, the execution in Collell, the friends in the woods, and the young Republican soldier that the end goal of the narrative does not revolve around finding the true hero but rather around creating the desired ending for the story. However, in this third part, speculation takes over, and the long-awaited conversation between Cercas and Miralles skirts around the issues of the war and focuses on the more abstract concepts of heroism and death.

The text suggests early on that the meeting between Cercas and Miralles will create the ending of the novel in question. Bolaño, a published and respected writer, acknowledges the importance of a good story when he says, "todos los buenos relatos son relatos reales" but he adds that even if Miralles is not the person Cercas hopes he is, it does not matter to the story. The art of writing something "real" depends on the fabrication of a good story. Cercas interrupts his friend because he guesses that Bolaño will suggest "si no es él, te inventas que es él,"

Chapter Four

which is exactly what happens in the end of the novel. Without the proof he needs, Cercas creates a heroic figure that will give his novel the appropriate ending and in doing so he interprets history, imagining what might have happened. Even when he asks Miralles point blank if he was the soldier who let Sánchez Mazas go and Miralles answers "No" (205), Cercas refuses to give up the imaginary vision of what happened because the novel at this point is less about what happened at Collell than about the writer creating a story. In this case a re-reading of history does not demand that the facts check out or that there be proof but it is offered as another version, perhaps a lost version of what may have happened. Riera recuperates a lost version of the plight of the Jews in Mallorca and Chacón offers the lost voice of women during the Civil War, yet Cercas places the responsibility of historical recollection not on the historian but on the writer. While the other two writers unearth stories buried under the heavy layers of time, Cercas simply invents one.

As the end of the novel suggests, Cercas is in fact our hero. He comes to understand the flaw in his search for the truth: "la única respuesta es que no había respuesta, la única respuesta era una especie de secreta o insondable alegría, algo que linda con la crueldad y se resiste a la razón pero tampoco es instinto" (207–08). The hero has recognized his inability to conquer the historical truth and accepts that the invention is the answer. As he rides the train back to Spain, Cercas sees himself reflected in the window of the dining car as a failed journalist but a happy one. His mind then wanders to a story Miralles had told him of his service in Africa as he and other members of his troop marched through the desert. The parallel between the soldier fighting in an unknown country and the writer forging through unknown territory makes them both a kind of hero: one fights for freedom and the other writes for freedom. Cercas claims, "Vi mi libro entero y verdadero, mi relato real completo" (209). Even though he is plagued by uncertainty, he understands that an interpretation of history will serve to tell the story of Sánchez Mazas and Miralles and that it is perhaps better than what "really happened." The novel ends with the image of the soldiers in Africa marching onward, "hacia delante, hacia delante, hacia delante, siempre hacia delante" (209). But these are also the words going through Cercas's mind as he rides home on the train eager to write down the story. The repetition of "ever onward" echoes Nietzsche's idea of history at the service of progress. History can only really be of use for civilization if it is first analyzed and criticized and then understood as part of the contemporary social fabric. The uses for life Nietzsche cites in his essay are the ideas of critical historical analysis and progress or change. Cercas's novel works in this vein to reposition notions of historical truth and ultimately to applaud the invention of possible historical circumstance and motives.

As Cercas mentions in the epigraph at the beginning of this chapter, the writer creates a mask that is and is not his own face.[5] The obligatory distance that writing and language establish between the author and his subject remains the key to understanding historical "truth." In *Soldados de Salamina*, the truth lies in the development of the story, and the hero is the writer. It is the nature of storytelling that defines narrative and, as Nietzsche reminds us, the story in history gives us a critical perspective of past events. The inclusion of references to "reality" outside the text such as the poet Sánchez Mazas, the page from his diary, and Javier Cercas as our narrator, brings to the novel dates, facts, and names that make up traditional historical documentation. Nevertheless, Cercas the author contests the reliability of such facts and creates a version of what may have happened. In doing so he reveals the tenuous relationship between history, language, and "truth," and ultimately we realize that for Cercas, truth lies in the difficulty of writing. His novel *La velocidad de la luz* is another reworking of history and investigates the intensity of individual sacrifice in the face of international war. Like *Soldados*, *La velocidad* is a text that summons to the forefront of historical narrative the importance of letters and personal anecdote in the reconstruction of what may have happened. Cercas embraces the Nietzschean idea that what may have happened can be more instructive than concrete knowledge of events, and in exploring the past he brings history to life through the experience of the writer.

La velocidad de la luz

La velocidad de la luz (2005), published after the enormous success of *Soldados de Salamina*, returns to many of the same

Chapter Four

themes of war, personal history, and writing that mark the work of Javier Cercas. Cercas splits the action of the novel between Spain and the United States, thus crossing national borders in an attempt to bring multiple cultural perspectives to the aforementioned themes. Instead of the Spanish Civil War, the Vietnam War is the conflict that provokes the writer to search for historical meaning through the individual experience of one soldier. The narrator of *Velocidad* echoes in many ways the narrator of *Soldados:* he is a frustrated writer, searching for a way to tell someone else's story and through the act of writing comes to realizations about the purpose and power of narrative. I will compare the two novels, focusing on how Cercas moves out of a specifically Spanish historical context to an international arena that complicates cultural representations of history, violence, and reality.

The narrator begins the story in a nostalgic vein that establishes the text as a vehicle for memory. "Ahora llevo una vida falsa, una vida apócrifa y clandestina e invisible aunque más verdadera que si fuera de verdad, pero yo todavía era yo cuando conocí a Rodney Falk" (15). The separation between the past and present and the emphasis on the passage of time suggest a change in the narrator's perspective toward his writing based on some past experience. The narrator alludes to various levels or versions of reality, an idea that evolves into one of the main themes of the novel. Just as in *Soldados* the reality of the past confronts narrative invention, and in line with a Nietzschean philosophy of progress, the liberties afforded to the writer provide valuable revisions of the past. However, in *Velocidad*, not only is the historical reality of the Vietnam War deconstructed but the reality, purpose, and integrity of the author/narrator is as well.

Cercas sets up parallel events that represent a connection between the narrator's present and Rodney Falk's past. Rodney's suicide at his home in Illinois and the car accident that takes the life of our narrator's wife and child both provoke a kind of awakening in the writer/narrator. The irony lies in the fact that only through the death of loved ones do the living come to appreciate their own lives, but in Cercas's novel the catharsis of writing and thus documenting becomes the antidote to the depression and overwhelming feeling of tragedy. Rodney is a shy and enigmatic figure who teaches Spanish at the University of Illinois where the narrator is completing his PhD and teaching as well. The two become friends as they meet twice a week at a local bar so the narrator can help Rodney with his rudimentary Catalan. Yet the two routinely end up talking about writing and about the pleasures and pitfalls of pursuing a career as a novelist. As a premonition of what will come in the future, Rodney warns "si te empeñas en ser escritor, aplaza todo lo que puedas el éxito" (67). The pitfalls of the successful writer come to epitomize the narrator's story that we read in *Velocidad* because once he becomes successful with the publication of his first novel, his life spins out of control and only by turning inward to write Rodney's story, the story we hold in our hands, does he realize how central the act of narrating is to the writer's identity.[6]

Even though the time frame, characters, and historical relevance are completely different in *Soldados*, the narrative's power to reveal possible truths about past events remains the same in *Velocidad*. The narrative experiment that allows the reader to slowly piece together a writer's motivation unfolds in both novels and shows the importance of the story but also of the act of writing. If we witness the struggle of the author to compose the story and experience similar levels of confusion, misinformation, and lack of motivation, then the final product we read becomes more valuable because the struggle of the author has been made transparent. The narrator of *Velocidad* comes to terms with his own destructive behavior not when he understands Rodney's suicide, but when he is able to *write* Rodney's story and give him the sense of transcendental permanence the novel provides. Thus, the novel struggles with two opposing ideologies: the identity of a wartime hero and the truthfulness of his story. Cercas deals with the same themes as in *Soldados*, but in *Velocidad* we confront the atrocities of war committed by the supposed hero. Through the eyes of the narrator, the reader sees the fabrication and falsification of identity in the kind of monumental history posited by Nietzsche, which is the glorification of events and victories. Cercas describes the connection between the two novels in an interview with Carlos Rodríguez Martorell: "*La velocidad* is a type of complement to *Soldados*. This happens to me with all my novels; in a way, the novels I write either rebut or complement my previous works.

Chapter Four

And, as you said, *Soldados* speaks of the possibility of good, while this one speaks of the reality of evil and the impossibility of redemption" (1). Cercas dismantles the idea of heroism personified in a soldier as he slowly uncovers the narrative quality of "reality" that eventually becomes history. Rodney's father and wife add layers of testimony to the events in his life as they recount to the author their own versions of Rodney's wartime experience. The narrator expects that Rodney's first-person account of events during the war will clear up any doubts and questions the narrator has, but it only confuses him further and leads him to speculate on the nature of the hero. If *Soldados* proclaims that only the dead are heroes, then in *Velocidad* the very nature of heroics comes into question. The text strips the individual of historical importance and points to the narrative construction of the hero.

After years of thinking about Rodney and dealing with his own fame and personal failure, the narrator decides to write to Rodney in an attempt to gain his trust and permission to write his story. The confrontation between subject and writer comes to a climax as Rodney and the narrator sit in a dingy hotel lobby in Madrid in the middle of the night, talking. Based on some letters that Rodney's father had given to him, the narrator feels a sense of urgency to write Rodney's story and when he presses Rodney for information about a certain episode in a small village named My Khe, Rodney becomes defensive. Specifically, when the narrator affirms that he feels "responsible" to tell the story, Rodney separates himself and his personal history from the fabricated story the writer will invent. He realizes that any retelling of the events will be true only in part, and that the writer is necessarily bound by perspective to give an inaccurate account. He says to the narrator: "Pero si tanto te importa puedo contarte algo que te deje satisfecho. ¿Qué prefieres? Conozco muchas historias. Y yo también tengo imaginación. Dime qué necesitas para que tu historia cuadre y te hagas la ilusión de que la entiendes. Dímelo y te lo cuento y acabamos, ¿de acuerdo?" (178). In this instance the character calls to task his author, pointing a finger at the multiple possibilities of truth and the uncertainty in historical narrative.

Nevertheless, Rodney does tell the narrator that as an act of retribution for a suicide bombing that killed two US soldiers, a platoon went to a nearby village and massacred the entire population. The narrator reacts with disbelief and can only express himself in his writing through irony, such as when he says good-bye to Rodney: "no acerté a decir nada, porque sólo podía pensar en que era la primera vez en mi vida que abrazaba a un asesino" (186). The narrator takes the high moral ground in judging his friend as a murderer, and this clearly separates the narrative voice from the object of the story. The implication is that Rodney deserves the mental anguish and suffering he experienced after the war as a kind of cosmic payback for his participation in the massacre. This moralistic value judgment of Rodney's behavior during war is the inversion of the scene between the Republican soldier and Sánchez Mazas in *Soldados*. In one instance, the brutality and violence of war overtakes the character, while in the other, a small moment of humanity crosses the political and military divide and saves a life.

The narrator is stunned that his friend was and possibly still is capable of killing innocent women and children, but this is the "truth" he was seeking at all costs, to understand Rodney's personal history and the role the soldier played on the larger stage of American history. With this episode revealed, the narrator's preconceived ideas of Rodney as a hero become confused and tainted with a story about what "really" happened. Just as the narrator struggles with his feelings toward his friend and with this new knowledge considers him an assassin, the reader links the unreliable and unstable image of Rodney to the act of narration and writing. For if the narrator cannot comprehend the "truth" that he wants to use in a novel about Rodney, then the novel we hold in our hands is also a product of fabricated histories and, as Rodney suggests, a good imagination. Cercas compounds the complexity of historical writing by questioning his own character's past: is Rodney making up the story of the massacre? Is he embellishing it to give the narrator a good story? Also the narrator's confusion at the moment of believing and then writing the "truth" translates to the novelistic genre that specifically deals with history. The blending of national and personal history with story, characters, and plot emphasizes the impossibility of knowing the past.

Nevertheless, the fictionalization allows the reader to grasp alternative versions of history. Rodney was presented as a war hero and through the narrator's intentions to write his story we see the inversion of heroics. Rodney, in a symbolic inversion, comes to represent all that is chaotic, violent, and savage about war. The traditional notion of the hero is constructed through Nietzsche's idea of monumental history; that is, the brave soldier who fights battles and wins or sacrifices his mind and body in the name of his country. Cercas inverts the formula and, in writing the underside of history represented by the tragic, embarrassing massacre that was to be silenced and forgotten, he unearths a different version of the war and of Rodney as hero. The hero has become a murderer through the retelling of history.

However, the act of writing down Rodney's story reveals the theoretical implications of the narrative. When the narrator decides to write Rodney's story, he can only compile notes from secondary sources. He goes to see Rodney's wife, Jenny, who recounts Rodney's final weeks at home and his decline into complete solipsism and detachment. The narrator is intrigued by her story, for it is a story, a retelling of events, and he promises to redeem Rodney's life by writing yet another version or interpretation of the story. In the previously mentioned interview, Cercas claims that in *Velocidad* there is no possibility of redemption; however, by writing Rodney's story, the narrator does redeem himself and give voice and meaning to his friend's suffering. The duality of narration comes to the forefront in the final sections of the novel in that the act of storytelling is compounded through various versions and then reproduced in the novel itself. This metatextual musing on the importance and necessity of "documenting" the invented past through narrative is a central structural device in *Soldados* as well. Both the character Javier Cercas from that novel and the narrator from *Velocidad* save themselves through the act of writing another's story and producing a piece of literary history. In *Soldados*, Cercas deals with actual historical events and people such as the Civil War and Sánchez Mazas, while in *Velocidad* he has abandoned the concrete and created a historical figure in Rodney and certain events that may or may not have taken place during the Vietnam War. However, the production of a literary rendition of the historical nods to the importance of unearthing alternative versions, as Chacón and Riera have also done, and giving voice to the unnamed soldier.

History and the Hero

War as a theme in the novels is particularly important, as it often produces a rupture in identity and social reintegration. The effects of war on a society and individuals are devastating, and especially in *Velocidad* the anguish of trying to recuperate meaningful relationships with others and in turn with society becomes unbearable. Jenny tells the narrator about Rodney's decline after the media had been to the house asking him about war crimes committed by the special Tiger Force unit. Once again the hero is seen as a criminal paying for his crimes thirty years after the act. The idea of reopening the case against the Tiger Force unit points to the uneasy relationship between history, facts, and reality. The impact of unsuccessful forgetting and trying to hide the obvious mental and psychological disturbances created by horrific images and events during wartime ultimately become too much for Rodney. The hero turned assassin becomes martyr as Rodney hangs himself in his home. The consequence of not only the criminal actions during the war but covering up the "reality" and illegality of those events becomes an unbearable burden for the solider.

In the one stilted conversation Jenny has with her husband during his final days, she asks him pointedly if he is afraid. Rodney finally responds: "Con una brizna de alivio, como si acabaran de rozar con la yema de un dedo el corazón escondido de su angustia, Rodney dijo que sí" (270). He goes on to explain enigmatically that he is afraid of his wife and of her son and sometimes of himself. Jenny is confused, even bewildered by his confession and sees this as the final act of resignation on his part. The fear of family and loved ones is the manifestation of a complete inability to identify with social structures and institutionalized relationships, yet Rodney's complete psychological isolation echoes the experience of the narrator after losing his wife and child in a car accident and ironically the withdrawal from society is what connects the two characters. The radical and tragic separation of the individual from social constructs produces insurmountable anxiety and Rodney kills himself, while the narrator delves into writing Rodney's story in order to vindicate the fallen soldier and vindicate himself as a writer.

Earlier in the novel the narrator contemplates his own fame that has driven him away from his family and to a life of endless partying and self-destruction. He remembers that years ago Rodney had told him to be careful of fame because it changes one's self-image and interaction with others. The narrator comments on his own situation with hindsight when he admits: "El resultado fue que le perdí el respeto a la realidad; también le perdí el respeto a la literatura, que era lo único que hasta entonces había dotado de sentido o de una ilusión de sentido a la realidad" (201). This observation can be seen to represent the crux of the novel: the interplay between reality and writing. The narrator equates losing respect for reality, or the innumerable versions of it, with losing respect for writing, implying that the written word is indeed one form of "truth."

Reality and writing are scrutinized in the novel, but it is the idea of the hero that comes under the greatest fire. Cercas creates a story around an imperfect hero in *Soldados* yet the show of human decency that spares the life of the Fascist Sánchez Mazas serves as the axis of the novel and posits that the legacy of the fallen hero lives on in the written history of the war. The duty of the writer is to expose the humanity behind the patriotic façade of wartime heroics. In *Velocidad*, however, the hero takes on a much more ominous characteristic. Rodney is the fallen soldier that does not die heroically in battle but rather by his own hand years after the war has ended. As a representative of the veterans, he is a troubled man with a shadowy past that, once uncovered, proves to be stained with the blood of innocent victims. His emotional and psychological suffering come to the forefront when the writer attempts to record his story. Thus, in this case, the writing of history reveals an ugly side of humanity, the unexplainable atrocities committed during wartime. The hero becomes assassin but is redeemed not through his suicide as one might conclude, but rather through the telling of his story. Rodney's heroic act is giving our narrator a reason to write, for through the act of writing he redeems himself and gives form and some sense of meaning to Rodney's life as well. The written word that creates a "truth" saves the narrator by giving him a story to write while it simultaneously preserves at least one version of Rodney's life.

By taking on the cultural notion of the hero, Cercas creates a dialogue between his two novels. With war as a backdrop and the nature of historical writing conceived as contrived and manipulated, the novels in question pose cultural questions of the effects of war on the individual and collective memory. In accordance with Nietzsche's ideas on the progress inspired by fictionalized accounts of past events, Cercas re-creates historical spaces within the narrative that suggest not only alternate versions of the past but rather multiple and varied perspectives of the past. While this seemingly unending cacophony of voices may undermine the notion of clarity and "real" knowledge about the past, it ironically concludes with just the opposite. Through the theoretical discourse of multiplicity in historical perspectives the reader comes away with a greater appreciation of diversity. Just as Chacón and Riera propose previously silenced viewpoints of the past, Cercas uncovers the silence that lies behind the rhetoric of war heroics by debunking the myth of the stereotypical brave, unwavering soldier.

The authors in this first section give voice to the silenced historical perspectives by emphasizing the malleable nature of historical discourse that insists that the text continue to evolve and exist beyond the confines of a determined time and space framework. The categories of historical narrative that challenge traditional ideas of monolithic history are only the starting point for an open-ended conception of history that permits revision upon revision of traditional historical models, such as war, women, the hero, and ultimately good and evil. Carme Riera, Dulce Chacón, and Javier Cercas bring cultural questions to the forefront of contemporary fiction in Spain by challenging notions of history and presenting through literature a myriad of lost voices. These representations of culture invite readers to contemplate the disjointed and often contradictory versions of history and ask that they be considered as productive and progressive instead of erroneous. By analyzing the past and seeing it as a continuum with the present and future, we may come to partially understand the very complex nature of culture and society constructed from the essence of human nature.

Part 2

Hyperreality or Creating Culture

In this section of the study, I move away from a strict sense of historical representations of culture and toward a contemporary notion of the historical present. Many critics have noted that the contemporary literary production of the Generation X in Spain revolves around an axis of historical neglect and outright rejection. The youth movement that characterizes the Gen X writers is firmly located in the hedonistic present and identifies with cultural globalization markers such as mass-produced and mass-marketed video, film, and music culture. However, while I agree with the idea that the Gen X steers away from historical comment of any concrete nature, such as references to the Spanish Civil War or History in general, I do find that the works are rooted in a very concrete historical present. The Gen X novels are intent on recording contemporary culture in a meticulous way; the references to popular culture as well as the attitudes of the young protagonists reflect a determined effort to document through literature the pulse of contemporary Spanish experience.

While the novels of the first section in this study by Carme Riera, Dulce Chacón, and Javier Cercas treat History as a narrative and look to redefine the nature of the historical novel, the Gen X writers turn away from History and look to the present in an effort to reconcile the novel with globalization. Narrative becomes the tool that is able to represent culture through language, and the young authors in this section look to the novel as a genre that serves not only as a literary artifact but also as a cultural artifact that captures a particular moment in time. In his essay "The Value of Narrativity in the Representation of Reality," Hayden White confirms the importance of narrative in the formation of historical discourse. The Gen X novels follow White's assertion that the nature of narrative "is to invite reflection on the very nature of culture and, possibly, even on the nature of humanity itself" (1). The exploration of humanity and the lack of a meaningful moral compass play a large part in the development of the Gen X genre. Young protagonists disillusioned with society step away from the self-victimization and self-pity found in mid-century novels such as Luis Martín-Santos's *Tiempo de Silencio*, where Pedro, the protagonist, finds himself paralyzed by a stagnant society festering under oppression and lack of resources. The young characters of Gen X novels turn inward and away from any political commentary or existential questioning about their isolation and instead wallow in a destructive solipsism. Nevertheless, the novels touch a nerve that is common to contemporary, postmodern society: we are all together in our isolation. The novel that demands that a reader participate in the construction of the narrative insists on the interpersonal connections between the text and the extratextual.

The importance of the Gen X lies in the link between narrative and the rapidly growing technology that seems to define contemporary artistic production. The connection between video culture and literature reifies the importance of narrative through the novelistic genre. Representations of culture in the novel link narrative to globalization because contemporary experience, which is the subject of the Gen X novel, transcends national borders, and a new sense of a global community is formed. In the spirit of Benedict Anderson, this imagined community depends on a specific "language" of uninhibited access to information through the Internet and the resulting instant intellectual gratification. The common ground is a virtual plane of existence, and thus the imagined community meets with Baudrillard's hyperreality in that the referent is purely fictional. The artifact that remains behind to document this phenomenon must be the narrative, the novel itself. Narrative is the link that connects the multifaceted world of a globalized cultural identity that seeks to express itself and ultimately document its development and dissemination.

The novels I analyze in this section by Lucía Etxebarria, Ray Loriga, and José Ángel Mañas present an intensified version of the novel, a novel that embraces language as a generational characteristic and moves easily through cultures and modes. For example, Mañas uses English song lyrics to locate his characters within a certain underground culture that reflects a generational attitude toward individual identity. Loriga also exploits the symbolic value of popular music culture but synthesizes written and cinematic language through his narrative and work in film as a director and screenwriter. Etxebarria focuses on the virtual nature of relationships inspired by the Internet, which provides a false sense of community between characters but also leaks into the extratextual relationship between implied author and reader.

Baudrillard maintains that the lack of a definitive referent in contemporary culture has created a kind of "hyperreality" in which nothing is what it seems, and our existence becomes determined by simulacra of what is "real."[1] "Reality" ceases to exist as a definable term in the Gen X novels. Just as History in the last section leads to a questioning of narrative and language, "reality" in this section destabilizes traditional notions of identity and culture. Through violence in its many forms (physical, emotional, psychological, and textual) the Gen X novels propose a different approach to a "reality" that is born of technology. A hyperreality that relies on mass-reproduced images would seem to lack any sense of a solid foundation and thus perpetuate the fractured, inconsistent identity that is characteristic of postmodernism. The lack of "true" self-knowledge leads many of the young protagonists in the Gen X novels to act out in violence as a way of recognizing the very real nature of the human body.[2]

In the chapters that follow, I look at the different kinds of violence found in the Gen X novels and how this leads to an alternative view of literature and film. The technology that takes a front seat in the cultural representations found in these novels reflects both an appreciation of and a warning against the overwhelming effects of globalization. The novel becomes a document that records the fast-paced present and the rapidly changing dialogue between literature and "reality." Roland Barthes notes in "Introduction to the Structural Analysis of Narrative" (1966): "What takes place in a narrative is from the referential (reality) point of view literally *nothing*; 'what happens' is language alone, the adventure of language, the

Part 2

unceasing celebration of its coming" (qtd. in White, *Content* 37; italics in original). The event in the novel is narrative, "language alone," as Barthes claims. Therefore the novel records a virtual reality that may or may not exist, and it is language that creates the hyperreal narrative.

The concept of hyperreality goes hand in hand with the notion of globalization in that the boundaries between cultures seem to come crashing down. The world becomes virtual as individuals access information without leaving the comfort of a favorite chair in front of the computer screen. Cultural exchange as a form of global capital increases the visibility of artists and writers around the world, yet cultural specificity necessarily delineates much of the cultural exchange as exotic, establishing a binary relationship between subject and "other." This positionality within the virtual reality is what forces the writers to confront ideas of national identity, or what it means to be "Spanish." The assertion of a very specific colloquial register enhances the novelistic experience and adds an aural and contemporary dimension to the created identities of the characters. In the Gen X novels the geographic specificity of the language used comes across as an identity marker and thus becomes a cultural representation at the most basic, textual level.

Ray Loriga, Lucía Etxebarria, and José Ángel Mañas are widely considered the forerunners of the Gen X literary movement. In the novels that appear in this section—*Caídos del cielo*, *El hombre que inventó Manhattan,* and the film *La pistola de mi hermano* by Loriga; *De todo lo visible y lo invisible* by Etxebarria; and *Historias del Kronen* and *La pella* by Mañas—the cultural capital of hyperreality transforms the texts into spaces of multimedia experience. The emphasis on video, music, film, and virtual role models creates a revolutionary literary space that challenges the reader yet ultimately embraces the novel as the one textual artifact that can contain it all.

Chapter Five

Television, Simulacra, and Power in Three Works by Ray Loriga

> Other generations had wars and social movements to unite them, but for Xers, television is the common experience.
>
> Rob Owen
> *GenX TV*

Television plays a crucial role in defining popular culture and, as Rob Owen explains, crosses cultural boundaries, creating a common perspective. Although Owen is writing about Xers in the United States, his observations pertain to the Spanish Generation X as well. Ray Loriga, considered one of the forerunners of the Generation X literary movement in Spain, in his first novel, *Lo peor de todo* (1992), tells the story of a disenfranchised youth struggling with family problems in a fast-paced, consumerist society. The first-person narrative, fantasies of violence, and ubiquitous North American capitalism (the protagonist works in a McDonalds) define, in part, the narrative style and content familiar to readers of Spain's Generation X.[1]

Nevertheless, Loriga has developed and expanded Gen X themes of disgruntled youth, family tension, and popular culture. His career has been dynamic as well as prolific.[2] Loriga has successfully tapped into the importance of image, video, and cinematic language in his novels, bringing this consciousness of form to his films. His activities as author, screenwriter, and director complement one another and inspire a new literary language. In his works, Loriga criticizes TV's superficiality and the erroneous sense of community it creates. This chapter will analyze the ways in which Loriga uses both visual and verbal language to reveal manipulative television ethics. Television produces images that seduce viewers with a created, false

Chapter Five

reality that shifts power from the actual events to the televised re-creation.

In order to better understand Loriga's contribution to the Gen X movement in Spain, I will focus on the relationship between written and visual language in *Caídos del cielo* (1995) and in the film adaptation written and directed by Loriga, *La pistola de mi hermano* (1997). The novel and its film version exemplify the difference between visual and verbal forms of communication. While the characters and plot remain the same in the adaptation, the style and tone of each work is markedly different. However, in order to locate these texts within the shifting parameters of the Gen X movement, I will briefly consider the polemics of naming the contemporary literary movement in Spain and of Spanish television.

Christine Henseler points out that Spanish Gen X authors are more concerned with redefining literary language than perfecting it. She describes the cover of Loriga's novel *Héroes* (1993), where the author appears holding a bottle of beer and sporting a skull ring and long hair. Loriga appropriates the marketing machine as he sells the relationship between author and text as part of "the territory of virtual reality, worlds infused with simulated truths where life [con]fuses with art and art confuses reality" (Henseler, "Pop" 694). In Loriga's case, art and life again become one and the same in his recent novel *El hombre que inventó Manhattan* (2004). Loriga lived in New York City for five years with his family and left shortly after the September 2001 terrorist attacks. *El hombre* takes place in Manhattan and presents itself at times as a real autobiography and, at others, as only a fantasy. The narrative voice in the novel assures us that the events are fiction, and then immediately insists they are not: "todas [las historias] son inventadas aunque muchas, la mayoría, son ciertas" (16). This crossover between life and art has long been at the core of Loriga's literary project.

However, even though Loriga has capitalized on the Gen X image of literary rebellion and self-promotion, he has criticized the notion of a generation of writers: "lo de la generación X, Mañas y demás, creo que era muy artificial puesto que éramos gente que tenía muy poco que ver en lo literario y que además no teníamos ningún contacto personal" ("Hombre" n.pag.). Loriga compares his literary generation with what he considers the more legitimate Generation of 1927: "Existía un lugar de encuentro, era gente que se conocía … había un núcleo … cuando yo empecé a publicar no conocía de nada a ninguno de los escritores que luego me pusieron como compañeros de ruta y sigo sin conocerlos" ("Hombre" n.pag.). Other "members" of the Gen X group have expressed similar feelings of disengagement.

On January 15, 2004, at a roundtable discussion at the University of Valladolid, contemporary Spanish authors Juan Bonilla, Marcos Giralt Torrente, and Lucía Etxebarria raised the question: Was there ever a Generation X in Spain? Etxebarria confirms that the term originated with Douglas Coupland's book *Generation X: Tales for an Accelerated Culture* (Ferrari 259). Coupland describes a group of isolated and estranged young people living in the United States. They are satisfied to settle for a McJob, defined as undemanding employment that simply pays the bills (5). Coupland's benevolent Generation Xers have little to do with the violence, sexual promiscuity, and hard drug use characteristic of the Spanish Gen X.[3] The authors at the roundtable discussion conclude that there never was a Generation X in Spain. Etxebarria affirms that the current group of writers lacks a formal manifesto and they do not ascribe to a common literary legacy. She also suggests that publishers invented the term to sell certain authors, such as Mañas and Loriga (Ferrari 259). Juan Bonilla warns against confusing a historical generation with a literary group (Ferrari 260). He also points out that the contemporary writers grouped together as part of the Generation X never put forward the name to identify themselves; on the contrary, the label was forced upon them.

However, most critics will agree that the term Generation X accurately defines a group of Spanish writers and the literary spirit they embody. Loriga has said that "todos los escritores reniegan de ser metidos en una generación" ("Hombre" n.pag.) and perhaps it is the work of the critic and not the author to conceptualize literary movements. Nevertheless, I think it is important to address the issues brought up by the authors. Their reactions to the term reveal the fragile relationship between the author and the market. For these young writers working on a global stage dominated by the Internet, image is an intrinsic part of selling books. Perhaps the globalization of the Spanish book market and the immediate access to image via the Internet can be considered additional characteristics of the Spanish Generation X. Commenting on current television production in Spain, Richard Maxwell observes: "cultural politics of nationality erupt onto the global grid of market culture" (271). Similarly, the specific traits of the Spanish Gen X movement give the authors a unique and marketable appeal to a global audience. They are at once Spanish (national) and international because they allude to British and American films, music, and books in their works. The need to expand and clarify the term Generation X affirms its importance to the contemporary Spanish literary scene.

The historical relationship between television and the viewer also influences Spanish Gen X literature. As Barry Jordan points out, under Franco's dictatorship television programming and other media outlets were strictly controlled by the state, and this "paternalistic legacy" would complicate later attempts to separate televised content from centralized state control (364). For example, the role of television during the transition to democracy was to "explain to the public the problems of the national economy (so as to avoid the association between democracy and economic instability, a serious problem in the early 1980's)" (367). Thus, television under Franco and during the transition was a tool of the state, employed to convince the public of certain political ideologies. More recently, Spaniards have protested the lack of legislation controlling the amount of sex and violence on TV as well as the dominant foreign ownership of all Spanish mass media (Jordan 367; Bustamante 360).[4] We see in Loriga's work that television is not just a source of entertainment, but also a political tool that wields the power to influence and manipulate the public's worldview. Loriga's fiction seeks to deconstruct television's mediation between personal perspective and social reality.

Although he focuses on television as a cultural marker, Loriga also addresses the broader context of contemporary Spanish cultural production in his works. The emphasis on the visual, the urban settings, and youth stems from an artistic tendency to look toward the future, instead of reflecting on past national disasters such as the Spanish Civil War and resulting Franco regime. However, Loriga and the Gen X writers are not apolitical;

their politics are enmeshed with an evolving cultural identity that finally allows the freedom *not* to address history or politics in their writing. The climate of criticism in Gen X writing bears a shift from the political to the personal. In the works studied here, Loriga seeks to tease out the personal conflict between the individual and, what he seems to consider, overbearing cultural production.

The contrast between the novel *Caídos del cielo* and the film *La pistola de mi hermano* stems from the relationship the reader/viewer establishes with the text. The novel presents a fast-paced narrative with jumps in location and time that require the reader to reorder the series of events. The narrative frenzy and chaos culminate in a scene on the set of a talk show that reveals the carnivalesque nature of television reporting. In the novel, the younger brother tells the story of how his older brother kills a security guard at a convenience store and then steals a car to escape from the law. In his haste to escape, the older brother speeds off with a young girl in the car. The narrator complains about how the media misrepresents his family but he can only speculate about what really happened. He pieces the story together through conversations with the girl only after his brother is shot and killed. The narrative perspective creates a source of doubt in the story, for readers do not have access to the main events. The young narrator must re-create them from the girl's recollections and bogus TV reports.

In the film, however, we follow the brother on his road trip and see the events unfold first hand. The element of doubt surrounding the younger brother's perspective is absent from the film. The camera work echoes the linear narrative and does not jump around frequently but is steady and focused. Loriga uses many single-shot scenes where the camera does not move but stays in one place, highlighting the importance of the dialogue. He does not cut from one speaker to the other in a traditional shot/reverse shot sequence but stays on one speaker while we hear the other's response off screen.[5] Loriga also uses slow motion at moments of high energy to underline emotional bonds instead of physical speed.

Loriga's movie creates a dialogue between television and film regarding violence in society. The story offers a glimpse into the startling manipulation of events by televised reporting

Chapter Five

and the alienation of misunderstood youth. Loriga questions the origins of violence in society: Is violence produced by society or do individuals react violently to a society that alienates and degrades them? At one point in the film the main character has a brief but revealing conversation with the girl as they both watch a boxing match on TV:

> —¿Crees que es culpa de la televisión?
> —¿El qué?
> —Todo.
>
> (La pistola n.pag.)

The girl does not respond, leaving the viewer to ponder the curt answer. Although the film does not exonerate the individual and blame television for "everything," the murderer in the story is portrayed as vulnerable, scared, and unable to understand his (or anyone else's) actions. Loriga juxtaposes brutal violence with adolescent awkwardness that leaves the reader/viewer wondering about the emotional price the individual must pay to fit in socially. He explores the mishandling of television that promotes sensationalism and creates a false reality while seducing viewers into believing in the power of violence.

Television newscasts edit and thus often falsify violent episodes in order to shock or at least impress the audience. TV automatically censors information with time limitations placed on news programs and talk shows as each story is carefully revised and packaged for immediate consumption. In this way events are "cut off from their antecedents and consequences" (Bourdieu, *Television* 7). The factual information of any given event becomes less important than the dramatic rendering of that event that will stimulate and attract television viewers. Broadcasters show what they believe will reflect the general public's interest and "the television screen ... becomes a sort of mirror for Narcissus, a space for narcissistic exhibitionism" (14). The simulated event is presented in a two-minute story on the evening news and "ultimately television, which claims to record reality, creates it instead" (22). Sharon Lynn Sperry has observed: "Television news is a blend of traditional, objective journalism and a kind of quasi-fictional prime-time story-telling which frames events in reduced terms with simple, clear-cut values" (131). Her assertion that television news is structured to complement the narrative shows framing the newscast reveals the implicit censorship involved in transmitting factual information in short, fictionalized segments. Therefore, television is not a mediator between the human gaze and society (Navarro 3), but rather the images on television create a virtual reality. Loriga shows this process in the novel through the narrator's confusion, and the process of fabricating misinformation becomes the axis of the narrative structure. The narrator grapples with his own perceptions of his brother, information from the girlfriend, and the many versions of his brother presented on TV.

In the novel, the young narrator criticizes the way in which the television press handles his brother's story. When a reporter asks him if his brother ever shot a gun at him, he confides to the reader "los de la tele son la hostia" (15). He also exclaims: "lo que me jodió es que los de la televisión dijeran que era marica sin conocerle" (16). The TV reports invent a personality that has nothing to do with the older brother but attracts viewers. They create a sensationalistic story with an intriguing character, hoping that viewers will follow the escapades of "el loco de la tele" (17). On the other hand, the narrator feels privileged when "en el informativo semanal nos dedicaron casi media hora" (34). The conditions and outcome of his brother's story gain importance with the amount of time televised. Therefore it seems logical to the younger brother that he and his mother make the requested television appearances.

The description of the narrator and his mother preparing for a talk show reveals the marketing strategy and general sensationalism that support "informative" shows. The show is called "Todos somos uno," suggesting the collective nature of the television experience. The "fabuloso mundo de la familia" (83) extends beyond the studio to the household and includes the vast, faceless audience tuned in to the program. Moreiras mentions the "information invasion" that collapses the private and public spheres into one disorienting space. The television "obliga al sujeto a modificar radicalmente su concepción y, más importante aún, su experiencia del espacio y del tiempo, de lugar y de la historia, en fin, de la propia cultura" (200). Television allows the invasion of the private sphere by the public in a seemingly harmless way. But the images on TV do not faithfully represent the public sphere, and in the novel the family's plight is embellished to incite the audience that ultimately ridicules the mother's testimony.

The narrator comments on the use of makeup that covers the physical ugliness of the presenter (Loriga 83) and how the makeup artists "me despeinaron un poco y me cambiaron la cazadora de mi hermano por una roja más vistosa" (84). The presenter assures the audience that the narrator is wearing his brother's jacket, which we readers know is a lie, and the mother's desperate attempt to vindicate herself on television only provokes the crowd: "Mamá mientras tanto trataba de convencer a todo el mundo de que ella a pesar de todo era una buena mujer y de que yo era un buen chico y que lo de mi hermano era un caso aislado, pero nadie la creía. PORQUE TODOS SOMOS UNO" (84). The chanting crowd drowns out the mother's protests like a Greek chorus announcing the fall of the heroine. The calculated presentation strips the mother of an explanatory voice, for without her guilt, the audience would have no scapegoat and no catharsis. The information presented by television journalism, according to Loriga, does not inform, but seduces in a dangerously mind-numbing way. The presentation is geared so that the viewer can actively participate in a virtual ritual of self-aggrandizement in Bourdieu's space of "narcissistic exhibitionism" (*Television* 14).

The collective agency of television produces an image of the assassin that mythifies his existence. He is labeled the "angel of death" by the press, thus combining the beautiful and the morbid. His real identity becomes fluid and unimportant once the TV image takes hold. "The continual temporariness of identity has a corrosive effect: the search for identity results in the erasure of identity. Yet it is not an existential crisis. Identity may be fleeting but it is also instantly replaceable" (Klodt 51). The televised re-creation of a particular identity replaces the brother's true identity. Even when the boy's futile escape from social structures is truncated and he is caught by the police and killed, the fabrication of the story continues to serve as a false referent that spurs on the fame of the girl and of his family.

Bourdieu points out that market-driven economics and competition push television journalism to the sensational, shocking, yet easily digestible bytes that will attract an audience. Today's "multichannel landscape is not a world of infinite diversity but rather a sophisticated marketplace that aims to attract demographic groups with spending power" (Spigel 16–17). Reality is sacrificed for a slick, sexy appearance (Bourdieu, *Television* 19–20). When Loriga transformed his novel into a film, how could he at the same time present these events effectively and avoid the television excesses he deplored?

Not surprisingly, then, a slick, sexy seduction of the viewer is missing from the film. Given the opportunity to represent visually the talk show described in the novel, Loriga decides to resist the temptation of the visual, and instead he makes a film that is poignant and visually poetic. He does not try to capture the fast pace of the verbal narrative but instead shoots a calm, understated film. The film lacks the expected rapid car chase and violent, chaotic editing that might portray the confusion at the store when the brother shoots and kills the security guard. Loriga shows that film is a narrative art and that the visual does not have to be the typical onslaught of information seen on television. His control of the images and calculated technique produce a slow pace that counters the television ethics he criticizes. Nevertheless, some television shows do have a slow pace and certainly many films contain high-speed car chases, so the opposition that Loriga sets up is not between television and film but rather the sedate filming style that he uses to tell a violent story stands out as an innovative choice. Montserrat Lunati points out the cinematic quality of the novel in which the "rhythm of the narration follow[s] the pace of the escape" (428). The choppy, rapid pace of the written narrative is slowed down to create a more contemplative tone in the film.

Loriga achieves this through three fundamental camera techniques: single-shot scenes, pan, and slow motion.[6] Loriga uses single-shot scenes and pan shots frequently throughout the film while he uses slow motion sparingly. I will analyze scenes that demonstrate the importance of the camera as a tool of visual language that establishes mood in the film. Even though Loriga is dealing in a visual medium, he chooses not to exploit the visual in order to make a hyperbolic statement. Instead he explores the literary and poetic uses of image in order to complement and not simply reproduce his own literary work.

The talk show scene described in detail in the novel does not appear in the film. In fact the presence of television in the film

Chapter Five

is subtle at best. A television set appears in several scenes, most notably when the older brother and girl are talking in a motel room. They are not watching TV, but the blue screen flickers as if it were a silent observer. At one point, we see a medium shot of the brother as he picks up a chair and bashes in the screen of the TV set. Just before he destroys it, the camera pans slowly to the girl asleep on the bed. The smooth camera movement suggests inclusiveness and we see the girl wake suddenly as the TV is destroyed. She runs to embrace the brother and thus closes the physical and emotional gap between them. The emotional symbolism of the filming is achieved through a medium shot that does not cut from one character to the other. This moment of rage and frustration reveals, according to Loriga, "el miedo que él tiene" and shows that the young assassin "en el fondo es un tío asustado" (Beilin 207). This intimate moment in the motel room is one of the few violent scenes in the film, and Loriga chooses to eschew the obvious camera and editing techniques that would emphasize and exaggerate the power of the image. Instead of a tight close-up or a cut to the girl's startled reaction, his use of the pan shot at a distance removes us from the brother's outburst. When we see the girl jump up from the bed and embrace him we too can feel the need to accept and understand his frustration. We long for the close-up shot that will reveal to us his hidden emotions just as the girl longs to break through his stoic façade and understand his true feelings.

The single-shot scenes and pan shots give a smooth, seamless feel to the conversations in the film. Also, the single-shot scenes reveal the importance of the dialogue because the camera movement does not distract the viewer. In a sequence of single-shot scenes that take place in the motel room, the viewer is forced to concentrate on the dialogue by the lack of movement on the screen. The low light and stillness of the actors emphasize the focus on dialogue. These scenes create an intimate atmosphere, and the two characters reveal innermost secrets about their pasts. The scenes include both characters; while one is talking, the other is included in the frame and is completely focused on the speaker. In this way Loriga highlights the subtle art of listening, suggesting that we viewers take a cue from the camera's stillness and listen as well.

In the first scene of the sequence, the brother and the girl are watching boxing on TV. They sit at opposite ends of the screen facing the camera. The brother expresses his self-doubt and alienation from society when he asks her "¿A veces no tienes vergüenza?" He confesses that his smile, the way he walks, even his hair embarrass him. The flicker of the TV illuminates their faces, reminding us of its presence in the room and in their lives. The young man's self-consciousness is exacerbated by the glow of the television screen that often emits images impossible to emulate. The scene then cuts to another medium shot of the two characters sitting on the floor with the TV on in the background. Again, their conversation takes center stage as the girl explains her sexual adventures with a foreigner. In the next medium shot, the girl is seated on the bed looking down as she explains a particularly strange and humiliating sexual experience she had, and we see the brother in the background, watching and listening to her.

The girl clearly dominates the conversation, and her revealing language takes the place of the anticipated sex scene. Lunati notes that the sexual dynamic exists in the novel as well, and we see an "affirmative representation of masculinity defined against the girl's amorality" (442). Likewise in the film, even though they kiss passionately, he ends up masturbating alone in the bathroom. Through their words they become more intimate than they could through sex. The camera language creates an intimate feel as well; the frame encloses them both, tightening the claustrophobic space. Even in the short scene when the girl is washing her face in the bathroom, her voice-over continues as we see the brother through the bathroom door, sitting and waiting for her. They are always filmed in the same frame in a single shot. In this way, Loriga visually echoes their emotional solidarity by keeping them together in the same frame instead of cutting from one character to the other.

On the other hand, an earlier scene of the two brothers driving their mother's car reveals an interesting contradiction. This scene can be read as a foreshadowing of the danger that the brother will encounter when he steals a car and flees from the police after shooting the security guard. The boys ask their mother if they can borrow her car to go out for the day. As they leave the house, she calls to her older son, "Oye, tú, chico malo, conduce con cuidado." The scene cuts to the boy recklessly driving the mom's station wagon in an abandoned dirt lot. They turn fast corners and skid out of control. However, the driving

Chapter Five

scene is shot in slow motion with quiet guitar music and lilting female vocals. The scene of rebellion is transformed into a tender moment of sibling bonding. We see the car slowly spinning out of control and then the shot cuts to a front view of the brothers smiling, laughing, and having innocent fun. Of course this peccadillo will become even more poignant when at the end of their outing together the older brother will murder a stranger and eventually face his own death. The relationship established early in the film between the brothers is highlighted in the car scene as the actions take back seat to the filmic technique. The slow motion footage forces the viewer to concentrate on the facial expressions of the characters and injects the scene with nostalgia.

The slow motion differentiates the scene from the rest of the film and heightens the sense of urgency, since we know from the beginning that the older brother will die. The car ride is revealed as a special memory for the younger brother when we realize in a later scene that he has been relating to the police all the information we have been witnessing on screen. His version of the day's events leading up to the shooting includes this romantic notion of innocent rebellion with his older brother. Loriga clearly seeks to shed some positive light on the older brother. Despite his bad judgment in killing someone, he was a "normal" kid who enjoyed spending time with his little brother.

The juxtaposition of youth and corruption, of innocence and violence, lies at the heart of the film. In a revealing sequence, set to pulsating punk rock music, we watch the brother shoot the security guard, run out of the store, jump into the first car he sees, and speed away. A sudden cut in the music and image brings us back to the store, where we see a small white dog splattered with blood tied to a colorful airplane ride. This abrupt cut to the blood-covered dog is a visual metaphor for the incongruity of violence and youth. The white dog symbolizes innocence and the blood on his coat suggests that society's violence is omnipresent and inescapable. We see this dichotomy as well in the prodding police officer as he hounds the mother and younger brother. He claims that he does not want to hurt anyone but shoots the older brother anyway out of a sense of duty. In Loriga's work, institutions with power, such as television and the police force, alienate and corrupt young people. He suggests that the innocence of youth does not stand a chance in the face of such social machines.

Nevertheless, Loriga is not the kind of author or filmmaker to preach to his public about the evils of corporate society. He includes violence in his works in order to explore human fascination with it. He claims: "Creo que la violencia es parte fundamental del ser humano" (Beilin 206). In the same vein, his criticism of television serves as a criticism of society's apathy toward violence in general. "La televisión no tiene culpa de nada. Es un espejo. La sociedad ve en la televisión lo que se merece" (206). The novel and film make evident the fictional nature of many television newscasts and challenge accepted cultural expectations. Just as defenders of television assert that violent images on TV do not incite violence in the viewer but reflect the violence already established in society, Loriga does not blame television for violence, but he does go to great lengths to reveal the manipulative power of the image. John Corner defines the moving image as always edited and tailored to fit into the figuration and flow of television aesthetics (29).[7] Loriga extends this concept of flow to novel and film in which he creates an open dialogue between content, meaning, and representation.

El hombre que inventó Manhattan (2004)

Loriga has developed in more recent works a sense of virtual or hyperreality in his novels that moves away from television violence to the very human emotions directed toward the superficiality of identity. In this way, he creates a simulacra of reality based on very human expectations. The interest in cultural dynamics of the "real" and the virtual exist in his novel from 2004, *El hombre que inventó Manhattan*, but in a more lyrical style that moves away from typical Gen X themes. The notion of "reality" in *El hombre que inventó Manhattan* appears mediated through cultural forms other than television. While the pace and style of this novel are markedly different from *Caídos*, the preoccupation with appearance and culture remains the same. Nevertheless, death in this novel becomes an overriding metaphor for illusion. *El hombre* boasts a much more complicated structure with intricacies and surprises, while

Chapter Five

the characters seem more fleshed out and less urgent in their actions. Described as "brilliant and moving" (Echevarría, "Melodías" n.pag.), Loriga's novel highlights his narrative wit and talent. However, the discomfort experienced by the individual in a social system based on appearances and display functions as a unifying theme of both *Caídos del cielo* and *El hombre que inventó Manhattan*.

In *El hombre* the metaphor of simulacrum is extended to the writing itself. The novel weaves together the radically different experiences of several inhabitants of New York City. Through serendipitous connections the individual characters together create a disturbing mosaic of urban existence. Death and sex, recurring themes in Loriga's work, are the fundamental links that connect the various lives in the novel. The structure continuously plays with simulacrum in the sense that information is withheld, then revealed as a truth, and finally disproved. Beauty as a simulacrum becomes a caricature of itself, for no longer is the illusion dangerous, threatening, or morbid. Rather the instability of time and space that television inspires in the subject of *Caídos* becomes the basis of experience and the only viable way to relate to one's surroundings in *El hombre*. Television as a cultural formulation of false reality gives way to the inner world of fantasy of each character. Imagination creates the simulacrum that sustains it. Unlike the fantastic imaginations of the Spanish literary character Don Quijote, who based his fantasy on novels of chivalry, the simulacrum of hyperreality has neither referent nor moral end. The illusion is perpetuated only by its own falseness. Loriga presents New York City as the ultimate simulacrum, a place that only exists as invented by those who live there. The novel revolves around the idea of otherness and the foreigner who is destined to build his own impressions on preconceived fantasy and imagination.

A large number of the characters in the novel are immigrants, including a Romanian superintendent, Korean beauticians, a Mexican actor, a European businessman, and the Spanish narrator/author Ray Loriga. The narrator informs us in the final chapter that he and his family lived in Manhattan for five years (187), which is the case of the author, who reveals in an interview that indeed he had returned to Madrid after living in New York for five years ("Hombre" n.pag.). The point of departure for the 36 vignettes that make up the novel is the suicide of superintendent Gerald Ulsrak. The novel deals with the vulnerability of the immigrant experience and begins with a play on names and interchangeable identities that throw the following events into a dubious light. Identities are unstable, blurry, and inevitably created, as Loriga describes at the beginning of the novel:

> El hombre que inventó Manhattan se hacía llamar Charlie aunque su verdadero nombre era Gerald Ulsrak, estaba casado y tenía dos hijas. A lo mejor sólo una. Se decía que la mayor de las niñas era hija de otro hombre ... Gerald Ulsrak había nacido en un pequeño pueblo en las montañas de Rumania y siempre había soñado con un sitio mejor, Manhattan, y un nombre distinto, Charlie. (9)

The narrator decides to pay homage to the life and times of Charlie upon his suicide by relating the stories that form part of Charlie's dream of a better place and a different name. The narrator affirms that all of the stories "son inventadas aunque muchas, la mayoría, son ciertas" (16). Charlie's suicide by hanging that provokes the telling of the stories looms over the narrative, reminding the reader that the truth of the dream does not exist and the subsequent chapters represent an imagined reality.

The simulacrum of death lies within the fabricated reality of the novel. Death cannot be understood because the referent is intellectually impossible to comprehend. In Loriga's novel, death is not a metaphysical or spiritual experience, but rather another kind of performance. The novel involves the bizarre and mysterious death of piano salesman Arnold Grumberg. One morning, as Arnold steps out of the doorway of his piano store with a cup of coffee in his hand, he suddenly faints and falls on the broken porcelain cup, which cuts his neck, killing him instantly. In the rehab center where Arnold previously had spent some time, the other patients who knew him comment on his sudden demise: "un hombre no se cae sobre una taza de café y se corta el cuello, sin más" (73). The characters question the circumstances of Arnold's death and doubt the possibility of such a mediocre demise. This discussion also highlights the comical aspects of Arnold's death. A man who had survived years of alcohol abuse and rehab mysteriously

Chapter Five

dies from something as mundane as a coffee cup? Arnold's death is not somber but rather whimsical and provocative in how it creates fiction within the novel. The performance demands participation from the reader and from within the text. Other characters and the reader fill in the gaps, grasping at straws to understand what really happened.

Toward the end of the novel, the mystery only becomes compounded as Molly, a barfly once rejected by Arnold, arrives home to her apartment and throws away a small figurine muttering that "El Señor Misterioso" (175) has served his purpose. The "voodoo" doll surfaces as the likely explanation of Arnold's death. Loriga relies on the supernatural to undermine a logical explanation by Western standards of what really happened to Arnold. Was he killed by a coffee cup or by voodoo? Arnold's death remains not only unexplained but also complicated by multiple perspectives and a possible motive. At best the cause of death is an accident or an unconventional case of voodoo at the hands of a disdained lover. Death and destruction remain ambiguous markers of illusion in Loriga's novel.

In the haunting chapter "Two Towers," Arnold Grumberg wanders lost and disoriented around the World Trade Center. He tries to cross from west to east without having to detour all the way around the two towers but instead he gets lost and overwhelmed. Loriga's reconstruction of the devastated site of the September 11, 2001, terrorist attacks pays particular homage to the massiveness and impenetrable quality of the buildings that, ironically, has been proven illusory. Arnold's inability to pass through the towers, his frustration, and ultimate resignation (he stops in a strip club) accentuate the actual absence of the structure. By not directly mentioning the events of 9/11, Loriga skillfully re-creates the space and time in all its banality. Everyday complications of concrete and cement attest to the minuscule stature of a person who "se encamina hacia Broadway para después asumir el reto de cruzar de una vez por todas el corazón de esas dos torres infranqueables" (143). Because Loriga never mentions the destruction of the towers, the reader is left to fill in the gaps between the fictional reality and what we know to be true. The author chooses to maintain the illusion of permanence and create a simulacrum that is at once disturbing yet, in a sense, comforting. Here the text relies heavily on a cognizance of the historical, extra-textual circumstance for a complete understanding of the narrative. The chapter would not exist in the same way if the World Trade Center still stood. Loriga plays with notions of absence, contextualization of fiction, and simulacra to a poignant end as he reconstructs the destroyed and makes the reader complicit in this act.

Death is presented in the novel as a construction fabricated in the minds of others. The whole novel *El hombre que inventó Manhattan* hinges on the untold dreams of a man who committed suicide; thus the novel itself is an illusion, or a mosaic of the non-existent American Dream. Death becomes the ultimate simulacrum in the hyperreal because it cannot possibly represent something else. Death as a means, not as an end, becomes completely self-reflective in the sense that it becomes void of religious or moral implications and serves to perpetuate life and inevitably itself. From Charlie's suicide to Arnold's strange accident, death serves as a springboard for narrative. It does not signal an end of life but rather a beginning, an impetus for the story. In this way death is only the illusion of an end and, much like beauty, seduces the reader into a complicit relationship of decoding the narrative. Death serves as a narrative tool urging the story forward not in an attempt to identify a murderer, as in a suspense novel, but rather to uncover reality itself as a construct.

In the final chapter of *El hombre* that serves as epilogue, the narrator/author places the immigrant experience squarely within a context of simulacra. The expectations of a new place and the preconceived notion that change will bring happiness are at the heart of the journey. The dreams of the immigrants found in the pages of Loriga's narrative act as a mirror for life in general. He explains: "Con el tiempo se empiezan a sufrir los rigores de la fantasía. Se cambia una tiranía por otra. Se adueña uno del simulacro" (187). The tyranny that unquestionably dominates society resides in the simulacra that must be endlessly renewed and exchanged. Whether beauty or death, the illusion manipulates the subject into believing the false reality. The young narrator of *Caídos del cielo* and Arnold Grumberg and Gerald "Charlie" Ulsrak from *El hombre* see the simulacrum before them and inevitably fall prey to its omnipotence.

On the other hand, Loriga's works are not an apocalyptic vision of the contemporary extreme. The author's humor and wry criticism of social mores reveal a cynical yet lighter tone. His

Chapter Five

use of simulacra in both *Caídos del cielo* and *El hombre que inventó Manhattan* explores how accepted concepts of "reality" and death are fabricated by social institutions such as television and the novel itself. However, he insists that people create fantasy from a need to believe in the permanence of the illusory. The creation of a fictional reality is itself a form of simulacrum, and Loriga seems aware of the metatextual nature of his writing.[8] As an author immersed in hyperreality where image and violence seem to dictate behavior, Ray Loriga offers a variety of narrative discourses that comment and criticize, yet at the same time celebrate the contradictory elements of contemporary culture.

    The variety of visual and verbal language in his novels and film reveals Loriga's interest in how form creates mood. He has said, "[en] una novela lo primero nunca es una trama, sino un tono" ("Entrevista" n.pag.). While Generation X writers are often associated with television and film techniques, Loriga's directional choices in the movie based on his own novel show us that this is not just a thoughtless appropriation, but it can be a profound and critical meditation about the possibilities of different genres. His vision of television as a tool of cultural production also brings together larger ideologies of consumerism, image, violence, and power.

Chapter Six

Textual Violence and the Hyperreal in *De todo lo visible y lo invisible* by Lucía Etxebarria

> ... ¿por qué nadie le pregunta a javier marías, o a antonio muñoz molina que por qué no tienen protagonistas mujeres? porque estamos tan acostumbrados al androcentrismo que el protagonista hombre nos parece la norma, y la protagonista mujer, la desviación.
>
> Lucía Etxebarria
> <http://www.lucia-etxebarria.es>

Lucía Etxebarria's public persona has overshadowed, at times, the value of her literary production.[1] In line with Ray Loriga's skepticism outlined in the previous chapter, Etxebarria remains another cautious member of the Generation X in Spain. Even though Etxebarria is somewhat of a media darling in Spain and manipulates the press and Internet to her advantage, she has openly denounced the Gen X label as a marketing tool for publishing houses to promote authors such as Loriga (Ferrari 259). In her chatty confessional about the writing business, *La letra futura*, Etxebarria castigates the press for inventing animosities between writers. She notes that at one point in her career "tuve que leer en no sé cuántos sitios que yo me llevaba fatal con el pobre Ray Loriga, contra el cual ningún encono alberto excepto la lógica envidia derivada del hecho de que su matrimonio sea feliz, su mujer una belleza y su hijo una monada" (71). Notably she mentions nothing about the success or relevance of his work and she seems to pity "poor" Ray for not being her friend. Nevertheless, Loriga's cynicism toward the Gen X label and Etxebarria's openly critical, some may say hypocritical, opinion of the press, as seen in the epigraph to this chapter, are evidence

Chapter Six

of the growth and movement away from any one tendency in contemporary Spanish letters.

This chapter will present an analysis of Etxebarria's 2001 novel *De todo lo visible y lo invisible,* a text that consciously plays with and intentionally confuses ideas of reader and textual "realities." It will also look at the problematic representation of women within the Gen X rubric and specifically in the novel and in Etxebarria's representation of women on her personal Web page. The cultural representations of female and gender link the novelistic genre to the narrative of the Internet, where the female body becomes a displayed and exploited sight/site.

As Christine Henseler notes, Etxebarria has "enchanted and bemused some, angered and alienated others" ("Ecstasy" 109). The controversy surrounding her self-promotional Web site, nude photo spreads, and generally antiestablishment antics has attracted not only the media's attention but the attention of critics as well. Somewhere beyond the cacophony of Etxebarria media coverage lie her texts. Despite what one may think about her public persona, her award-winning novels offer a unique glimpse into the trappings of twenty-first century female identity. Through the incorporation of contemporary cultural references, feminist and gender issues, and a keen sense of what it means to be living in the twenty-first-century, Etxebarria has produced novels that embrace and challenge the notion of reality.

Several critics including Akiko Tsuchiya and Christine Henseler have approached her works as vestiges of a culture clash between literature and the publishing market. The presence of Etxebarria in the media, through her Web site, many interviews, or the notorious nude photos of her in *Dunia,* confirm the author's ideology that a malleable image is an important tool in self-promotion, which in itself sells books. Nevertheless, the relationship between her body and her body of works always remains outside of the textual realities she creates in her novels. The ever-changing persona that she presents to the market and media cannot alter the textual specificity of her works. As Henseler points out, Etxebarria seems intent on changing the dynamics between author and reader and she uses the media to force readers to reconsider the traditional relationship between reader and writer. The intimacy that Etxebarria seeks with her public is no where more apparent than in *De todo lo visible y lo invisible*. The violence that is typical in Etxebarria's narratives in the form of self-deprecation, rape, and drug and alcohol abuse moves to the syntax in this novel and becomes a textual manifestation of the psychological violence in the novel.

All of Etxebarria's novels revolve around individual isolation and a misunderstanding between established social contracts and individual desire. Her characters often lose themselves in alcohol or drugs in the search to identify their place in society. Her narratives dwell on the body as a locus for change and the site of abandonment. Jessica Folkart describes the overriding metaphor of the body in Etxebarria's novel *Beatriz y los cuerpos celestes* as a site of containment: "all the spaces in this text house bodies in pain, where physical pain becomes an expression of or a diversion from psychological pain" (45). Folkart expertly analyzes the novel in terms of narrative structure and reveals the complex play between Beatriz's pain and the power of language. Folkart explains, "the narrator resorts to the written Word to utter her existence into being and to comprehend it as an ongoing process of dialogue with a reader, yielding a new perspective on the bodies involved" (50). Thus the physical pain that Beatriz suffers must be displaced to the text in order to reestablish her sense of self. It is this kind of textual violence that comes to the surface in *De todo lo visible y lo invisible*. The protagonist, Ruth, inflicts pain on herself through several suicide attempts and resorts to physical violence when she cracks a bottle over the head of her estranged lover, Juan. Yet the rupture and dislocation of the narrative manifests itself in the structure of the text. The violence Ruth experiences leaps off the page, as the disjointed narrative depends on footnotes, on visual aids, and on the "author's" interruptions to complete the fictional reality.

Baudrillard claims: "Simulation is no longer that of a territory, a referential being or a substance. It is the generation by models of a real without origin or reality: a hyperreal" (*Simulacra* 1). He refers to the postmodern notion that art is independent of reality. Contemporary art does not reflect or try to represent reality in any way; it is self-referential, or fully self-contained. Just as television in Loriga's works creates a reference point that guides the actions of the characters, Lucía

Chapter Six

Etxebarria tackles problems of representation, truth, and fiction in *De todo lo visible*. While Loriga criticizes the media for institutionalized misrepresentation, at the same time he realizes the profound effects that television and media have on the everyday dissemination of information. In his novels, the characters do not compare their lives to those represented on television, but rather television becomes the "reality" to which they aspire.

Etxebarria also creates a virtual reality within the novelistic genre and builds a self-sufficient literary world through two nonconventional narrative tropes: first, she uses footnotes throughout the novel and second, within the text of the footnotes, she suggests that the protagonist is, in fact, a real person. This game between fictional and actual identity becomes a satirical commentary on the reality of the novel. The notion of "reality" in general is challenged in both Loriga's and Etxebarria's works; however, Etxebarria seems to rely heavily on narration and textual space to question specifically the role of author, narrator, and reader. In this case, Etxebarria not only creates a voice for the implied author, thus placing herself in the text, but insists on drawing her protagonist out of the textual space and into the world of marketing and media that has come to define in part her own public persona. The confusion between the character's fictional life and her supposed existence in "our" world outside of the story allows the reader to participate on various levels in the creation of the literary project. We are observers of the actions and reactions of the characters in the novel but at the same time we permit the author to cross normal boundaries of narrative decorum. Not unlike the characters in Carme Riera's *La meitat de l'ànima*, Etxebarria's characters seduce the reader and confuse traditional notions of fact and fiction. The playfulness of the footnotes and visual cascading of words on the page may seem gratuitous to the storyline, but in an effort to reveal various levels of experience, of what poet William Blake called the realms of the visible and invisible, Etxebarria carefully constructs a reading of the novel through the deconstruction of narrative.[2]

Another innovation of the novel is Etxebarria's use of textual violence or the disruption of normative reading patterns. In *De todo lo visible y lo invisible*, Etxebarria explores violence thematically and structurally. The novel revolves around the doomed love affair and multiple suicide attempts of famous film director Ruth Swanson. Ruth plays the role of the "other woman" in her relationship with Juan, and this drives her to self-destruction. The emotional violence becomes physical when she tries to end her life. Fame also violates Ruth's space and identity. The constant judgment of her art, lifestyle, and physical appearance by strangers leaves her exposed and vulnerable to the superficial opinions of others. But what is most intriguing about Ruth's story is the structural violence of the narrative, as will become evident in this analysis. Violence in this sense is used to refer to visual aberrations from normal paragraph structure, the constant metatextual musings of the implied author, and the use of footnotes in a work of fiction. These textual ruptures in turn create a narrative reality and an extra-textual reality at the same time; that is to say that Ruth Swanson is our protagonist but Etxebarria insists that she lives in our world as well. The text supports both a fictional reality and an extra-fictional reality, thus reflecting Baudrillard's "hyperreal."

The first example is the cascading syntax found throughout the first part of the novel suggesting Ruth's coming in and out of consciousness as she lies in a hospital bed recovering from her second suicide attempt. The stylistic recourse has been described as a narrative tool that "expresa el proceso de hundimiento y recuperación, tras un intento de suicidio" (Goicoechea 119). The thematic violence of the narrative is reflected in the disjointed structure on the page. The word *bajando* is repeated in decreasing font size and reads from right to left five times in the first chapter. Reading from right to left instead of the standard left to right forces us into an alternate way of reading and interpreting. Not only are we reading backwards, but also this act symbolically refers to the alternate reality of Ruth's subconscious that we become privy to through this nontraditional way of reading. The broken sentence signals a rupture in the fictive reality, allowing us to enter into subconscious thought and see that the conscious and subconscious are tenuously linked through language. The other moments of rupture occur when the word *subiendo* reads from left to right and in increasing font size. This pulls us back into the narrative reality out of the depths of Ruth's subconscious.

The increasing and decreasing font size suggests an aural complexity as well. The decreasing font size of *bajando* eventually reduces the narrative voice to a whisper, and we can hear the real world fading away as Ruth's inner thoughts come to life. Just the opposite is true for the increase in font size with the words *subiendo*. We are drawn back into the surrounding noises and distractions of social interaction of everyday life and reality. However, this phenomenon is inverted as the words *bajando* appear twice reading from left to right and the words *subiendo* appear twice from right to left. The wordplay creates a visual pattern important to the text that suggests both fluidity and rupture. The breakage that appears in the text forms a pattern that connects the larger paragraphs. In this way Etxebarria has managed to combine contradicting terms and make the narrative read as one long thought process. The author uses jagged sentences to unite two distinct worlds residing in the mind of one protagonist. The syntactical manipulations reflect Ruth's psychological instability and the fissure between her emotional state and her reality. The motion of the words on the page suggests interaction between reader and text and subsequently a movement to different levels of meaning.

Ruth moves from her subconscious (invisible) to the conscious or visible world around her. The reader becomes involved not only in the psychological process of Ruth's recovery but also in the ups and downs of her physical recuperation as well. The emphasis on the mind's capacity to move from one realm of consciousness to another is reflected in the physical words on the page. Just as Folkart has pinpointed the importance of the body as locus of experience in *Beatriz*, in *De todo lo visible* as well the body becomes equivalent to a visible space of emotional experience. The narrator repeatedly refers to Ruth's physical appearance, her clothes, the brilliant red color of her hair, and the general discomfort she feels about her own body. The preoccupation with looks and particularly the predominantly female dissatisfaction with body type translates to the readerly experience. Ruth's criticisms of her own body correlate with the disruption and unsettled reading provoked by the cascading words on the page. Significantly, the pages with the broken text and cascading words appear early in the book and set the tone for a nontraditional reading of the text. The stage is set for ground breaking in the very literal sense of breaking the paragraphs within the text and also in the sense of requiring a new and different interpretation of the relationship between form and content.

Etxebarria also injects meaning into form in the same way as does Dulce Chacón in *La voz dormida*. The juxtaposition of official documentation and narrative exposé creates a multi-layered version of a certain event or experience. Chacón uses letters and testimony from women serving time in the Ventas jail contrasted with state-issued documents outlining the same events. As discussed in Chapter 3, the commingling of various discourses creates the notion of unlimited versions of history, and while the many parts would seem to make a whole, the incorporation of political, institutionalized language into the poetic narrative of the novel serves to emphasize the impossibility of re-creating or knowing the "truth."

Etxebarria employs this same mechanism in *De todo lo visible* to underline the severe rupture between Ruth's emotional journey in and out of consciousness while recuperating in the hospital and the official documentation that coldly and concisely defines the situation. The first few pages of the novel introduce us to Ruth in a cloudy state of mind, drifting in and out of a dream world. The novel opens with Ruth's musings: "Duermo, duermo, duermo, duermo, soy un árbol, un vegetal, y pienso, pienso, pienso, pienso ..." (17). The crescendo of the cascading word *subiendo* draws her out of her dream and immediately a third-person narrator takes over: "Cuando Ruth abre los ojos no alcanza, al principio, a entender lo que pasa" (17). The different psychological levels are marked not only by the words rupturing the paragraph on the page but also by the appearance of a new narrator, a removed omniscient observer who relates the action.

Four pages later the narrator disappears altogether and Ruth's formal hospital admission papers appear in the text. The short lines of information reject any notion of reflection or interpretation as the words and numbers are probably typed onto an already existing form. The address of the clinic appears at the top of the form and subsequently we read "INFORME DE URGENCIAS" (21), which declares the intention to give the date, time, and name of the patient; the intent is to inform only. The form includes a social security number and address. Written below this information is: "mujer, 33a. M.C. Intoxicación medicamentosa. Paciente traída por el 061, que refiere que la paciente se ha tomado 65 c de Orfidal y 45 c de Lexatín hace 5 h. La paciente se niega a que se la ponga SNG y se niega a colaborar" (21).

Chapter Six

The numbers, names of the drugs, and official diagnosis present a contrasting version of the events. The lack of commentary and precise clinical analysis of the situation heightens the sense of confusion and brings into the narrative an outside assessment of the situation. As readers we no longer have to rely on Ruth for information or trust her version of the story. This document gives us the supposed facts and in doing so exposes the sharp contrast between hospital protocol and personal experience.

While Chacón's novel urges the reader to rethink the nature of history, *De todo lo visible* presents alternate versions of present "reality." We rely on Ruth's version of her hospital experience to ground us in the text and provide insight into the nature of the character, yet with the inclusion of a hospital document the narrative becomes caught between two versions of reality. The novel creates its own reality, with the document acting as a touchstone for everyday experience. The hyperreality of the novel becomes self-sufficient because the fictional experience is supported by an official-looking document.[3] The document reflects administrative procedures for admitting patients to the clinic and includes practical information such as the person's name, address, date of birth, and the current date. "Ruth de Siles Swanson" appears on the form, and we see before us her birthday, her address, and her social security number. The incorporation of a character into an official-looking document that displays her address (Calle Echegaray) and other pertinent information plays with the creative narrative convention. Ruth is presented as a person who lives in Madrid and claims all of the rights and privileges of a citizen. The clinic Etxebarria cites in the novel, Fundación Jiménez Díaz, does exist at the given address Avenida de los Reyes Católicos 2, 28040 Madrid. Therefore, our protagonist finds herself with official documents admitting her to a clinic that does exist and in this way the line between fact and fiction becomes blurred especially in the sense that we have both a testimonial account of the events and the entrance papers "confirming" the time and date of Ruth's arrival. The official document placed beside the unofficial, muddled recollections of the patient plays with the mixing of actual information and fictional invention. In this way, Etxebarria creates a self-sufficient textual space that does not distinguish between facts inside or outside of the textual boundaries.

Textual Violence and the Hyperreal

Another textual invasion that distracts the reader's attention is the curious use of footnotes throughout the novel. As a way of interjecting new information and creating a certain, intimate relationship with the reader, the footnotes demand that the reader's gaze and attention be redirected to the bottom of the page. This abrupt shifting of eyes and mind gives the novel an academic feel since it is usually only in scholarly works that we see footnotes.[4] Etxebarria employs this form in her novel, thus giving the text several levels of meaning. The fictional reality becomes compounded in the footnotes that refer to the characters as if they had a relationship to the world outside the narrative space. Etxebarria combines fact and fiction in her use of footnotes, and the narrative discourse takes on multiple layers of meaning and "reality" as the footnotes expand the characters' lives beyond the fictional world they occupy. Through this kind of narrative rhetoric, Etxebarria creates layers of reality from within the novel and creates a metatextual commentary highlighting the constructedness of narrative and of the reader's relation to it.

Rhetoric designed to seduce the reader into narrative compliance has appeared throughout the history of Spanish letters. One only has to think of the *Quijote* or, more recently, *La familia de Pascual Duarte* to see evidence of the author distancing himself from his work through extratextual framing of the narrative. Etxebarria's use of notes to gloss her own text serves not to distance herself from the narrative but rather to blur the division between created and lived reality, or between narrative voice, implied author, and real author. Wayne Booth describes the implied author as "the intuitive apprehension of a completed artistic whole" (73) or the voice that establishes tone throughout the narrative. The tone or attitude the narrative voice takes toward her subject creates a unique fictional reality that guides the reader through the moral quagmire of interpersonal relationships. Tone allows the reader to form an opinion about the actions and reactions of characters in the novel with the help of the narrative voice that represents the overriding viewpoint and attitude of the implied author.

The tone of *De todo lo visible* vacillates between apologetic and ironic, presenting Ruth as a survivor yet at the same time as self-destructive. The footnotes in the novel break dramatically

Chapter Six

with the narration, and we hear the implied author's voice rise distinctly above the narrative as it makes references to "real" people, provides us with the protagonist's e-mail address, or chides a character's ignorance. The narrative ramifications of footnotes as a structural transgression in the novel create a different kind of authorial presence. Etxebarria plays with the idea of confusing the "real" with the implied author. By drawing the reader out of the narrative space and reality into a footnote that cites familiar places, names, and facts, the author momentarily dupes the reader into thinking she hears the author's voice guiding her through the text. This momentary lapse of narrative structure induced by the use of the academic footnote connotes a momentary rupture of the fictional reality created by the implied author.

In this sense the implied author becomes a scrim that seems to reveal the presence of the "real" author lurking behind the scenes. "[T]hough the author can to some extent choose his disguises, he can never choose to disappear" (Booth 20). But in this case, Etxebarria uses a trope that makes the reader believe in a false intimacy with the main character of the novel and by extension with the author herself: she does not want to disappear but wants to remain fully engaged and present in the text. By breaking down the metaphorical walls that divide reader/author/character, the text allows for moments of familiarity that seem sincere until the structure of the novel re-emerges and places reader, narrator, author, and implied author neatly back into place. Etxebarria knows her readers well. She understands the need to connect on a personal level with the characters of a novel, and in a calculated move that invites the reader further into the narrative structure, she creates false intimacy between them.

Nevertheless, the text exists intact as a system of narrative devices that incorporates metanarrative commentary in order to create a self-sufficient world or fictional "reality" that alludes to readers' personal experience. The nature of the notes is at times informative and at other times critical. Two notes comment on the redundancy in the text. The voice of the implied author appears in the note offering textual commentary and aligning herself with the observations of the supposed reader. In the main body of the text appears: "Juan anotaba cada infidelidad a Biotza con meticulosa obsesividad culpable; etcétera, etcétera" (283). Here we run into the superscripted numeral 1 and we read the footnote: "Vale, vale ... Esto ya lo habíamos dicho." On the next page, after a lengthy analysis of the problems in Ruth and Juan's relationship, we read note 2; "También lo habíamos dicho." This type of footnote found throughout the novel anticipates the reader's reaction to the body of the text and, in a kind of metatextual criticism, highlights the repetitiveness of the text. In bringing to light this fault, the implied author scolds the narrator for potentially boring the reader. The intimacy created between reader and implied author emerges in the tone and physical textual space, for the footnote is a separate text removed from the main body that pulls the reader into a world of multiple narrative realities constructed in the novel.

In other cases the notes bridge the gap between the novelistic reality and the reader's reality by alluding to popular cultural icons. For example, the protagonist Ruth remembers certain events at Shangay Lily's birthday party. The footnote explains, "Polifacético y subyugador personaje muy conocido en el ambiente artístico de Madrid. Actor, escritor, tertuliano de radio, presentador de televisión y unas cuantas cosas más, amén de feminista convencido" (303). The footnote is anything but objectively informative. The added note on Shangay Lily fails to cite specific information about his birth or published works but instead provides only a personal evaluation of his contribution to popular culture. The comment highlights the presence of Lily in Spanish culture but fails to give the reader any concrete information about him. Therefore the bridge between Ruth's association with Shangay Lily and the person who lives and works in Madrid is the intimate and complimentary tone of the narrative voice in the footnote. The footnote text presents Lily in a positive light with a certain attitude instead of offering factual information. The cultural specificity of the footnote demands that readers be familiar with the works and presence of Shangay Lily in order to fully appreciate the implications of the attitude projected in the text.[5] His extroverted sense of self that comes from years of struggle and rejection because of his sexual orientation has become Shangay Lily's trademark. His keen sense of humor and humanity have made him widely popular in Spanish television and in the press. Ruth's friendship

Chapter Six

with such a personality in the novel elevates her persona to the level of the stardom enjoyed by Shangay Lily. Ruth reaches beyond the borders of her fictional life and into the realm of a Madrid social scene populated by highly successful artists. The footnote alluding to the great achievements of Shangay Lily in terms of Spanish cultural production firmly place the reader's sympathies with him as well.

Another cultural reference specific to Spanish artistic production provides a more blatant transgression of novelistic boundaries. In the main text Ruth's film is harshly reviewed as pornographic and uninspired. Her reputation is damaged, but the film does extremely well at the box office and is chosen as one of the few films of first-time directors to be shown at the Cannes Film Festival. The footnote that follows this episode in the text claims: "Esta historia está basada en un hecho real: Dunia Ayaso y Félix Sabroso rodaron *Fea* con un millón de pesetas" (91). The footnote goes on to explain how the filmmakers both applied for VISA credit cards and used the line of credit to make the film after their bank loans had been rejected. Unfortunately their film was never produced professionally but the footnote states: "En cualquier caso, si queréis obtener una copia en vídeo de esta obra magna, podéis contactar con Félix Sabroso a través de la siguiente dirección de *e-mail*: amorylujo@infonegocio.com" (91). The familiar tone of the footnote with its use of the second-person plural and the e-mail address breaks with the narrative tone of the body of the text. The direct address to the readers immediately creates a community outside of the narrative. The reader is not alone with the text but part of a larger connected group that has immediate access to the "real" filmmaker through digital technology. The novel uses e-mail correspondence in this way to heighten the sense of intimacy not only between the implied author and reader but also between readers themselves. This break in the narrative action adds to the multilayered structure of the novel, creating a specific discourse of interrelationships that ultimately define the textual space. The reader becomes complicit in generating textual reality that in this case draws on fictional characters and allusions to "real" stories that heighten the sense of intimacy between fiction and "reality."

The collaborative efforts of reader and narrator to build the textual reality of the novel produce a version of Baudrillard's

Textual Violence and the Hyperreal

hyperreal. As mentioned earlier, the hyperreal is a self-sufficient system that creates its own references without problematizing the accuracy or "truth" of the information shared. Etxebarria does not concern herself with the accuracy of the information provided. As noted with her inclusion of Miss Shangay Lily and the two filmmakers mentioned, these figures provide a symbolic bridge between the text and the current cultural production in Madrid. The referent itself is less important than the fact that it appears in a novel as a tool to create a narrative world that seems to totter between fiction and fact. The footnotes that refer to the text are a mechanism of self-referentiality that gives the text an illusion of authority. The footnotes seduce the reader into taking part in the circular notion of the hypertext.

Another example of a footnote that uses e-mail as a tool to call the reader to action plays with various textual levels of meaning and illusion. The footnote explains an e-mail address found in a letter written by Ruth and reproduced in the body of the text. Early in the novel, the letter plays an important role in Ruth's seduction of Juan and in the textual seduction of the reader. The narrative voice in the text assures us that this letter represents Ruth's attraction for Juan and that she feels attracted to him "porque confirmaba su propia existencia" (153). The letter appears as a separate document that reproduces these feelings of dependency and attraction. The written words confirm Ruth's feelings, and the letter survives outside of the text as a "document" passed between the two characters. For Ruth it is not necessarily Juan who confirms her existence but rather the letter that represents her feelings toward him. The act of writing and then sending the letter confirms her feelings and existence, while on a metatextual level the "document" confirms her existence within the realm of the textual reality.

The play on text in this section multiplies as we read the narrative voice, Ruth's voice in the letter, and the second narrative voice in the footnote. Ruth closes her letter by writing: "no tengo teléfono, o más bien, nunca lo cojo, pero tengo una dirección de e-mail: ruthswanson@espasa.es. Puedes enviarme un e-mail, o si no tienes cómo hacerlo, escribirme a casa" (153). Immediately after the e-mail address a superscripted number 1 indicates a footnote. Is this footnote part of Ruth's letter meant for Juan to see or only for us readers of the novel? We jump down the page to the footnote that addresses us readers in the

145

Chapter Six

informal vosotros declaring, "La dirección existe, y podéis escribir a Ruth si queréis. Pero ella nunca os responderá. Eso sí, yo leeré las cartas, y le transmitiré los mensajes" (153). We recognize part of the e-mail address as that of the publisher of the book we are holding in our hands, Espasa, and this adds an official mark to the fictionalized e-mail. Obviously Ruth is a character in a book, but the publisher Espasa certainly exists. Yet the voice of the footnote assures us that any effort to contact Ruth is already futile as there will never be a response. And who is the "yo" in the footnote? Who will read the e-mails and forward them to Ruth? The use of the first person draws attention to the constructedness of the narrative, for there is an "author" or presence that seems to be overseeing the course of the narrative. But at the same time, this effort to become intimate with the reader provides a distancing step that allows the fictive world to take on a life of its own while excusing the flesh-and-blood author of any fictional improprieties. The "yo" of the footnote will read and pass on to Ruth all the e-mails sent to the given address, acknowledging the separate identity of author, narrator, and protagonist.

Nevertheless, contrary to the stylized efforts to forge a "real" identity for Ruth, her existence is thrown into dubious light. The voice of the footnote explains that Ruth will never respond, suggesting that she is incapable of responding. The word "never" puts finality to the fiction and confirms for us readers that Ruth is of course a character in a novel. The text mocks the role of the reader, for who would ever believe that footnotes in a novel were truthful and send an e-mail to a protagonist's address? Yet the inclusion of this footnote stands as a testament to the successful seduction of the reader and the blurring of fictional and nonfictional realities. The author here cleverly reminds us that Ruth and her story are, in fact, fiction. She assumes we have fallen somewhat prey to the extratextual devices that claim otherwise and the e-mail address that can never be answered by Ruth. The fictional nature of the character snaps the reader back into the fictional reality of the text.

All of the narrative elements that create the rhetoric in *De todo lo visible* lead to a new way for the author to relate to her audience. The intimate tone and direct address in the novel build a multitiered narrative that plays with established literary relationships between author, implied author, narrator, and reader. Etxebarria breaks down these barriers and changes the way we read the text by decentering traditional notions of structure and discourse. The discourse or, according to Seymour Chatman, the way we read relates to Booth's tone of the implied author. The attitude toward the subject of the novel becomes the attitude toward the reader in Etxebarria's footnotes. The notes usurp the narrative space and place the reader directly into the novel as an accomplice to the narrative act. Henseler observes that Etxebarria's personal Web site foments this intimacy between author and reader. Personal data and anecdotes appear on the Web site, but "[m]ore important than the information that Etxebarria publicizes is that readers enter a new kind of relationship with the traditionally absent author" ("Ecstasy" 119). This new kind of relationship between reader and author is apparent in *De todo lo visible* as well. The absent author, who is never completely absent from the text according to Booth, emerges not as the flesh-and-blood writer but rather as an ideology toward the text. This is indeed the virtual author who leaves fingerprints on the structure and discourse of the novel by multiplying her identity so that the reader becomes seduced into thinking that our author has allowed us into a private "reality."

The self-contained reality of the novel becomes a space of a virtual relationship. Unlike Loriga's or Mañas's works that directly allude to the virtual nature of society by citing film and television in a narrative space, Etxebarria exploits the virtual aspects of e-mail as a form of instant communication that creates a false intimacy with a fictional character. The virtual aspect of culture as explained by Baudrillard converts the representation of something into the referent, making the image or reproduction the reality of the event. In Etxebarria's novel, the structure becomes the referent, and even though she incorporates cultural artifacts and people into the narrative, their role is strictly to augment the textual "reality" so as to make it seem more commonplace and current to us readers. The referent is the fictional text, and this is the basis of the novel's hyperreality. Instead of trying to imitate reality or everyday life, *De todo lo visible* recreates a world that revolves around and exists through various layers of text and narrative voice. The artistic need to present cultural phenomenon such as the novel, or writing in general, in challenging ways can attest to the thriving literary production in contemporary Spain. While at times negatively criticized in Spain, Etxebarria has come to the forefront of the group of contemporary authors who test boundaries and push limits. As Henseler has pointed out, some critics and readers see her manipulations of the media as shameless self-promotion, while others find great value in her dedication to analyzing an unjust society for women and minorities and confronting polemical feminist issues. The conversation can be expanded to include her unique handling of narrative structure and style. The playfulness with which she approaches the text reveals a certain alliance between the "high" art of writing literature and the influence of popular culture.

What can we conclude from this use of footnotes and visual cascading syntax in Etxebarria's novel? First and foremost, the visual exercise of the novel—of reading up and down, forward and backward, and jumping to footnotes within the novel—suggests playfulness within the literary genre. Second, it brings a discourse of violence and rupture to a syntactic level. The violations of the page, the paragraph, and the narrative flow all reflect the emotional and psychological violence that pushes Ruth to act out through suicide. And lastly, this kind of experimental writing blurs the boundaries between author, text, and reader. We are invited to participate in creating the text in numerous and unexpected ways.

Etxebarria and Internet Ethics

Lucía Etxebarria is well known for her polemical approach to reconciling fame and ethics. She rejects the role of ivory tower academic in her nonfiction work and explores the violence brought on by low self-esteem in her novels. The female body as eroticized fetish is a loaded image that draws on deeply embedded cultural renderings from a male point of view. Both the circulation of a particularly negative discourse and the female stereotype previously discussed in her novel *De todo lo visible y lo invisible* suggest a problematic relationship between female identity and autonomy. The push toward self-realization is evident in Etxebarria's works, and at times her means intended to defy patriarchal control reach an extreme that pushes the reader outside of what is "comfortable" and "socially acceptable." This is perhaps even more relevant when considering her Internet ethics.

In one section of Lucía Etxebarria's official Web site the question "¿Es usted feminista?" appears superimposed over a black-and-white photograph of a topless blonde model kneeling down with her hands between her legs and head seductively thrown back. The image evokes the sensuality of many Marilyn Monroe photographs; however, the question "¿Es usted feminista?" seems to contradict the fetishized representation of female sexuality. The section contains carefully researched information and statistics on gender inequality in the workplace, rape, and anorexia, to name only a few topics. However, each news item is projected against a backdrop of nude photographs of women, some well-known Hollywood actresses. For example, the viewer reads the information about socially rendered gender stereotypes against a fuzzy black-and-white photo of a topless Kim Bassinger. "Mujeres y Trabajo" is projected over Sharon Stone in a transparent bathing suit. The section begins with the results from a survey asking married and single people if they are happy or not (single women seem to be the happiest) and this information is superimposed over a photo of Madonna lounging around completely naked. The images and composition of this portion of the Web site present provocative messages about the social (patriarchal) construction of female identity. The images of women's bodies within the feminist context shock the viewer into reevaluating the exploitation of female sexuality by a dominantly patriarchal society. The juxtaposition of scientific data relating the problematic condition for women in society with erotic images of the body is a powerful statement on the destructive results of the male gaze that sees women only as sexualized objects.

Etxebarria takes liberties as an author, a public figure, and a woman to appropriate erotic images of women and place them in a context that reveals how female sexuality is manipulated by the media. The statistics on domestic abuse, rape, and eating disorders become more potent and more disturbing when combined with the exploitation of the female body eroticized as "other" through the male gaze. Nevertheless, by fusing together the mainstream sexual images of women with hard statistical facts about female suffering in virtually all sectors of society including family and the workplace, Etxebarria sends a very different message. Viewers realize their hypocritical nature as people who are programmed to see the female body as erotic yet ignore the "reality" of women's lives in society. The female eroticized body has become commonplace in advertising, yet the plight of women suffering abuse and low self-esteem seems to be silenced in many sectors of social discourse. Michel Foucault explains the intent to repress sexuality in modern societies: "What is peculiar to modern societies, in fact, is not that they consigned sex to a shadow existence, but that they dedicated themselves to speaking of it *ad infinitum*, while exploiting it as *the* secret" (35; italics in original). However, the images of women's bodies on Etxebarria's Web site do not relegate the sexualized body to a shadowy existence, for we see the body exposed and displayed; instead, the meaning of female sexuality and the body as fetish is confused by the context. Sex and female sexuality is portrayed as *the* secret because the bodies contradict the written information: the visual seduction, by introducing ambiguity into the meaning of the words, alters the reading of the text. We are forced to reconcile the images of mass media consumption with the startling statistics of marginalized and abused women.

In her novels, Etxebarria seems to follow a similar path of mixing signals and confusing the erotic with the political in an attempt to appropriate female identity within a patriarchal society. The need to work through the postmodern crisis that leaves the individual isolated occupies the narrative space of the novel. On her Web site, she claims in an interview that self-inflicted violence is a problem of self-esteem, and in her novels this lack of self-esteem is clearly a result of being female in a patriarchal system. Catherine Ross has studied sex, drugs, and violence in Etxebarria's first novel *Amor, curiosidad, prozac y dudas,* and here the body becomes a site of repression in that drug use alters reality temporarily for the protagonist. Ross also points out the self-inflicted violence inherent in drug use when she describes the youth represented in the Gen X novels as depicted "always [to be] in search of something—usually something self-destructive—that makes everything else matter" (157). The negative repercussions of self-destructive behavior on female identity are at the core of *De todo lo visible* as well. The novel can be read as a feminist statement of women's struggle in the workplace and in society, but also the propagation of a negative stereotype throws the protagonist's self-realizations into a dubious light.

The lack of female agency and problematic identity in relation to the female body seen on the Web site emerges also in *De todo lo visible*. When Ruth is fading in and out of consciousness after one of her suicide attempts, the narrative voice moves between a dreamlike stream of consciousness and the harsh reality of getting to the hospital on time. As she is loaded in to the ambulance "como un supositorio, por la parte trasera" Ruth thinks to herself "esto es serio" (20). She goes on to ponder in her foggy state: "no pienso volver a abrir los ojos pase lo que pase, quiero ser árbol, quiero ser árbol, ya no quiero ser ninfa" (20). The word *ninfa* 'nymph' suggests a Modernist interpretation of the female. The woman turned into fetish by the male gaze strips the individual literally and figuratively of her identity. The nymph is a timeless, eroticized invention of female sexuality, and the ethereal, unreal quality of a nymph entices male desire through the impossibility of possessing her. If a woman sees herself as a nymph—defined by male desire and destined to be elusive—then her own sexuality becomes obfuscated, for once she recognizes her own desires, she no longer fulfills the male fantasy; she becomes human and ruptures the very construct of the fetish.

To further emphasize the importance of the nymph that runs throughout the novel, the cover of the 5th edition printed by Espasa provides an image. The nude woman with flames of red hair and the daisy in her hand is Ruth, her red hair indicating Irish ancestry and the flower, her love of daisies; both remind her of her deceased mother. The cover harkens back to the full frontal nudity of women on Etxebarria's Web site. Henseler writes about precisely this kind of marketing of female writers in Spain, explaining that Etxebarria appears in her study because Etxebarria "moves the discussion of the female body in narrative to the body (of narrative) in the publishing industry" (109). Henseler also says, "One could claim that Etxebarria is attempting to re-appropriate that space that some have considered 'prostituted' or contaminated with female bodies (of narrative)" (116). Alternative viewpoints and perspectives unique

Chapter Six

to the female experience are populating the public spaces once unavailable to the female writer, but the tools and methods that promote the "new" discourse are the same loaded stereotypes as always. The protagonist of *De todo lo visible* reminds the reader of many stereotypical preoccupations women are supposed to have, ranging from the materialistic to the emotional.

Therefore, the value of a critical reading of the representations of women in Etxebarria's novels and Web site is that such a reading forces us to once again renegotiate the relationship between cultural representations of individual identity. What may seem contradictory in Etxebarria's texts opens up a discussion on the symbolic value of images and how women's bodies are represented, both verbally and visually. The violence in the novel directed toward Ruth's body and psyche as well as toward the text itself, paired with the statistics citing violence against women superimposed on the erotic female bodies online, all create a discourse surrounding socially constructed female identity. The important connection between the novel and the virtual space heightens the awareness of a hyperreality to which the text refers. The violence to women, to the word, and to the image can all be read as cultural representations of protest because they are presented within a discourse of empowerment. However, much of the criticism that falls on the created persona "Lucía Etxebarria" can be attributed to the inconsistent language of her actions and words. For the purposes of this study, I have focused on the texts themselves and not on the media spectacle surrounding the public persona of the author. Etxebarria's novel is a unique work that cleverly crosses boundaries of the text/reader relationship. The inclusion of e-mail addresses, contemporary figures, and specifically the hospital forms bring a contemporary historicity to the text that echoes the actual letters and documents included in both *La voz dormida* and *Soldados de Salamina*. The mixing of different linguistic registers creates a dynamic text that reaches across time and space while emphasizing the literary importance of cultural artifacts.

Etxebarria certainly plays a media game but by bringing attention to this in her narrative and pubic persona she embodies the irony of hyperreality. The body is tangible yet can be represented as malleable and transformative, just as identity, especially female identity, is based on cultural markers that shift and change depending on their context. The power of the text lies in the limitless possibilities of representation that are constantly renewed and regenerated. Etxebarria is a master of the media and of the manipulation of her own image, but she also captures the essence of the irony that is the foundation of the hyperreal.

Chapter Seven

(Inter)Textuality in José Ángel Mañas's *Historias del Kronen* and *La pella*

> Smells like teen spirit
> Nirvana
>
> Esmelslaiktinspirit
> José Ángel Mañas
> *Historias del Kronen*

José Ángel Mañas's *Historias del Kronen* (1994) remains one of the most important representations of Gen X literature in Spain.[1] The novel has been widely studied, mainly by North American critics, and despite a lukewarm reception by the Spanish academy, the novel was cited by the Madrid daily *El Mundo* as one of the top one hundred Spanish novels of all time (*Pella* jacket). Several critics of the novel have noted that the decadent portrayal of Spanish youth is representative of a general political apathy at the end of the twentieth century. In 2008 Mañas published *La pella*, which deals with similar issues of drug abuse and general malaise among Spanish youth. However, a notable presence of the implied author in *La pella* harkens back to the narrator Javier Cercas of *Soldados de Salamina*. This study does not propose to compare *Soldados* and *La pella*, but to point out the overt presence of the implied author in *La pella* that gives it a distinctly documentary-style voice and adds to the play between author–implied author–reader that we have observed thus far in this study. First *Kronen* will be explored as an example of intertext and illusion and then compared to *La pella,* which uses the authorial voice to establish a reciprocal relationship with a complicit or, in Umberto Eco's terms, a "model" reader.[2]

Chapter Seven

Historias del Kronen

In *Kronen* the characters' violent behavior stems from an aversion to the responsibility inherent in family and friendship and from a disregard for the historical. Nevertheless, if we carefully analyze the novel's intertextuality and Roberto's testimony that redirects our reading of the text, the overriding moral criticism comes into full view. Also, the hyperreality constructed through intertextuality creates a novelistic space in which the characters define themselves through existing literature and film. Just as Lucía Etxebarria incorporates references to the "real" world outside the novel in *De todo lo visible y lo invisible,* Mañas uses other texts to illuminate the inner thought process of the protagonist, Carlos. *Kronen* relies on several levels of polisemantic expression, which in turn emphasize the complex act of interpretation. Ultimately the novel can be read not as a handbook for disgruntled youth but rather as a counter example of excessive behavior in contemporary youth culture. The intertextuality and epilogue in the novel warn against imitating destructive behavior found in popular literary texts and therefore, *Historias del Kronen* becomes a critique of itself. Not only does Mañas warn the reader against the emotional and physical destruction that results from imitating violence but also he pinpoints the danger of the seductive pull of visual and verbal texts.

While Mañas's model reader will come away from the novel with an implicit moral stance condemning the characters' behavior, Mañas's narrative technique of interweaving popular texts in order to seduce the reader deserves closer attention. As a mode of analysis I will locate the intertexts in the novel within a theoretical framework that ultimately places the responsibility of interpretation on the reader. Similar to the extratextual tropes employed by Etxebarria in *De todo lo visible* and by Carme Riera in *La meitat de l'ànima, Kronen,* in a less overt way, uses other texts to reveal to the reader the unreliability of language. The text does not propose a "truth" about video culture, American culture, or Spanish youth culture, but rather through the indirect criticism of globalization found in the novel, it questions both visual and verbal language as a means of expression and identification. The protagonist, Carlos, looks to visual media such as film and video to fill the communication gap that leaves him afloat in a culture that rejects stable identity. Dorothy

Odartey-Wellington points out the criticism of mass consumption seen in Gen X novels, where there is "a preoccupation with the diminished, destabilized, or dislocated subject in the global media and economic environment ..." (27). *Kronen* focuses on the precarious nature of identity and through representations of contemporary culture, it seeks to redefine the function of the novel and its various parts.

Randolph Pope analyzes the book's epilogue in "Between Rock and the Rocking Chair: The Epilogue's Resistance in *Historias del Kronen*." He cites the innovative way in which Mañas uses the epilogue to uncover fundamental aspects of the text as a whole. Not the usual recap of events or tidying up of the plot, the epilogue in *Kronen* introduces the traumatizing effects of two "disquieting secrets" (116), namely, a sexual transgression and a murder. Instead of wrapping up the narrative, this epilogue opens up a narrative space for further interrogation, and as Pope claims, "this may be the moment in which the text transfers its questions to the reader and critics" (120). The epilogue redirects the perspective of the narrative by first telling of Carlos's vacation in Santander and then introducing a dialogue between Roberto and his therapist. The transfer of narration from Carlos to Roberto's observations filtered through an interlocutor creates a parallel between the textual and metatextual meanings in the novel. Carlos represents the narrative quality of the text, as he is the driving force behind the story, while Roberto represents a reaction to the discourse or mode of narration. Roberto criticizes Carlos's actions and his dependence on pop culture for role models. Thus, the epilogue inverts the narrative mode of the novel and, as Pope points out, the epilogue of *Kronen* becomes the key to interpretation and inverts the traditional novelistic form.

Many critics of the novel have focused on the masochistic tendencies of the main character, Carlos. In his desire to combat boredom, he pushes his body to horrifying limits. Yaw Agawu-Kakraba calls *Kronen* "literature of insurgency," suggesting that the novel rebels against tradition and establishment and must be appreciated in these terms. In the same vein, Germán Gullón and Nina Molinaro highlight the body as the epicenter of hedonism, excess, and isolation. These critics suggest that through excess and addiction, the characters conceal a deeper ontological crisis while placing all consciousness of identity in the material body. Toni Dorca, Santiago Fouz-Hernández, and Isabel Estrada see the characters' moral and spiritual vacancy as a way of revealing the emotional crisis of contemporary Spanish youth where solidarity, principles, and relationships fall victim to superficial pleasures and solipsistic behavior.[3] María T. Pao presents a provocative reading of the novel as "blank fiction" and sees in it a warning of North American consumerism.[4] However, through Roberto's confession and remorse shown in his conversation with the therapist in the epilogue and through the presence of extensive intertextuality, the novel succeeds in incorporating contemporary cultural icons while condemning not consumerism but rather uninformed readings of popular culture. The identity crisis of urban youth can be traced to specific antecedent texts, and the misinterpretation of these texts leads to destructive imitation of their protagonists. *Kronen* ultimately criticizes certain behaviors that dominate its pages, such as Carlos's obsession and imitation of literary forms that become dangerously demented when seen through Roberto's eyes in the epilogue.

Mañas seems to idealize Carlos's violent reality with his seductive, fast-paced, first-person narrative. But what steers the final reading of the novel is the context invoked by the epilogue that frames the events. The epilogue functions as a subversive closure that undermines the tone and first-person narrative of the body of the novel. In this sense, we readers are enlisted as textual and intertextual sleuths. In spite of Carlos's repugnant actions throughout the narrative, he is appallingly confident and inspires admiration in the eyes of his friends. The double bind of the attraction/repulsion the reader feels toward Carlos is given a voice in the epilogue through Roberto. However, Roberto is convinced that he will see Carlos again and apparently forgive him. Therefore, the reader is left to ultimately accept or condemn the behaviors exhibited in the novel, for Roberto has already forgiven his friend for his misdeeds.

We see in *Kronen* that meaning is a slippery slope when the textual indicators are confusing, ambiguous, or contradictory. For Wolfgang Iser, the vacancies or gaps in meaning are fundamental indicators to the reader who must make narrative connections. Therefore, doubts cast by inconsistencies in the

(Inter)Textuality

text direct the reader to meaning. The encoded or implied reader exists in the text through clues that the "real" reader detects and pieces together. For example, in the culminating scene of the narration, all voices other than Carlos's are represented by empty parentheses "( )" (215–23). This textual rupture points to the importance of what is not said in reconstructing the meaning of the scene.[5] Christine Brooke-Rose uses the term "encoded" reader to identify that part of the text that serves to illuminate interpretation, suggesting that the real reader breaks the code by correctly differentiating overdetermined or obvious codes from underdetermined ones. She claims that the function of "underdetermination is to blur. The encoded reader is then required to cooperate actively, to be hypercritical" (134). This technique of encoding a reader allows the author to imagine the interpretive ability of a real reader and indicate through absences or codes what the real reader will contribute to the narrative. In Mañas's novel, film and literature work side by side to seduce the young protagonist and provoke in the reader a sense of familiarity. The melding of intertextuality and encoding produces a shockingly "real" account because the referents are part of a collective reality that forces the reader to adapt the narrative to her own experience.

Mañas creates a complex game of misinterpretation where the reader, both implied and real, falls victim to the narrative just as the protagonist is lured by visual texts such as film and television. Carlos is seduced by the cultural subversion of snuff films, pornography, and violence transmitted through various forms of mass media. The reader, in turn, is seduced by the nature of Mañas's vivid descriptions and colorful dialogue. Yet *Historias del Kronen* is not a novel merely "conforme a las consignas de un mercado que actúa como incitador constante de una dinámica expeculativa" (Echevarría, "Oiga" 9).[6] The embedded self-criticism of violence in art that Mañas achieves in the text relies on the manipulation of both character and reader that he suggests is characteristic of an over indulgent, saturated mass media culture.

Historias del Kronen is Carlos's frenetic account of unbridled hedonism during summer vacation in Madrid. His relationships and daily activities revolve around buying, selling, and using drugs, and spontaneous sexual encounters. The narrative is

Chapter Seven

told in first person, and as Carmen de Urioste points out, similar to other protagonists of Generation X novels, Carlos has a voice that carries "un patente valor testimonial" ("Narrativa" 460). This testimonial voice expresses particular concerns of urban youth at the end of the twentieth century and places the subject squarely within a contemporary cultural framework. Readers identify with Carlos because his constant references to popular music, film, and books place him within a familiar contemporary reality. Carlos bases his behavior exclusively on certain movies, novels, rock lyrics, and rock groups such as *A Clockwork Orange*, *Henry: Portrait of a Serial Killer*, *American Psycho*, The The, and Nirvana, which represent for Carlos a world where sentimental relationships do not exist and only violence and immediate gratification matter.[7] What shocks the reader about Carlos is that his fascination with violence moves beyond the mere representative level abundant in pop culture and turns into physical, verbal, and psychological abuse. The key aspect of Carlos's relationship to violence is the link he creates between his reality and that of popular films and novels. The epilogue, which presents the only other perspective of the summer's events, is a conversation between Roberto and his therapist. While other characters try to sway Carlos from his destructive behavior, Roberto's session is the only conversation free from Carlos's commentary and judgment. The confessional tone of the session reveals Roberto's critical view of Carlos's unaccounted-for actions and flippant attitude.

Another important aspect that distinguishes Carlos from some of his peers is that he does not have to work to party and buy drugs. Carlos is a university student, and apparently a good one because he passed all of his courses in the spring and does not have to prepare any exams for the fall semester. Therefore, while "Carlos's indolence, antisocial tendencies, misogyny, and obsession with violence and sadistic sex do not reflect wholesale the lives of his peers" (Pao 250), neither do his social position and class. Manolo, the bartender who works in the bar Kronen, is a member of the group of "friends" and claims: "Qué bien vivís, hijoputas. Mientras los demás curramos para ahorrar unas pelillas para pagarnos el verano, vosotros ya tenéis el chaletito esperando" (177). Wealth allows Carlos to consume drugs, sex, and violence in excess. His family provides him with shelter, money, and a car, all of which, ironically, seem to foster in him a false sense of liberation from family ties and responsibility. Carlos's lifestyle actually depends on his family's wealth as well as on their apparent ignorance of his activities.

Carlos yearns to escape the mundane, upper middle-class reality that he thinks plagues his parents. While he complains about their constant attempts to control him, he blames them for the general apathy of his generation. "Ni siquiera nos han dejado la rebeldía ... lo que nos falta es algo por lo que o contra lo que luchar" (67). The fictional reality of film and novels represents for Carlos not only an escape from his routine life but also an obsession, something to believe in and "fight" for. The films and books that inspire him become fetishes that provide an outlet as a simulacrum of subversion. This literary culture provides a site of resistance against the established social norms represented by Carlos's family and prioritizes immediate gratification over any kind of group solidarity (Corbalán 209). However, as Carlos continues to idolize the destructive behavior of his literary counterparts, the text becomes self-reflective and reveals that Carlos is another in a long line of literary hooligans. Mañas carefully builds Carlos's obsession with cinematic and literary violence by revealing his perverse interest in several shocking scenes that distract him from his day-to-day existence. Carlos describes his delight in the violence from *A Clockwork Orange*:

> [E]s una de mis películas preferidas, un clásico de la violencia. Mi escena favorita es cuando Alex y sus amigos están violando a la mujer del escritor. Alex corta con tijeras el traje rojo de la cerda mientras los otros sujetan al escritor, obligándole a mirar. Alex está cantando Aimsingininderein y le da patadas al compás de la música. (32)

A friend recommends *The Texas Chainsaw Massacre* to Carlos and says: "A ti te encantaría Carlos. Es un tío en Texas que se dedica a matar con una sierra eléctrica a toda la gente que pasa por su casa, y lleva una careta que se ha hecho de pieles humanas" (92). The inclusion of these popular films reaches out and touches the reader's reality by referring to a context larger than the narrative reality contained in the book, but more importantly these allusions work to guide our reading of the novel. The

Chapter Seven

short descriptions provoke a moral reaction from the reader. For even if Carlos is impressed, the great majority of readers finds it morally offensive to celebrate rape and murder. The familiarity of the texts in the novel allows the reader to negatively judge Carlos's enthusiastic approval of such graphic violence. However, it is important to note that the films mentioned are highly valued works of cultural subversion. The artistic merit of the socio-political criticism implied in the subversive content paired with the highly stylized forms of representation garner respect for these works in academic and critical circles as well. *A Clockwork Orange*, published in 1962 by Anthony Burgess, has become a canonical work for its groundbreaking treatment of violence, youth, and the torturous corrective measures employed by authorities. Stanley Kubrick's 1971 film adaptation received accolades for representing the underground life of disturbed youth through the stylistic effects of costume, editing, and montage. Therefore, Carlos's appreciation of the work is warranted on a certain level, which produces a troublesome relationship between Carlos's objectionable behavior and his recognition of the value of consecrated art forms.

The commonality of themes in the aforementioned texts and in *Kronen* is important because it places Mañas's novel squarely within a certain rebellious literary tradition: an aesthetic of violence that aims to shake up and disturb traditional notions of literary decorum. Mañas takes up where Burgess and Kubrick left off; *Kronen* stands as perhaps the best example of contemporary Spanish literature that incorporates mainstream English and American ideologies of youth violence. Boredom, emotional isolation, and the meaninglessness of life push these young characters to the edge of sanity. The protagonist of Kubrick's film, Alex, describes himself and his friends as eager to enter into a drug-induced state in order to carry out their violent acts. The link between behavioral aberration and drug consumption begins at the outset of Kubrick's 1971 classic film. The first shot is a close-up of Alex, and as the camera draws away to reveal five friends sitting in the milk bar in silence, Alex's voice-over claims:

> There was me, that is Alex, and my three droogs, that is Pete, Georgie and Dim. And we sat in the Korova Milk Bar trying to make up our rassoodocks what to do with the evening. The Korova Milk Bar sold milk plus—milk plus vellocet or

> synthemesc or drencrom, which is what we were drinking.
> This would sharpen you up and make you ready for a bit of
> the old Ultra-Violence. (*Clockwork*)

The similarities between the film and *Kronen* are evident at the opening of Mañas's novel with the group of friends gathering in a favorite bar, Kronen, as they plan their nightly activities that undoubtedly will include some sort of violence. Mañas's novel opens with the same tone found in *A Clockwork Orange*: "Me jode ir al Kronen los sábados por la tarde porque siempre está hasta el culo de gente" (*Kronen* 11). The bar serves as a meeting point, a public space where the antisocial male can pretend to belong and find release from boredom through alcohol, drugs, and violence. This parallel creates a link between the two texts and on a discursive level exemplifies the spirit of imitation that guides the narrative.

Similarly to *A Clockwork Orange*, Bret Easton Ellis's 1991 novel *American Psycho* has been both praised and condemned for revealing the twisted mind and violent tendencies of the protagonist. Nevertheless, it held both the American popular readers' and critics' attention in the early 1990s.[8] Patrick Bateman, the protagonist, reflects on his lack of interpersonal connections, and his words echo Carlos's own feelings of isolation and his rejection of emotion:

> There wasn't a clear, identifiable emotion within me, except
> for greed and, possibly, total disgust. I had all the character-
> istics of a human being—flesh, blood, skin, hair—but my
> depersonalization was so intense, had gone so deep, that the
> normal ability to feel compassion had been eradicated, the
> victim of a slow, purposeful erasure. (282)

Alex from *A Clockwork Orange*, Bateman from *American Psycho*, and Carlos from *Kronen* are contemporary literary heroes that idolize marginalized, violent behavior because it undermines any sense of traditional morality or social responsibility. The fact that Carlos bases his behavior on established literary models gives him a kind of legitimacy as he continues the legacy of his violent predecessors. What lies at the base of this male identity crisis is perhaps the threat of displacement in the dismantling of a highly patriarchal society.[9]

Chapter Seven

Nevertheless, Mañas does not seem to eulogize his literary predecessors, but rather he shows Carlos to be so deeply affected by his longing to imitate a negative attitude and thus belong to a marginalized sector of society that he loses the ability to distinguish between art and life. Artistic reality within *Kronen* and Carlos's reality become even more blurred when he describes to his friend Roberto the key elements of "Esnafmuvis" ["snuff movies"]. They are "unas pelis que están ahora de moda en las que filman a un tío o a una tía, normalmente una puta o un chavalito, se los follan y luego les matan. Pero de verdad, y delante de la cámara" (93). The violence enacted for a cinematic end confuses the boundaries between literary symbolic violence and truly erratic, threatening behavior. The legal, social, and moral transgressions of snuff movies represent the link between film and reality that fascinates Carlos. His obsession with cinematic violence reflects his own life experience drained of all sense of human compassion. After a particularly aggressive sexual encounter, Carlos smiles and thinks, "Ha sido igual que una peli porno" (79). Ironically, once the violence in his own life becomes "real," and when he lashes out physically and not just in his imagination, his life seems more artistic, more meaningful and valid, like a film or novel that represents some form of achievement and permanence.

The incorporation of popular culture in the literary text points to the fragmented identities of postmodernism.[10] Carlos appropriates the attitudes of various fictional characters and thus bases his own behavior on fantasy. He declares: "La cultura de nuestra época es audiovisual. La única realidad de nuestra época es la de la televisión. Cuando vemos algo que nos impresiona siempre tenemos la sensación de estar viendo una película" (42). With this juxtaposition of video culture elaborated in the novel by the protagonist and in the extraliterary reality of the reader, Mañas enters into a game of genre revealing the falseness of Carlos's assertion by drawing attention to himself as a writer. The novel we hold in our hands that conveys the information about the highly developed and influential video culture remains fundamental to the dissemination of popular culture; in other words, the information we receive from Carlos is completely dependent on the novelistic genre. The video culture here is transmitted through the novel, and even though

(Inter)Textuality

we understand Carlos's obsession with the visual, Mañas seems to privilege the narrative space as a complex interweaving of language and image.

In the novel, the intertextuality builds a sense of literary and artistic awareness that becomes intrinsic to the evaluation of Carlos's character. The artistic forms he embraces as subversive and antiestablishment seduce him in a very conventional way. As he tries to emulate the protagonists, he becomes less an individual and more a type: "Carlos suffers from the illusion of uniqueness at the same time that he is read as representative of the pessimism of Spanish youth" (Pope 121). Along with a general pessimism, Carlos embodies the rejection of historical meaning in culture. His thirst for immediacy and self-gratification blinds him to the cultural repercussions, either positive or negative, in the works he idolizes. Carlos refuses to intellectualize and distance himself from the violence in the works, and this reveals his lack of sophistication as a reader that leaves him vulnerable to the text. He willingly follows the text as his behavioral guide and thus conforms to a literary type. The fact that we are reading a novel about a person who reads texts, both verbal and visual, is a key to understanding the metatextual moral message and the counter-example made explicit in the epilogue.

The event that provokes Roberto's visit to the therapist that appears in the epilogue involves the death of one of the young friends. The narrative action of the novel culminates in a birthday party for Fierro, who is a diabetic unable to consume alcohol but, because his health condition poses a high risk, Carlos still wants to get Fierro drunk to celebrate. The scene quickly dives into a vortex of violence as Carlos, high on cocaine and alcohol, ties up Fierro and proceeds to pour a bottle of whisky down his throat. Fierro falls from the chair onto the floor in convulsions, faints, and eventually dies. The first-person narration completely dominates at this point as all other voices are suppressed, indicated only by empty parentheses: "Pero no digas bobadas. ¿Cómo va a estar en coma? Si no era más que güisqui. ( ) Pero no, Miguel. ¿Para qué vas a llamar a una ambulancia? ( ) No está más que un poco borracho, como debe estar ... Mierda de Fierro. Otro débil" (222–23). The rambling, almost incoherent, drug-induced monologue flippantly relates

Chapter Seven

the horrible tragedy unfolding in the text. The empty parentheses are visual affirmations of what Iser calls "vacancies" and are elements of narrative that control the process of communication (112). The blanks force the reader to create the narrative and propel the action forward without the help of language. In this way Mañas incites the reader to action, for we must ignore Carlos's incoherence in order to reconstruct the true meaning of the scene. His denial of Fierro's impending death: "no está más que un poco borracho," alarms the reader who quickly realizes the gravity of the situation.

However, the most disturbing aspect of this event surfaces in the epilogue. Carlos seems oblivious to the severity of his actions that caused Fierro's death and also ignores Roberto's anguish and fear. In the beach town of Santander, Carlos finds a new friend, Julián, who replaces Roberto as his new buddy, which becomes explicitly clear as Carlos symbolically tosses a letter from Roberto into the garbage. The new friendship and disinterest in the past suggest that the vicious cycle will continue, and Carlos will make and break his relationships without any thought or appreciation of the bonds of true friendship.

Even though Carlos is emotionally anesthetized, the epilogue provides a set of new and intriguing textual clues that subvert the context of Carlos's first-person narrative. Pat Rogers has described a particular kind of ending or epilogue in literature where "the author is walking backwards out of the narrative ... by reversing the perspective or redirecting the angle of one vision on events" (85). With this reversal of perspective, often neat, tidy endings are abandoned for open-endedness and a narrative appreciation of the unknown. Such is the case with Roberto at the end of *Kronen*. He closes the novel wondering how he will act when he inevitably runs into Carlos after his vacation in Santander: "No sé cómo voy a reaccionar al verle" (238). Thus, the clear lack of both narrative and moral closure, for we never know if Carlos will be held responsible for Fierro's death, gives the reader even more room for speculation. Not only are the signs and codes of the text contradictory in the epilogue, but also the reader is forced to leap into the future and imagine the encounter between the two friends. Roberto's concern about his unstable friendship with Carlos becomes more intriguing when he expresses his latent desire to see him again: "Creo que Carlos vuelve el lunes a Madrid. Seguramente le veré en el Kronen" (238).[11] Even though Roberto has been warned by his therapist to avoid contact with Carlos, this ending introduces a new set of conflicts that Mañas has decided to leave unresolved. Rogers explains: "modern discussions of closure deal almost entirely with refusals of closure, imperfect or bogus closure, or those unconvincing final gestures which Barthes sees as 'unmasking' the false sense of repletion in the classic bourgeois text" (88). Rogers pinpoints the narrative chaos created by an epilogue that does not tidy up narrative gaps or ambiguities. This structural chaos demands a "rereading" or rearranging of textual facts in order to piece together a meaningful narrative.

The importance of the epilogue lies primarily in its position within the narrative as the final part of the story that the reader hears. What seals the narrative remains as the freshest, most recently recorded images in the reader's mind. Unlike in the body of the novel, there are several voices in the epilogue and an additional perspective in the lyrics of the song that close the novel. In the epilogue, we first hear the familiar tune of Carlos's central narrative presence with his negative and disrespectful tone. The following exchange between Roberto and his therapist creates a dialogue in which the characters pose questions and prod for answers. Roberto's voice expresses a completely different attitude toward the previous actions of the novel. Roberto speaks with his therapist and even though we do not read his inner thoughts, through this dialogue his opinions are free from Carlos's judgmental eye. In previous cases Carlos adds commentary to conversations he has with others. For example, when his friend Nuria suggests "hay más cosas que tu pequeña vida egoísta ... Tienes miedo a sufrir y lo escondes haciendo sufrir a los demás ... no quieres asumir la responsabilidad de tus actos" (149). Carlos does not say a word but gets up from the table where they are eating and leaves. However, we read his internal thoughts: "¿Por qué coño se empeña todo el mundo en psicoanalizarme? ...Ya he aguantado suficientes sermones por hoy" (149). It is precisely this reaction that is missing in the epilogue. Roberto's conversation with his therapist remains undiluted by Carlos's negative comments.

Roberto makes clear through his confessional tone to his therapist that he has suffered from Carlos's actions. Roberto

Chapter Seven

was present at the party when Fierro was forced to drink the whisky and is tormented by his death. He claims: "Yo no podía dejar de sentirme culpable, era increíble lo mal que me sentía … Fierro ha sido la víctima de nuestros jueguecitos mentales" (236–37). Roberto's feelings produce a blatant moral contrast at the end of the novel compared with Carlos's incoherent ramblings at the scene of the crime and his disinterest in the consequences. Furthermore, Roberto's reflections acquire the power of transference, similar to the practice that displaces personal (negative) emotions onto the psychiatrist. Mañas creates a type of textual transference: Roberto's concern regarding Carlos's behavior is transferred to the reader and suggests a moral criticism of the novel. Roberto represents the moral high ground and perhaps the skeptical reader's own sentiments toward Carlos and his seemingly irrational actions. The tables are turned, and Roberto's disillusion adds emotion and morality to a novel that otherwise lacks a sense of balance between action and consequence. Roberto brings the narrative to a more human level, that is, the reader has access to the internal struggle of an individual who witnessed and was complicit in a murder. Roberto describes his friendship with Carlos to his therapist: "No nos contamos nunca nada. No comunicamos, ¿comprende? Por eso vengo a verle, para poder contarle a alguien mis movidas" (233). Roberto explains that communication helps him to understand his emotions, and this basic act of speaking and confession produces a human contact lacking in his relationship with Carlos. The emphasis on interpersonal communication in the epilogue can be seen as a criticism of the isolating video culture so revered by Carlos in the main body of the novel.

The epilogue also links Roberto's suffering to the influence of pop culture and the intertexts already mentioned. Roberto pinpoints the immense importance of the novel *American Psycho* and its effects on Carlos and the rest of the group. Mañas chooses to highlight at the end of his novel the influence of another novel and not of film or music.[12] This can be read as a self-conscious warning of the power of the novel in general or perhaps of the novel we hold in our hands. Roberto says: "Matar a alguien era una idea que Carlos tenía metida en la cabeza desde hacía tiempo. Aquello le excitaba y no dejaba de darme la coña. Sobre todo después de leer Americansaico" (237). The therapist asks him to describe the novel, and he continues:

> Un libro. Un libro cojonudo. La única novela que Carlos soportaba. Me influenció mucho en una época. Bueno, nos influenció a todos. Todo aquel rollo que llevábamos nos embruteció tanto que a nadie le pareció rara la idea de Carlos. Yo creo que si Carlos nos hubiera propuesto matarle, tampoco nos hubiera extrañado nada. Creo que lo hubiéramos hecho. (237)

Roberto seems to realize the immanent chaos and resulting destruction when the boundaries between art and life are violated. He laments how the negative influence of literary violence in general, and *American Psycho* in particular, has drained the group of friends of any sense of moral responsibility, and killing has become a pastime, not strange or outrageous to anyone. One novel cannot be held responsible for Fierro's death, but the text indicates that emulating certain types of art can lead to destructive consequences in life. Therefore, Carlos's behavior reaches an undesirable extreme and becomes a lesson to the reader on how not to read a text. One could conclude that Carlos is a disingenuous reader and has misinterpreted the irony of *American Psycho* and in doing so creates a model of how not to approach a text.

Roberto's dialogue with his therapist reflects the reader's musings as he questions Carlos's and the other friends' violent actions and expresses guilt and remorse over their destructive outcome. The attitude that concludes the novel is not focused on the violent acts, but rather on the reflections and questioning of violence that entraps the young characters in a self-destructive cycle. Moreover, Roberto's reflections on the effect that other texts exert on the youths' behavior question the boundaries between art and life and prioritize a rereading of the novel as a way to understand and perhaps escape the cycle of violence.

Mañas suggests that literature, art, and film can produce a dangerous confusion when the line between the character and the individual becomes blurred and indistinguishable. Roberto reveals the tragic consequences of confusing reality with art when he sums up his story: "Eso era lo que Carlos decía siempre: que la vida era como una mala película" (237). Roberto's criticism of Carlos's actions and his consciousness of his own moral anguish concerning Fierro's death recuperate the lost sense of humanity of Carlos's narration. Therefore, if we read the epilogue as a humanizing frame of Carlos's actions we can understand the counter example of his conduct dominated by intertexts of fantasy and fiction.

It may not be a surprise that Mañas's more recent works turn away from the overt appreciation of violence and tend to carry a heavier moral message. As a contrast to Carlos's unflinching nerves of steel, the characters in Mañas's latest novel, *La pella*, seem to realize the inherent dilemma the individual must face when personal pleasure is placed above family and social responsibility.

La pella

Published in 2008, *La pella* was promoted as Mañas's return to the "universo realista que fue el escenario de sus primeros éxitos" (*Pella* jacket). The return to his signature style labeled "dirty realism" comes after he published in 2007 a historical novel on the life of Alexander the Great, *El secreto del oráculo*. While *La pella* does recall certain tendencies of his earlier novels such as a penchant for dialogue and mapping the course of the narrative action through the streets of Madrid, the newer novel is noticeably different in that the main character is concerned with the consequences of his actions. *La pella* can be read as a literary counterpart to the moral void apparent in *Kronen*.

When *Kronen* was named a finalist for the Premio Nadal in 1994, Mañas was only 22 years old, the youngest writer ever to be nominated for the Nadal; yet Rosa Regás, now the director of the Biblioteca Nacional, won the award that year for her novel *Azul*. In an article aptly titled "Veinteañeros, audiovisuales y psicópatas," published in *La Vanguardia* on January 8, 1994, Llàtzer Moix tentatively describes the emerging youth movement in Spain as an inevitable trend in Spanish literature and cites an unnamed juror on the Nadal committee as saying "es tradición del Nadal hacer apuestas de futuro. Veremos si Mañas lo tiene" (Moix 1). From the initial moments of his literary success, Mañas was expected to do great things as if he had to earn the respect that was thrust upon his work with the Nadal nomination. However, Mañas seems to embrace the popularity of his first novel, which marked his career as a writer and has allowed him to experiment with other genres such as the detective novel

Caso Karen and the aforementioned historical novel (Jorge Pérez 1). Nevertheless, the style and tone of *Pella* imitates the urban and generational dialect of *Kronen,* reminding the reader of the author's unique sensitivity to postmodern isolation and popular culture.

La pella closely reflects *Kronen* in both thematic and stylistic ways. While Mañas's other novels, such as *Soy un escritor frustrado* (1996) or *Caso Karen* (2005), deal with violence and murder, they avoid a distinctly generational approach. Both aforementioned novels have older protagonists, one a university professor and the other a police detective, who struggle with identity issues stemming from their professional dissatisfaction. In *La pella*, Mañas returns to the youth culture located in the streets and surrounding neighborhoods of Madrid, focusing the narrative on drug-related interactions and petty theft. The narrative often gives way to a writing style and lexical manipulations reminiscent of *Kronen* that destabilize the text and disrupt the reading process. For example, words in all capital letters suggest yelling over loud music in a crowded bar, and words are invented based on phonetic renderings of foreign words. This process of changing the appearance of the visual text on the page is similar to what Etxebarria does in *De todo lo visible y lo invisible* by changing the lines and font size on the page. This lexical manipulation of the text draws the reader into the experience of constructing the story in a visceral way. By playing with the visual aspect of *La pella*, Mañas reminds the reader of these very same elements found in *Kronen,* thus creating an intertextuality that crosses both thematic and stylistic lines.

La pella also plays with the role of the implied author. Toward the end of the novel, a character appears named Mañas who is interested in writing the story of the events and characters in the novel we have just read. Similar to but not as developed as the presence of Javier Cercas, the narrator/protagonist of *Soldados de Salamina*, the appearance of Mañas in the text blurs the traditionally established boundaries between reader and author. As studied in previous chapters, the presence of the author in the work questions the boundaries of reality and fiction. The author creates a meta-version of himself that appears in a fictional work and thus invents a character based somewhat in "reality" but that becomes independent of the writer and

Chapter Seven

enclosed in the text. In the following analysis of *La pella*, I will look at the privileging of the upper class, the presence of the author in the text as a means of metafictional commentary, and the impact of the stylistic aberrations found in the novel.

La pella is the story of Borja and Kiko, two characters who previously appeared in Mañas's *Ciudad rayada* (1998). Jorge Pérez notes the consistency of character and place in *Kronen*, *Mensaka* (1995), *Ciudad rayada*, and *Sonoko 95* (1999) as the key to the intertextuality that locates the action and development of the metanarrative in a specific time and place, thus forming a "narrativa que se genera en los espacios intersticiales de una España inmersa en un complejo proceso de revisión y negociación de su identidad nacional" (34). In this sense *La pella* can be considered as the fifth installment of the sequence initiated by *Kronen* in 1994. Mañas's on-going literary project roots itself firmly in the Spanish capital and emphasizes the importance of the urban setting that defines his characters. The text names specific streets, neighborhoods, and freeways that suggest a web of possibilities for movement and freedom. As Kiko drives his Vespa through La Elipa, the geographical markers establish an image of national importance: "se saltó al menos dos semáforos antes de salir a Marqués de Corbera y cruzar la Emetreinta, rodeando a continuación las oficinas de Televisión Española para incorporarse a O'Donnell" (91). The movement across the major freeway that circles Madrid, the M30 or "emetreinta," marks the entrance into the heart of the city. Kiko passes from the periphery into the center just as he lives on the outside of Borja's upper class world and tries to move symbolically into his privileged space.

The primacy of location in the novel stems from the problematization of the "other" that appears in *La pella* and in the previous novels of the series. "Estos 'otros' que inquietan al sujeto ... se definen en otros niveles que van más allá de lo político-legal, y que afectan a la identidad biológica, social y cultural" (Jorge Pérez 46). The "others" that disturb a concept of national unity and identity are identified in the previous novels, specifically in *Ciudad rayada,* as "chinos, putas, guiris rubios, maricas, moros y vejestorios" (Jorge Pérez 46). The fear of the "other," reflected in the pejorative name-calling, suggests a lack of autonomy and the need to lash out and blame the "other" for tainting an imaginary form of "pure" identity.[13] However, as Kiko's entrance into the national capital indicates, he must penetrate the social and cultural reality represented by the affluence of Calle O'Donnell and the surrounding neighborhood. Thus, because of his socio-economic status, he becomes the abject "other" for Borja, the force that he is drawn to obsessively but will ultimately reject. The negative, or rejected "other" that is necessary to define the individual moves from a national invader to a pariah living within the national community. Kiko is the undesirable thief and drug addict that Borja eventually will turn over to the police in order to clear his own conscience and ultimately save his sense of identity within the familial circle.[14] The cultural representations of class in this novel point to an inherent discrimination against the poor and the triumph of the wealthy in a superficial, market-driven economy that reproduces itself in a hierarchical society.

The friends share the same ambition to make easy money selling drugs while living the life of a rock star surrounded by music and beautiful women. When a drug deal goes wrong, Borja re-evaluates his life at the urging of his family and mainly his cousin, Nico, and his consequent redemption leaves Kiko recuperating from a beating in the hospital. The moral message of this novel is much less enshrouded than that of *Kronen*. The text indicates Borja's doubts about his illegal lifestyle from the very beginning. Kiko's reckless behavior is juxtaposed with Borja's measured personality as is their socio-economic status throughout the novel. It is this aspect of the novel that sets it apart from the rest of Mañas's work. The emphasis on the privilege of money and the power of family bonds that ultimately rescue Borja from his life of crime points to a more tempered, conformist vision of youth culture. This turn away from the unabashed freedom of expression and disregard for social norms found in *Kronen* suggests reconciliation with society and less adulation of the violent tendencies of Gen X youth.

Borja is a kinder incarnation of Carlos from *Kronen,* even though the two characters are similar in many ways: they both are university students, they live in upper-middle class families, and they both are drawn to the trappings of Madrid's underground drug culture. However, Borja's family directly influences him, while Carlos ignores his parents and sister.[15] *La pella*

Chapter Seven

makes a clear moral distinction between classes where *Kronen* does not, because although Borja goes along with Kiko's plans for selling drugs, he judges his actions throughout the novel. The basic difference between need and want seems to separate the two friends in their attitude toward stealing and drugs. Borja wants to party, do drugs, and be part of an alternative world because he is bored with his life, while Kiko, on the other hand, sees the drug sales as a means to survive on the streets and to pay off debts.

When the two friends find themselves in a pinch and need fast money to pay off one of the primary dealers, Kiko comes up with a scheme to take some pills and sell them in Italy, where they can make more money than on the streets of Madrid. Borja agrees with this plan but on the way to the airport they clash over Kiko's methods. As they race toward the airport on the freeway, Kiko asks Borja to cut him some more lines of cocaine. Borja begins to prepare the lines but his wallet falls to the ground and as he reaches down to pick it up he notices that the cables under the steering wheel of the car have been cut. He then realizes that the car they are using to get the airport has been stolen and in a somewhat ironic moment of moral superiority Borja chides Kiko for stealing the car, demanding that Kiko stop the car so that he can get out. As he rolls down the window to throw the bag of pills that they are going sell out of the car, he says to Kiko, "¿Cómo me haz podido hacer ezto? ... yo aquí contigo, como un subnormal, con zetecientaz pastillaz en el bolzillo, metido en un coche robado ..." (62).[16] Ironically, and perhaps somewhat unbelievably, Borja is ready to abandon the drug deal because he finds it unacceptable to be in a stolen car. Nevertheless, for Kiko, the moral ambiguity of the situation is less important than the solidarity implied. The idea of two friends off on an adventure means more to him than the possible consequences, and the ends justify the means if he can score enough money to pay off the dealer. Therefore, the moral hierarchy established by Borja over the car disregards the economic problem at hand and overshadows the fact that Kiko wants to help him out of a tight spot.

Since Borja is ready to reject the plan because Kiko has used a stolen car to successfully gain them quick access to the airport, the issue is less about the money he owes the drug dealer, Nacle, than about his own moral conscience. His economic status allows him to think, and ultimately know, that the money he owes will appear from somewhere. If need be, he can ask his cousin or another family member for money, which is in fact what he ends up doing. For Kiko, this possibility simply does not exist. He does not have the luxury of family money to back him up, and therefore he steals out of "necessity." He convinces Borja that they must go through with the plan because he has made a personal sacrifice in the name of friendship and solidarity.

The disparity of social classes appears throughout the novel, often suggesting that with economic status comes security. For example, Borja plays tennis at an elite club with his cousin Nico. In an effort to get Borja accustomed to "una actividad física y una vida más sana," his family has arranged the tennis match with his physical and mental health in mind. The text makes a point of comparing the cousins in terms of what they are wearing. Nico looks very professional in "zapatillas y ropa de marca, raqueta cabezona Rossignol de grafito de alta calidad," while Borja wears "bermudas desgastadas ... Adidas viejas y su raqueta destensada no impresionaban demasiado" (85–86). The importance of appearance is obvious at the tennis club but also to the narrative, as it suggests that economic status allows for the luxury of leisure time. Borja can play tennis with his cousin Nico, while Kiko must steal a car during his time off so that he has a way to get to the airport. The dichotomy of social mores plays out in the narrative as it reveals the disastrous outcomes of inappropriate mixing of social classes.

Early in the novel Borja reveals his loyalty to his family when he arrives at a special dinner for his grandmother. The narration describes her as the aging matriarch of the family and the wealth passed down from generation to generation hangs symbolically around her neck in "el collar de diamantes que le había regalado su marido, poco antes de fallecer" (26). Thus the jewelry gains sentimental value as it represents not only wealth but also the solidarity of marriage and family. Even though Borja arrives late and has to excuse himself for failing to show up to the last family gathering, he notes that "la anciana, que intentaba mantener a toda costa las buenas relaciones, esbozó una sonrisa condescendiente. —Todavía tenemos que madurar bastante, Borjita ..." (26). Thus, the narrative establishes the

Chapter Seven

change that Borja will undergo as he comes to realize the importance of family and the dangers of running with the "wrong" crowd (class).

The problematic class division becomes evident at the end of the novel when Borja chastises Kiko for stealing expensive items to sell at the Rastro. Kiko spends the night at his girlfriend's house in a wealthy suburb and in a hostile act that puts money and drugs above sentimental relationships, he robs her family's house. Kiko somewhat innocently expects Borja to thank him for this risky act of kindness that will make more than enough money to pay off Borja's debt. However, Borja reacts in quite the opposite way. At the bidding of his always present and moralizing cousin Nico, Borja finds Kiko and demands that he return all of the stolen items to his girlfriend Marta's house. Kiko claims that this is impossible, since he has already placed the items for sale on the black market and he acts surprised that Borja is not impressed. At this moment Borja informs Kiko that he had everything worked out to pay back the debt: "ya lo había hablado yo todo con mi primo Nico y entre él y mi tío me iban a preztar el dinero, joder" (131). This moment in the text reveals the clear division and hierarchical nature of a post-consumer society in which symbolic power infused in the exchange of money for goods depends on the economic stability of some of the society's members. The connection to *Kronen* lies in the ability of the protagonist, Borja, to correct his bad behavior through available monies provided by family members, just as Carlos is able to pursue a life of hedonistic excess dependent on his family's economic status. The ability to buy his way out of danger places Borja in a privileged position, one that Kiko cannot even imagine. As a final insult, Borja labels Kiko and through language places him in a marginalized position in relation to the "dominant" or privileged culture. Borja says: "¡Pero mírate! Daz pena. Nico tiene razón: erez un pobre yonqui de mierda ..." (132). "Pobre" in this case has a double meaning because it suggests that Kiko is a pathetic person who cannot control his drug use and thus garners the sympathy of others, yet given the context of the narrative and the importance of money to resolving the narrative conflict, "pobre" also acquires a second socio-economic meaning. Kiko is poor in the sense that he cannot buy his way out of problems and that the only solution available to him is to steal from others. He lacks the economic means to fit into Borja's world and into the society that equates money with power and the rational. Furthermore, in order to restore order at the end of the novel, Borja and Nico go to the Rastro flea market every Sunday in order to "ir comprando uno por uno los objetos robados a medida que iban apareciendo" (133). The restoration of the physical objects as well as Borja's symbolic restoration to his family and appropriate class are gained through economic means.

The emphasis on money as a means to personal and collective stability reflects a certain cultural hypocrisy both in *Kronen* and in *Pella* because both texts end with a moralistic evaluation of youth and society. Carlos is the antimodel for urban youth because his behavior is despicable as reported by Roberto in the epilogue but also by the conclusions suggested to the implied reader who brings to the reading a specific horizon of expectations and a general sense of cultural norms of acceptable behaviors. The extreme manifestation of aberrant actions of violence addresses the cultural normalcy imbedded in the social fabric that in both novels is presented as desirable. On the other hand, in *Pella* the moral core of the novel is not confused by a subversive characterization of the protagonist nor is it revealed in a final epilogue but rather it exists as the main plot device of the novel. Thus, Borja can be seen as the inversion of Carlos because he realizes his error and comes to terms with his relationship with his family.[17]

The presence of the implied author in *Pella* replaces the self-exploratory epilogue of *Kronen*. Only through the reflections of Roberto does the reader gain insight into a moral criticism of Carlos's actions, yet in *Pella*, the presence of the authorial voice gives rise to a metatextual musing on the nature of writing. Again placed at the end of the novel, the presence of a different narrative voice, in this case a shift to first person, adds perspective and distance from the main action of the text. The authorial voice that comments at the end of the narrative brings the fictional reality a step closer to the actual creation of the text. The characters acquire a certain transcendental quality as the authorial voice comments on the resulting activities of each character reminiscent of the short biographies that appear after a film documentary that aim to bring the viewer up

Chapter Seven

to date on the characters' lives. In this way the novel becomes a stage of hyperreality, crossing a fictional line into a more journalistic style. For example, the narrator says: "Por su parte Kiko desapareció de la circulación durante un par de semanas e incluso dejó de ir a su curro donde, según tengo entendido, lo despidieron" (133). The interjection of "según tengo entendido" reveals the writer behind the text and also suggests doubt about the true whereabouts of Kiko. The text reveals that Kiko ends up in the hospital after a brutal beating in Tijuana. The novel ends with a short dialogue between Káiser, Kiko's friend, and a writer named Mañas.

Similar to Javier Cercas in *Soldados de Salamina,* Mañas cites himself as the author of the novel and includes a reference to his previous publication about the misadventures of Kiko and Borja, *Ciudad rayada.* Just as Cercas is the protagonist of his novel and in *La velocidad de la luz* makes numerous references to his first novel, *Soldados*, Mañas cites his previous novel, which confuses the fictional reality of the novel with that of "real" life.[18] Thus the hyperreality of the novelistic space is set against the reader's own knowledge of the author Mañas and his publications. The blending of the two worlds creates a novelistic space, much like *De todo lo visible y lo invisible* by Etxebarria that welcomes this confusion and places the author as implied author at the center of the text.

Another manifestation of the fusing of literary and extraliterary realities occurs through the incorporation into the text of recognizable brand names and what Carmen de Urioste calls the "'ruido' lingüístico producido por la sociedad contemporánea" ("Punk" 29). Similar to his other novels, Mañas captures the influence of a global economy in his phonetic renderings of certain commercial labels and youth phenomena. The impact of the local and the global comes to light in the way language is rendered in the novel. For example, the style is colloquial and reflects a certain age sector in a culturally specific locale. Words such as "chavalitos" (49), "tronco" (10), and "gillipollas" (59) reflect a distinctly peninsular Spanish register. The linguistic markers that indicate region and age are also supported by extensive descriptions of streets and bars that locate the text unequivocally in Madrid: "estaban en pleno Serrano ... de la calle Velázquez" (29) and "[e]n la glorieta de Bilbao, las lunas inmensas del Café Comercial, que hacía esquina con Sagasta …" (105). The importance of these references becomes clear as they are juxtaposed with the presence of international brand names and personalities.

The text opens with a description of Kiko that comments on his "Kirk Douglas" chin and describes his attire as "una sudadera con capucha con el logotipo de Adidas impreso en azul a la altura del pecho y las inevitables zapatillas New Balance" (9). Kiko is a walking conglomeration of regional and international identities as the recognizable brand names acquire a symbolic value in the culturally specific fictional reality of the novel. Even, Kiko, representative of the more unfortunate class, is touched, literally, by economic globalization. The sportswear becomes symbolic of a certain wealth inherent in the English language that corresponds to the English-speaking market. By comparing Kiko to Kirk Douglas and focusing on his clothes, the text presents a true cultural hybrid in Kiko, and he becomes representative of the narrative itself with its combination of local and international references. "[L]os ídolos rockeros: Bob Marley, Bob Dylan, Janis Joplin" (97) occupy the same textual space as "tres quintos de Mahou prácticamente vacíos" (45). A very popular beer in Spain (Mahou) would perhaps be unidentifiable to someone who had not spent time in the country, yet the immediate recognition of the rock stars is perhaps a more universally coherent social reference.

The isolated representations of Spanish pronunciation imposed on a foreign word imported from the global economy fuse together linguistically the ideas of global and local identity previously described. In one single word Castilian Spanish exercises a local influence on the imported identity. These cases are abundant in *Kronen* and form part of the created literary space that can be firmly located in Madrid of the early 1990s. Pablo Gil Casado explores at length the lexical manipulation in Mañas's works and points out that the practice forms part of the linguistic register that glorifies "la adopción de un lenguaje marginal" (79). Gil Casado traces the linguistic innovation seen in Mañas's work to that of Ramoncín (José Ramón Julio Martínez Márquez) and his work *El tocho cheli* from 1993, which locates the linguistic wordplay in the Barrio Salamanca that gained in popularity in the early 1960s (91). Together with

Chapter Seven

the innovations of the *cheli* argot, Gil Casado describes the phonetic renderings of English words as part of the linguistic register that signals "la marcada intención de hablar en clave" in the novels (94). Consequently the reader engages in numerous acts of deciphering the encoded language presented in the text and in this way participates actively in the construction of the linguistic register. While the characters enact a form of encoded dialogue, the text itself becomes a linguistic puzzle that constantly engages the reader not with plot twists or even character development but rather with linguistic innovations that are culturally charged.

The phonetic renderings of English words propose the importation of British and American culture at the same time clearly showing the Spanish appropriation of the word and the idea. For example, in *Kronen* the characters refer to the restaurant "Pizzajut" and the songs "laikaviryen" and "smelslaiktinspirit" (Gil Casado 93) that at once recognizes the influence of North American culture but makes the reference entirely Spanish in the pronunciation. In *Pella*, the neologism "jipjopero" describes a local bar that plays hip-hop music (49), and a drunk barfly is sarcastically compared to the popular 1940s film star "Jamfri Bógart" (101). In a similar vein in *Pella*, the orthographic representation of Borja's spoken dialogue suggests a lisp, because the "s" is replaced with a "z." In one example Borja exclaims: "Pero tú erez gillipollaz! ... Eztamoz removiendo mar y tierra para pagar laz pellaz, y vaz y pillaz todo ezto ..." (59). At this point the text demands that the reader step back and restructure the character's voice. In this way the presence of the implied author becomes clear in that there is an intense level of metatextuality that requires a constant interpretation on the reader's part. In the same ways that Etxebarria demands the reader step out of the fictional reality of *De todo lo visible y lo invisible*, Mañas creates a text that suggests an authorial presence yet leaves the decoding to the reader.

La pella can be read as a thematic and linguistic continuation of the representation of urban youth culture established most successfully in *Historias del Kronen*. However, in this latest novel, Mañas does depart from the more polemic and ambiguous morality of his earlier novel to present a resolution that includes a somewhat uncharacteristic move to socialized behavior seen in Borja's rejection of the drug world and his entrance into the family fold indicated by his friendship with his cousin, Nico. Nevertheless, many of the same elements that contribute to the novel as a cultural space of intertextuality and hyperreality connect *La pella* to the other Generation X novels studied in the second part of this book. The clear presence of the implied author that serves as a bridge between the textual reality and the readers' world becomes heightened in the Gen X novels as the written word competes with the ever growing audiovisual immediacy that saturates our daily lives. With all of the devices and technology that allow people to instantly "connect," the form and tone of the novel is bound to change. The cultural representations in Mañas's novels not only serve to provide insight into a specific time and space in the late twentieth and early twenty-first centuries of upper-class urban youth in Madrid, but they also remind us of the development of the novel as a genre. As is evident in all of the novels in this study, the text remains itself a cultural artifact, and in Mañas's case, the rich cultural content should not overshadow the importance of the genre. *Kronen* can be read as a literary warning against the perils of textual misinterpretation, and both novels in this chapter triumph in the creative lexical manipulations of language. The phonetic spelling of foreign and Spanish words, the incorporation of brand names into the flow of the narrative, and the unusual spellings that force the reader to become analytical in reconstructing the text are only possible in the written text.

In most Gen X works the role of the protagonist as hero comes into question. Just as Carme Riera, Dulce Chacón, and Javier Cercas question the identity of the historical hero during the Inquisition and the Spanish Civil War, the Gen X authors struggle with the isolation and detachment of the modern hero grappling with a hyperreal culture. The characters in the works by Etxebarria, Loriga, and Mañas see themselves reflected in some way in the cultural representations projected on television, the Internet, or the movie screen, and this reflection becomes not just referential but rather the core of individual identity. Thus, the "hero" of the Gen X novels does not participate in the construction of a social consciousness but in the creation of a virtual identity. Vicente José Benet describes this emptiness as a point of philosophical, historical, and parodic questioning of the

Chapter Seven

reality that surrounds the characters, resulting in an archetype that is symptomatic of contemporary culture (48). This contemporary culture can be described as a virtual or hyperreal experience that drives the narrative toward a vacuum that is ironically filled with contradiction and interrogation. Thus, the written word, the text, and the narrative represent cultural constructions that inform our readings of violence, "reality," and our own place within the contemporary extreme.[19]

Conclusion

As exemplified by the title of this study, the notion of culture is complicated and multifaceted. Cultural reproductions in the novel range from historical to textual violence, from documenting alternative historical voices to alternative present-day realities. Perhaps it is easier to understand *the cultural* instead of culture: "a cultural text is always part of a wider and more complex symbolic system, a field of struggle for the symbolic reproduction of a social reality that is ultimately elucidated at the political sphere" (Sarto, Ríos, and Trigo 4). An exploration of the political and its relationship to the cultural helps to understand the links between the various cultural references analyzed in the novels.

The Spanish government recently passed the *Ley de la Memoria Histórica de España*. This legislation offers a political backdrop to the importance of historical memory as evidenced in the first section of this study.[1] The law aims to recognize and compensate those who suffered violence and discrimination during the Civil War and resulting dictatorship. In very direct language the law addresses the unjust violence and "graves violaciones de Derechos Humanos cometidas en España entre los años 1939 y 1975" ("España" n.pag.). The law also deals eloquently with the complexity of national and personal memory, declaring that "[n]o es tarea del legislador implantar una determinada memoria colectiva" ("España" n.pag.), but rather personal memories of the victims and their families must form part of a new Spanish consciousness. On a theoretical level, the law recognizes the unjust and unbalanced reparations provided to the victims of the war and at the same time opens up an entire discourse silenced during the transition to democracy. This opportunity to literally unearth the past as mass graves are opened

Conclusion

and symbolically the past is exhumed from under years of soil forces the Spanish social consciousness to turn to the idea of historical revision. Therefore, the thread that ties together the various cultural representations in the novels becomes more apparent given the current social and political climate in Spain. The novel as document and historical witness to the past and present gains more immediate significance when the country is faced with a historical and political reconciliation.

The popular reaction to this law is perhaps best summed up in a quote taken from Carlos Cué's article from *El País,* in which someone present at the hearing shouted in triumph, "Hoy, por fin, se ha acabado la guerra" (n.pag.). This feeling of euphoria is inspired by a political gesture that symbolically affirms the marginality of the victims of the war and the failure on the part of the state to react appropriately to their loss; however, it has nothing to do with anything concretely accomplished by the law. The promise of reparation that is the most important logistical element of the law is actually secondary to the symbolic gesture inscribed in the law, documented in the press, and circulated as a discourse of recuperation of historical memory. Perhaps the same can be said about the novels in this study, because the individual work is bound to the larger social discourse that it helps circulate or, in some cases, rejects. The historical novels that present a reinterpretation of history function as a group to question the role of history in present-day culture and national identity. The novels of the Gen X are often criticized as not literary enough to warrant distinction, but the discourse of isolation in a hyperreality strikes a meaningful chord in a literary environment so heavily influenced by technology.

What Pierre Bourdieu calls a field of cultural reproduction would seem to support this notion of a conglomerate of works at a given time and space that operate in a similar, systematic way. In this system, the work or text loses individuality and becomes part of a larger discourse similar to Roland Barthes's idea of how the individual author fades out of sight from the text itself, which takes on meaning from social conditions and circumstances. Nevertheless, the value of textual analysis remains paramount, as the individual works are the cornerstones of any larger cultural discourse and necessary for the constant circulation of ideas. Bourdieu and other cultural theorists recognize the importance of the tensions that exist between cultural production and consumption. In a market-driven global economy, the product is not always consumed for its intended purpose, but rather as a symbol of status, leisure, or intellect, for example. In the case of literature, the consumption of a certain novel or author places the reader in a category that in turn denotes a complex mesh of identity markers. Thus, the consumer who reads the new historical novels is assumed not likely to read Gen X novels, as each category denotes a different population and cultural field. One is historical, national, and political, while the other appears to be apolitical, antihistorical, and apathetic toward the conscious formation of a national identity.

Nevertheless, this division is arbitrary, and as I have shown in the previous chapters, the link between cultural discourse and literary production resides in the malleable nature of the novel. Even though literature, television, and film are produced with specific audiences in mind, the end result is a circulating discourse on the value of art to undermine, parody, criticize, and examine not only culture but also the nature of writing and language. In the first section, the novels that take on History and reread the past through the lens of those sectors of society without traditional representation ultimately become critiques of contemporary modes of writing history. In *Dins el darrer blau*, for example, the text becomes a metadocument that implicitly recognizes the polemical nature and value of the actual documents of the *auto de fe* re-created in the novel. Riera states in the note at the end of the novel that her story is based on several existing documents that she consulted so that the novel would faithfully represent the plight of the Mallorcan Jews. In this sense, "reality" stands somewhere in the shadows of the narrative but is pushed aside by the novelistic genre that permits through narration an interpretation of events. However, as evidenced in the other novels in the first section and as elaborated by Hayden White and others, history can be considered the fusion of science and art and is always rooted in narrative. History is a story that needs to be told by a narrator using descriptive language that produces an imaginary in time and space. Thus, the work of the novelist becomes the work of the historian.

As Nietzsche claims, history is only useful when narrated because this permits the imagination to play a part in the retelling of events that leads to critique and evaluation. It is through the cultural representations found in literature and art that the critical observation of history demands reflection and permits an understanding of past mistakes that consequentially allows society to progress. In this spirit of progress, the authors of the historical novels seek to reinvent the nature of historical narrative in order to provide a Nietzschean approach to Spanish history. As history is retold through the novel, the room for imagination and invention grows considerably and leads to a literary reality that mixes fact and fiction. In this sense, the historical novels create their own version of hyperreality, or a reality that does not have a referent firmly rooted in "fact." The imagination that brings culture into the novelistic space links together the rereading of history and the rereading of reality in that the novel itself becomes an unstable space where language and meaning must be decoded, reassembled, and reevaluated.

The novels that represent contemporary culture also problematize the officiality of the written word. The "fact" and fiction of the novels of the Generation X are inseparable, for the narrative moves easily and constantly between a novelistic reality and references to international popular culture. The presence of the Internet, video, and film in the Gen X novels alludes to the changing dynamic of consumer culture, yet the novelistic space remains the most important vehicle to document the rapid change in communication. The apparent lack of a historical consciousness in the Gen X novels is replaced by an obsessive awareness of technological advances but, in both the historical and the hyperreal, the link between the literary representations and Spanish identity is key. In the study *Spain beyond Spain*, Brad Epps and Luis Fernández Cifuentes point to the traditional relationship between literary history and national identity. Traditional categorization of important literary works seems to work in tandem with tracing important historical and political moments that determine a sense of national identity (11). Therefore the study of marginalized histories may lead to a type of "unconventional" literary history, which the authors posit as already problematic, "one that appears to lie somewhere between paradox and illusion: an infinitely open, inclusive, and non-hierarchical compendium in which meaning shimmers and shines" (17). While this vivid description suggests a kind of utopic literary history, it sums up perfectly the relationship between the historical and hyperreal novels in this study: between paradox and illusion, between impossible history and virtual reality. The novels grounded in history actually convey a sense that history cannot be known, let alone understood in any comprehensive sense. Loriga, Etxebarria, and Mañas sustain the illusion of reality through texts that privilege other texts such as film, music, video, and the Internet. I do not mean to suggest here that the novels in this study depart from the canon or propose a "new" kind of literary history, but in the manipulation of the novelistic genre, the texts do propose a new way of reading and demand a different relationship between the reader and the novel.

I have relied on Jean Baudrillard's notion of hyperreality to convey a sense of postmodern isolation and illusion especially present in the Gen X novels. The intertextuality of *Historias del Kronen* and *La pella* points to a global system of images and a universal language of youth culture dominating the lives of the young characters that may ultimately unite people around the world. However, the tone in Mañas's novels is anything but conciliatory, and the video culture that Carlos embraces in *Kronen* only provides transitory pleasure that reproduces the fetishistic desire to consume more. Baudrillard gives a concise definition of this level of simulacra: "simulacra of simulation, founded on information, the model, the cybernetic game—total operationality, hyperreality, aim of total control" (*Simulacra* 121). "[T]otal operationality" suggests that the product or consequence is obsolete but the act of consuming or the desire, which can never be satisfied lest it cease to exist, becomes the "reality."

Ray Loriga addresses the fabrication of "reality," death, and genre in his works, which look at the superficiality of television and by extension, the human imagination. His texts perhaps deal less with the generational identity crisis than they do with the universal hypocrisy and cynicism of contemporary society. His move from novel to film lays bare the complicated nature of both written and visual languages. As mentioned, language becomes the space for experimentation where genre is redefined and meaning renegotiated.

The relationship between author and reader comes to the forefront in the work of Etxebarria as she manipulates the text

Conclusion

visually and thematically in order to cross the imaginary boundary between author, implied author, and reader. Her narrative directly addresses the reader and displaces the character from the novelistic reality, breaking down the conventional distance usually established between reader and text. Etxebarria's text remains assertive and transparent in its attempt to renegotiate the role of the writer in society. Through her contentious relationship with the press and her insistence on a brash, commercialized brand of feminism, Etxebarria has consciously built a persona around her works that effectively reflects the hyperreal. Or as Baudrillard might claim, the "imaginary power and wealth of the double—the one in which the strangeness and at the same time the intimacy of the subject to itself are played out" (*Simulacra* 95). Etxebarria embraces the double nature of her persona by denying herself the sacred privacy traditionally allotted to the stereotypical reclusive writer and assuring her readers through the mass media that she suffers from weight problems and depression: just like everyone else.

If the reader can come to understand the constructed nature of the cultural and by extension of the novel, then we can begin to see with a critical eye the ways in which literature and art convey certain representations of the world in which we live. The novel surely has not lost its entertainment value, but it also can be said that nothing that entertains is innocent or harmless. Whatever the artist's or writer's intentions, the text remains an entity representative of a specific time and place from which it cannot be fully separated. Through the works of the very different and at times contradictory styles that I have analyzed here, we can obtain a more complete picture of contemporary Spanish literary production. Through the cultural representations in the seemingly polar opposite narratives and the apparently contradictory styles of Carme Riera, Dulce Chacón, Lucía Etxebarria, Javier Cercas, José Ángel Mañas, and Ray Loriga, we can see the value of the differences and the surprising similarities that reveal the skepticism regarding an absolutist view of reality and history.

Notes

Introduction

1. Hyperreal and hyperreality are Jean Baudrillard's terms that describe an advanced capitalist, consumerist society in which images refer to other images or to themselves and the representation of reality becomes obsolete and subsumed by the creation of a hyperreality dependent on the circulation and interrelation of simulacra.

2. Amago's excellent introduction provides an overview of postmodernism and an alternative reading of the self-reflexive novel that "offers a functional, constructive alternative to the pessimistic worldviews" of some postmodern critics (14).

3. Novels such as Montero's *Crónica de un desamor* and *La función delta* deal with feminist issues of single, working women coming to appreciate their independence and sexuality. Her *Amado amo* is a criticism of a corrupt corporate work ethic. Millás deals with the junction between the personal and the public persona and interpersonal relationships in *La soledad era esto* and *El desorden de tu nombre*. His *El orden alfabético* also exposes the corrupt nature of business and politics. Muñoz Molina writes a metaphorical tale of betrayal and intrigue in the noir tradition in *Beltenebros*. Other important authors in this vein are Javier Marías, Belén Gopegui, Cristina Fernández Cubas, and Soledad Puértolas.

4. See Christine Henseler's excellent study *Contemporary Spanish Women's Narrative and the Publishing Industry* and articles by Akiko Tsuchiya and Carmen de Urioste.

5. Etxebarria was accused of lifting passages from psychologist Jorge Castelló's *Dependencia emocional y violencia doméstica* (2004) for her *Yo no sufro por amor* (2005).

6. This is the basis of Pierre Bourdieu's idea of cultural production as the economic world reversed. The popularity of the poor, starving artist who had the passion for and soul of survival rendered a certain value to the artistic production that was not based on economics or capital value but rather on a different set of cultural values. I will return to Bourdieu later in the introduction.

7. Barry Jordan and Rikki Morgan-Tamosunas edited a collection of essays, *Contemporary Spanish Cultural Studies*, that includes insightful and informative articles on the Valencian Institute of Modern Art, television news, the Internet, soap operas, and football, to name only a few.

8. From Baudrillard's *Simulacrum and Simulation*. The hyperreal exists when information ceases to refer to an actual event and is consumed, interpreted, and dispersed without regard to verisimilitude. Both Baudrillard and Bourdieu use television news as an example of the hyperreal. The information or "truth" of the event becomes secondary to the reporting and distribution of selected facts, such as in war reporting.

9. Ortega y Gasset, for example, clearly envisioned artistic intellectualism as rejecting popular culture. As Graham and Labanyi explain Ortega's case: "popular culture in its folkloric sense did not concern him" (7).

10. Lidia Falcón, "Violent Democracy."

11. See Chapter 5 on Ray Loriga for a more detailed account of these phenomena.

12. In Eco's *The Role of the Reader,* he defines the model reader as the reader the author has foreseen who is "supposedly able to deal interpretatively with the expressions in the same way as the author deals generatively with them" (7).

Part 1: History or Creating the Past

Chapter One:
Rewriting the Past as Cultural Capital: Sacred Violence in Carme Riera's *Dins el darrer blau*

1. All English translations of Catalan are my own.

2. See the Introduction for a more complete rendering of Nietzsche's ideas about history.

3. Carme Riera (Palma de Mallorca, 1948) published her award-winning first collection of short stories, *Te deix, amor, la mar com a penyora* [*I Leave You, My Love, the Sea as a Token*] in 1975. She then received the Prudenci Bertrana prize in 1980 for her novel *Una primavera per a Domenico Guarini* [*Springtime for Domenico Guarini*], the Ramon Llull prize in 1989 for *Joc de miralls* [*Mirror Images*], and the Josep Pla (1994) for *Dins el darrer blau* [*In the Last Blue*]. This novel has also been awarded the Joan Crexells Prize and the Lletra d'Or. It is the first novel written originally in Catalan to win the National Literature Prize in Spain. Other notable works by Riera are: *Qüestió d'amor propi* [*A Matter of Self-Esteem*] (1987) and *Contra l'amor en companyia i altres relats* [*Against Love in the Company of Others and Other Stories*] (1991). Riera published *Cap al cel obert* [*Toward the Open Sky*] in 2000, which was awarded the Serra d'Or Prize and the National Prize for Culture; *La meitat de l'ànima* [*The Soul's Other Half*] in 2004; and *L'estiu de l'anglès* [*The English Summer*] in 2006. Riera has also published scholarly works on twentieth-century poets Carlos Barral, José Agustín Goytisolo, and Jaime Gil de Biedma, among others. In 2000 the Generalitat of Catalunya awarded Riera the San Jordi Cross for her impressive contribution to and promotion of Catalan literature and culture. Several noted scholars have translated her works into English, including Patricia Hart (*Senyora ha vist els meus fills?* as *Madame, Have You Seen My Sons?*), Christina de la Torre (*Joc de miralls* as *Mirror Images*), Roser Caminals-Heath and Holly Cashman (*Qüestió d'amor propi* as *A Matter of Self-Esteem*).

4. See Jacqueline Cruz and Barbara Zecchi for revealing somewhat disturbing data about the increase of domestic violence in Spain.

5. Girard's theory of sacrificial violence is rooted in his ideas of mimesis. He posits, as a universal condition that upholds cultural structures and institutions, the notion that desire is based on imitation. The desired object itself holds no apparent value but the need to appropriate someone else's desire, to usurp the subject position, drives human nature, which is inherently violent. Girard formulates the triangle of desire whereby two rivals compete to obtain the object of desire. Desire, therefore, is cyclical, inorganic, and purely the imitation of someone else's initial desire. He distinguishes between "good' violence and "bad" violence: good violence channels this mimetic desire into a communal form of violence such as ritual sacrifice that ultimately maintains social order, while "bad" violence is vengeful, passionate, and leads to a cycle of killings. Girard sets forth his theory of mimetic desire in *Deceit, Desire and the Novel* (1961) in which he analyzes literary works by Cervantes, Stendhal, Dostoevsky, and Proust. In *Violence and the Sacred* (1972) he continues to expand on the idea by deciphering the nature of violence in culture and discussing the concept of the scapegoat.

6. As an example of this phenomenon, Girard claims that twins, in some societies, are seen as the harbingers of evil (57), for they disrupt the social symbolic system. He uses the term *desymbolism* to indicate a tragic event that disrupts the social order through nondifferentiation (65). He cites several literary examples where tragedy ensues when confusion, which he equates with the inability to differentiate, causes an inappropriate action to set off a chain reaction of violence.

7. For an explanation of Girard's triangle of desire, see note 5.

Chapter Two:
Reader/Text Solidarity in Decoding the Past in Carme Riera's *La meitat de l'ànima*

1. Maryellen Bieder affirms that Riera breaks away from the pack of contemporary historical fiction writers by "problematizing the construction and interpretation of history" ("Paradox" 171) and because she deals with the marginalization and silencing of women and of Catalan as a national language ("Paradox" 172).

2. All English translations from Catalan are my own.

3. Seymour Chatman discusses the relationship between story (plot) and discourse (style) as basic structural differences in *Story and Discourse*.

4. Eco defines this "larger picture" as the *macroposition* of the *fabula*. For example, if I say "Where is John?" the utterance suggests that I know someone named John and have a certain interest in his whereabouts that I reveal as unknown to me but hope that someone else may provide. This explanation is the *macroposition* of the *fabula*, which may or may not coincide with the *microposition* or the utterance itself. The *macroposition* can be seen as an abstraction of the *fabula*.

5. Kristeva discusses the fluidity of the subject that allows for more that one position within a socio-psycological construct. This idea decenters notions of hegemony and monolithic discourse in that it embraces change and movement. See *Revolution in Poetic Language*.

6. Stewart reveals the musing of a "defective" reading of the novel posted on a Web blog in August of 2005 titled "Carme Riera's Mother" that asks if anyone has any information about the mysterious bearer of the letters. As Stewart points out, this is proof of the "author/protagonist's success in convincing the reader that what she recounts is 'real'" (242).

Chapter Three
Women, Writing, and the Spanish Civil War in *La voz dormida* by Dulce Chacón

1. Ventas prison in Madrid opened in 1931 as part of the Republican reform plan and was run by the Director General of Prisons, Victoria Kent (Trueba Mira 314). During Franco's reign, the jail was considered a "warehouse for recluses," and 10 to 12 women were forced to share one cell. For accounts of the horrible conditions, torture, and day-to-day experience of the prisoners see Mercedes Núñez, *Cárcel de Ventas*. The prison was closed down in the early 1970s.

2. Dulce Chacón was born in 1954 in Zafra, Badajoz. Her poetry collections include: *Querrán ponerle nombre* (1992), *Las palabras de piedra* (1993), *Contra el desprestigio de la altura* (Premio de Poesía Ciudad de Irún 1995), *Matar al ángel* (1999), and an anthology called *Cuatro gotas* (2003) that includes the aforementioned texts. Her novel *Cielos de barro* (2000) won the Premio Azorín de la Diputación de Alicante, and *La voz dormida* was awarded the Book of the Year 2003 by the Premio de Librero de Madrid. Other novels by Chacón are: *Algún amor que no mate* (1996), *Blanca vuela mañana* (1997), and *Háblame musa de aquel varón* (1988). She also wrote a play in 1998, *Segunda mano*, and was preparing a script for a stage version of her 1996 novel, *Algún amor que no mate* ("Fallece" n.pag.). Chacón collaboró with Cristina Sánchez to write *Matadora* (1997), the autobiography of the bullfighter. It was a shock to the academy and to her readers when Chacón died at the height of her success as a novelist on 3 Dec. 2003 from pancreatic cancer.

3. See Shirley Mangini's excellent study for a compelling and complete account of women writing about their experience during the Second Republic and Spanish Civil War. Also, Mary Nash provides detailed historical accounts of women's experience in her groundbreaking research on women in Spain.

4. In 1938 women were "liberated" from factories and work (Bussy Genevois 191).

The government gave maternity bonuses and banned women from entering the professions. In 1938 the law on civil marriage was nullified and the divorce law repealed. From 1941 to 1946 laws were passed banning abortion, adultery, and concubinage. Women who lived as prostitutes were subject to prison and heavy fines, yet prostitution remained legal. A man could kill his wife and lover and only face banishment; if no one was killed, he was acquitted of adultery (191).

5. Juana Doña's testimonial novel, Tomasa Cuevas's three volumes, Sara Berenguer's and Dolores Medio's novels, and the aforementioned study by Romeu are examples of the body of work that provides insight into women's situation during and after the war. The names of the women incarcerated, the famed group of young girls executed known as the Trece Rosas, details of infant mortalities, and the squalid conditions of the jails appear in several of the texts, including Chacón's.

6. For an overview of other Civil War novels written by women, see Carolyn Galerstein's article in which she describes novels by authors such as Ana María Matute and María Teresa León.

7. This photo, "Miliciana with her child before she leaves for the battlefront," also appears in Shirley Mangini's study.

8. The men hiding out in the sierra have all changed their names to protect their identities. Thus Mateo was formerly Felipe, and Jaime formerly Paulino. Elvira breaks through the layers of identity when she tells Mateo that his wife, Hortensia, never called him by his code names, El Cordobés or Mateo, but she always referred to him as Felipe (262). Insisting on using his pre-war name maintains the intimate, unadulterated bond between Hortensia and Felipe, and it is this reality that Felipe/Mateo clings to while hiding in the mountains.

9. See Sontag's book for an illuminating analysis of war photography as fabricated history.

Chapter Four
The Impossible Invention of History and the Hero in Javier Cercas's *Soldados de Salamina* and *La velocidad de la luz*

1. Javier Cercas (1962–) has published *El móvil* (1987), *La obra literaria de Gonzalo Suárez* (1994), *El inquilino* (1989), *El vientre de la ballena* (1997), *Una buena temporada* (1998), *Relatos reales* (2000), *Soldados de Salamina* (2001), and *La velocidad de la luz* (2005). The author is currently Professor of Spanish Literature at the University of Girona and previously spent two years teaching at the University of Illinois at Urbana-Champaign.

2. See the Introduction of this study for a more detailed analysis of Nietzsche's ideas of history and progress as presented in his essay "On the Uses and Disadvantages of History for Life" from *Untimely Meditations*.

3. Nevertheless, the absence of historical consciousness in the Gen X novels is itself a political and social statement that judges the pertinence

of the historical in the present. Perhaps it is the lack of a connection to the past that pushes the younger generation into a moralistic void.

4. Roberto Bolaño (1953–2003) was a successful writer from Chile who spent years in exile in Mexico and in Spain.

5. José Saval explains that the narrative mask Cercas creates in order to inject himself as the narrator in the novel serves a structural purpose that works in tandem with the other names taken from the author's real-world experience (62). The structure and parallels that drive the text depend on this tension between reality and fiction, between biography and invention.

6. The narrator alludes to his wild success after publishing "mi novela sobre la guerra civil" (190), suggesting a reference to *Soldados de Salamina*, thus injecting the present work with a humility and realization that a repeat performance of the success and subsequent fame of his first novel is not to be expected.

Part 2: Hyperreality or Creating Culture

1. See the Introduction for a more detailed discussion on Baudrillard.

2. See Molinaro for an excellent study on the nature of the body in Mañas.

Chapter Five
Television, Simulacra, and Power
in Three Works by Ray Loriga

1. Generation X writers from Spain were born in the 1960s. Their works lack a notion of the historical and include crime, unemployment, drug addiction, video culture, and a disenchanted worldview (de Urioste 456). The other foundational novel of the movement is *Historias del Kronen* (1994) by José Ángel Mañas.

2. Loriga has published seven novels: *Lo peor de todo* (1992); *Héroes* (1993), which received the "El Sitio" Novel Award; *Días extraños* (1994); *Caídos del cielo* (1995); *Tokio ya no nos quiere* (1999); *Trífero* (2000); and *El hombre que inventó Manhattan* (2004). Loriga also wrote and directed the film version of his novel *Caídos del cielo,* titled *La pistola de mi hermano* (1997); and co-wrote the Pedro Almodóvar film *Carne trémula* (1997). Carlos Saura directed his script *El séptimo día* in 2003, and Loriga filmed *Teresa, cuerpo de cristo* in 2007.

3. Santiago Fouz-Hernández elaborates on the differences between Coupland's vision of the Generation X and Spanish narrative at the end of the twentieth century. Going one step further, Athena Alchazidu defines the Gen X in Spain as "neotremendismo" and convincingly ties it to mid-twentieth-century Spanish literature rather than to a foreign influence.

4. An example of the international influence on Spanish TV is the appointment of Maurizio Carlotti as Director General of Telecinco in 1994

(Smith 17). He restructured the station and championed innovative programming that resulted in a series of prime-time hit shows imitating US formats. See Smith's article "Quality TV?" for a more in-depth study.

5. Shot/reverse shot refers to the editing technique that creates a logical conversation in film. We see the speaker and then cut to the listener to see her reaction and response. Loriga often includes both conversing actors in a medium shot, which reduces the editing or cutting of the film and creates a seamless shot.

6. In a single-shot scene, the entire scene takes place without a cut in the film. The camera stays in a fixed place and actors move in and out of the frame. A pan shot is a shot that pivots from left to right or right to left without the camera changing its position. For details on camera and editing techniques see Corrigan, *A Short Guide to Writing about Film*.

7. Corner explains the important "mobile concept of flow" (61) posited by Raymond Williams in his benchmark study *Television: Technology and Cultural Form*. Williams sees all TV shows, newscasts, commercials, etc., as linked together to form meaning in a stylized sequence he calls flow instead of the static notion of individual program distribution.

8. In an interview with David Trueba, Loriga comments on the process of writing: "Inventas tu manera de leer, de acercarte a las cosas, de relacionarlas. Y, finalmente, te inventas tu manera de contar" ("Retrato" 3).

Chapter Six
Textual Violence and the Hyperreal in *De todo lo visible y lo invisible* by Lucía Etxebarria

1. Etxebarria has published fourteen books of fiction and essay. Her first novel, *Amor, curiosidad, prozac y dudas* (1997), was followed by the Premio Nadal-winning *Beatriz y los cuerpos celestes* in 1998. Other highlights are *De todo lo visible y lo invisible* (2001, Premio Primavera) and *Un milagro en equilibrio* (2004, Premio Planeta). Her most recent novel is *Cosmofobia* (2007).

2. In an interview with Escabias in 2000, Etxebarria explains that the title of her novel comes from Blake ("Entrevista" 202).

3. One must assume that the hospital form is a creation of the author too. Her effort to include practical information and empty spaces for the discharge time and date, as well as an address for the clinic suggests that Etxebarria is familiar with the clinic and with such forms.

4. Most scholarly works use endnotes so as to give the reader the option of flipping back and forth in the text or avoiding endnote supplementation altogether. With endnotes, the main text flows more easily without the distraction at the bottom of the page, but the interested reader must search to locate the pertinent information.

5. Shangay Lily (1963) has published four books, including the popular *Machistófeles* in 2002. His Web site, <http://www.shangaylily.com>,

reveals his dedication to gay rights through a witty and provocative diary and autobiographical sketch.

Chapter Seven
(Inter)Textuality in José Ángel Mañas's
Historias del Kronen and *La pella*

1. Mañas has published *Historias del Kronen* (1994), *Mensaka* (1995), *Soy un escritor frustrado* (1996), *Ciudad rayada* (1998), *Sonoko 95* (1999), *Mundo burbuja* (2001), *Caso Karen* (2005), *El secreto del oráculo* (2007), and *La pella* (2008).

2. See Chapter 2 for a more complete analysis of Eco's model reader.

3. Only Estrada pinpoints the problem as specific to males who resort to violence when unable to express the frustration of a rapidly changing social order. While "Generation X" refers to both males and females, the males in the novel act out in ways the women do not. An in-depth study of gender relations and representation in *Kronen* remains to be seen.

4. Pao describes blank fiction as fiction set in urban environments that "depict[s] characters' whole rejection both of the traditional constraints of job and family and of political or social ideals [that] dovetails with a sense of living at a remove from reality, produced in part by the ubiquitous presence of television, film and video" (245).

5. Odartey-Wellington makes the point that the parentheses work to focus our attention on Carlos, just as a director would choose to focus the camera on the main character and exclude other commentary or voices (31). She suggests that this connects the novel's structure to that of a film script, thus stylistically intertwining the two genres.

6. Rafael Rojas points out further negative criticism directed at young Generation X writers: "Los críticos refunfuñaban constantemente contra la idea de que la juventud pudiera ser en sí misma un valor literario e incluso los autores consagrados se revolvían contra sus menores, quién sabe si defendiendo su territorio, y así, Pérez Reverte criticaba a los jóvenes que relatan las apasionantes vivencias que uno experimenta tomándose una caña con los colegas ..." (<http://www.ociototal.com/recopila2/r news/kronen.html>).

7. The novel *A Clockwork Orange* (1963) by Anthony Burgess and the 1971 film version directed by Stanley Kubrick tell of the violent exploits of Alex and his gang of friends. *Henry: Portrait of a Serial Killer* (1990) directed by John McNaughton has been called an "excruciatingly disturbing, partially fact-based drama [that] follows [a] serial killer's grisly day-to-day routine. Its subdued style may disappoint Hollywood thriller fans, but the realistic performances [and] terrifying brutality have made it a cult favorite" (Reel.com review at <http://www.reel.com/movie.asp?MID=2149>). *American Psycho* (1991) is the story of a yuppie psychopath, Patrick Bateman, who murders victims indiscriminately. The

The formed by Matt Johnson in 1978 is an underground band that combines various musical styles. A verse and the chorus of "Giant" from the album *Soul Mining* serve as the epigraph of Mañas's novel and echo the spiritual crisis, not of Carlos, but rather of Roberto in the epilogue: "I'm scared of God and scared of hell / And I'm caving in upon myself / How can anyone know me / When I don't even know myself" (*Kronen* 10). The song also appears at the beginning of the novel and serves as bookends to the work emphasizing Roberto's critical tone. Nirvana struck huge success with their 1991 album *Nevermind,* and the single "Smells Like Teen Spirit" became an anthem of disgruntled youth of the 1990s.

8. Several noted critics praised *American Psycho* for its unabashed honesty and portrayal of brutality in 1980s New York City. Norman Mailer claimed: "The first novel to come along in years that takes on deep and Dostoyevskian themes. ... [Ellis] is showing older authors where the hands have come to on the clock. ... He has forced us to look at the intolerable material, and so few novelists try for that anymore" ("American Psycho"). Henry Bean, writing for the *Los Angeles Times Book Review*, says: "What's rarely said in all the furor over this novel is that it's a satire, a hilarious, repulsive, boring, seductive, and deadpan satire. ... Ellis is, first and last, a moralist. Under cover of his laconic voice, every word in his three novels to date springs from grieving outrage at our spiritual condition ..." (n.pag.).

9. See Isabel Estrada's work for an excellent analysis of the male identity crisis as presented in *Matando dinosaurios con tirachinas* by Pedro Maestre.

10. Ana Corbalán discusses the elements of the postmodern subculture in the novel and concludes that through personal and bodily transgression, the youth criticize dominant culture (210).

11. Roberto discusses his homosexuality with his therapist and confesses romantic feelings that he had for Carlos. He doubts that Carlos knows he is gay but admits "nunca comprendí por qué me besó aquel día en el concierto . . . Era por hacer la tontería, por transgredir o quizás para humillarme" (243).

12. *American Psycho* was made into a film starring Christian Bale and co-written and directed by Mary Harmon. Mañas does not mention the film version in his novel.

13. Jorge Pérez describes this concept of identity as "basado en el *Volkgeist,* ese espíritu populista que configura su identidad basándose en una supuesta pureza étnica, unidad lingüística, y una memoria histórica" (39).

14. See Kristeva for a discussion on the abject "other" that is defiled and at the same time desired.

15. In a scene from the film version of *Kronen* directed by Montxo Armendáriz, a drunk and stoned Carlos aggressively tries to kiss his sister in an elevator. This scene pushes his lack of respect for women and family over the edge as both, represented in the sister, are disrespected and perversely eroticized.

16. The use of "z" in place of "s" in Borja's speech suggests a lisp. I will comment on this aspect of language in the text later in this chapter.

17. Vicente José Benet points out a similar ending to the film *Mensaka*, where we witness the character's integration into "una realidad absolutamente convencional y de orden" (51).

18. See Chapter 3 for an analysis of Cercas's works.

19. I borrow the phrase "contemporary extreme" from the essay collection edited by Alain-Philippe Durand and Naomi Mandel.

Conclusion

1. For the complete text of the law, see "España: Ley de la Memoria Histórica." For an account of the public reception, see Carlos Cué, "La ley de memoria se aprueba entre aplausos de invitados antifranquistas."

Works Cited

Ackelsberg, Martha A. *Free Women of Spain: Anarchism and the Struggle for the Emancipation of Women.* Bloomington: Indiana UP, 1991.

Agawu-Kakraba, Yaw. "José Ángel Mañas's Literature of Insurgency: *Historias del Kronen.*" *Revista Hispánica Moderna* 55 (June 2002): 188–203.

Alchazidu, Athena. "Generación X: Una modalidad finisecular del tremendismo." *Études Romanes de Brno* 32.23 (2002): 99–108.

Amago, Samuel. *True Lies: Narrative Self-Consciousness in the Contemporary Spanish Novel.* Lewisburg: Bucknell UP, 2006.

Amar Sánchez, Ana María. *Juegos de seducción y traición: Literatura y cultura de masas.* Rosario, Arg.: Estudios Culturales, 2000.

"American Psycho." *Vintage Screening Room.* n.d. 15 July 2006. <http://www.randomhouse.com/vintage/screen/books/psycho>.

Amorós, Celia. "Violencia contra las mujeres y pactos patriarcales." *Violencia y sociedad patriarcal.* Ed. Virginia Maquieira y Cristina Sánchez. Madrid: Pablo Iglesias, 1990. 1–15.

Anderson, Benedict. *Imagined Communities: Reflections on the Origin and Spread of Nationalism.* London; New York: Verso, 1991.

Asunción Gómez, María. "Feminism and Anarchism: Remembering the Role of Mujeres Libres in the Spanish Civil War." Trans. Patricia Santoro. *Recovering Spain's Feminist Tradition.* Ed. Lisa Vollendorf. New York: MLA, 2001. 293–310.

Bakhtin, Mikhail M. *The Dialogic Imagination.* Trans. Caryl Emerson and Michael Holquist. Austin: U of Texas P, 1981.

Baudrillard, Jean. *Selected Writings.* Ed. Mark Poster. Stanford: Stanford UP, 1988.

———. *Simulacra and Simulations.* Trans. Sheila Faria Glaser. Ann Arbor: U of Michigan P, 1994.

Bean, Henry. Rev. of *American Psycho.* By Bret Easton Ellis. 1999. July 2004. <http://www.randomhouse.com/vintage/screen/books/psycho.html>.

Beilin, Katarzyna Olga. "Ray Loriga: Dudas y sombras." *Conversaciones literarias con novelistas contemporáneos.* Suffolk: Tamesis, 2004. 191–210.

Benet, Vicente José. "El malestar del entretenimiento." *Archivos de la Filmoteca: Revista de Estudios Históricos sobre la Imagen* 39.10 (2001): 40–53.

Works Cited

Benjamin, Walter. "Critique of Violence." *Reflections*. Trans. Edmund Jephcott. New York: Harcourt, 1978. 277–300.

Berenguer, Sara. *Entre el sol y la tormenta*. Barcelona: Seuba, 1988.

Beverley, John. Introduction to "La voz del otro: Testimonio subalternidad y verdad narrativa." *Revista de Crítica Literaria Latinoamericana* 18.36 (1992): 7–18.

Bieder, Maryellen. "Carme Riera and the Paradox of Recovering Historical Memory in *La meitat de l'ànima*." Glenn and McNerney 169–89.

———. "Cultural Capital: The Play of Language, Gender, and Nationality in Carme Riera." *Catalan Review* 14.1–2 (2000): 53–74.

Booth, Wayne. *The Rhetoric of Fiction*. Chicago: U of Chicago P, 1961.

Bourdieu, Pierre. *The Field of Cultural Production*. New York: Columbia UP, 1993.

———. *On Television*. 1996. New York: New Press, 1998.

Brooke-Rose, Christine. "The Readerhood of Man." *The Reader in the Text: Essays on Audience and Interpretation*. Ed. Susan R. Suleiman and Inge Crosman. Princeton: Princeton UP, 1980. 120–48.

Bussy Genevois, Danièle. "The Women of Spain from the Republic to Franco." *A History of Women: Toward a Cultural Identity in the Twentieth Century*. Ed. Georges Duby and Michelle Perrot. Cambridge: Harvard UP, 1994. 177–93.

Bustamante, Enrique. "The Mass Media: A Problematic Modernization." Graham and Labanyi 356–61.

Camí-Vela, María. *La búsqueda de la identidad en la obra literaria de Carme Riera*. Madrid: Pliegos, 2000.

Carbonell, Neus. "The Ethics of Dissidence: Resistance and Relationality in Carme Riera's *Dins el darrer blau*." Glenn, Servodidio, and Vásquez 218–30.

Cercas, Javier. *Relatos reales*. Barcelona: El Acantilado, 2000.

———. *Soldados de Salamina*. 2001. Barcelona: Tusquets, 2005.

———. *La velocidad de la luz*. Barcelona: Tusquets, 2005.

Chacón, Dulce. *La voz dormida*. Madrid: Alfaguara, 2002.

Chatman, Seymour. *Story and Discourse: Narrative Structure in Fiction and Film*. Ithaca: Cornell UP, 1978.

Cixous, Hélène. "The Laugh of the Medusa." 1975. *New French Feminisms*. Ed. Elaine Marks and Isabelle de Courtivron. New York: Schocken, 1981. 245–64.

A Clockwork Orange. Dir. Stanley Kubrick. Perf. Malcolm McDowell. Warner Brothers, 1971.

Colmeiro, José F. "Re-Collecting Women's Voices from Prison: The Hybridization of Memories in Dulce Chacón's *La voz dormida*." Glenn and McNerney 191–209.

Coll-Tellechea, Reyes. "*Dins el darrer blau* by Carme Riera: Memory's Future and the History of the Spanish Jews." *Models in Medieval Iberian Literature and Their Modern Reflection: Convivencia as Structural, Cultural and Sexual Idea*. Newark, DE: Juan de la Cuesta, 2002. 307–20.

Collera, Virginia. "Etxebarria afirma que en 'Ya no sufro por amor' cita a Castelló pero no plagia." *El País*, Cultura sec. 13 Sept. 2006. 27 Sept. 2006. <http://www.elpais.es/articulo/cultura/Etxebarria/afirma/sufro/amor/cita/Castello/plagia/elpporcul/20060913elpepicul_3/Tes/?print=1>.

Corbalán, Ana. "Subculturas jóvenes posmodernas: *Historias del Kronen* como medio de escape y resistencia." *Siglo XXI: Literatura y cultura españolas* 5 (2007): 197–213.

Corner, John. *Critical Ideas in Television Studies*. Oxford: Oxford UP, 1999.

Corrigan, Timothy. *A Short Guide to Writing about Film*. New York: Pearson Longman, 2004.

Cortázar, Julio. *Rayuela*. 1963. Madrid: Cátedra, 1984.

Coupland, Douglas. *Generation X: Tales for an Accelerated Culture*. New York: St. Martin's, 1991.

Crespo, Mariano. "Entrevista a Dulce Chacón II." *La Mujer Actual*. 19 Jan. 2006. 24 Sept. 2009. <http://www.mujeractual.com/entrevistas/chacon/index3.html>.

Cruz, Jacqueline, and Barbara Zecchi, eds. *La mujer en la España actual: ¿Evolución o involución?* Barcelona: Icaria, 2004.

Cué, Carlos. "La ley de memoria se aprueba entre aplausos de invitados antifranquistas." *El País Digital* [Madrid]. 1 Nov. 2007. 10 Oct. 2009. <http://www.elpais.com/articulo/espana/ley/memoria/aprueba/aplausos/invitados/antifranquistas/elpepiesp/20071101elpepinac_18/Tes>.

Cuevas, Tomasa. *Testimonios de mujeres en las cárceles franquistas*. 1982. 3 vols. Huesca: Instituto de Estudios Altoaragoneses, 2004.

Doña, Juana. *Desde la noche y la niebla (mujeres en las cárceles franquistas)*. Madrid: de la Torre, 1978.

Works Cited

Dorca, Toni. "Joven narrativa en la España de los noventa: La Generación X." *Revista de Estudios Hispánicos* 31.2 (1997): 309–24.

Durand, Alain-Philippe, and Naomi Mandel, eds. *Novels of the Contemporary Extreme*. New York: Continuum, 2006.

During, Simon. Introduction. *The Cultural Studies Reader*. London: Routledge, 1993. 1–25.

Eagleton, Terry. *The Idea of Culture*. Malden, MA: Blackwell, 2000.

Echevarría, Ignacio. "Melodías de Manhattan." Rev. of *El hombre que inventó Manhattan*, by Ray Loriga. *El País*. Babelia Literary Supplement 31 Jan. 2004. 6 July 2004. <http://www.elpais.es/articuloCompletohtml?xref=20040131elpbabese5&type=Tes&anchor=elpepisupbab&print=1&ddate=20040131>.

———."Oiga Usted, joven." *El País*. Babelia Literary Supplement 30 Oct. 1999: 9.

Eco, Umberto. *The Role of the Reader*. Bloomington: Indiana UP, 1979.

El Saffar, Ruth. "Unbinding the Doubles: Reflection of Love and Culture in the Work of René Girard." *Denver Quarterly* 18.4 (1984): 6–22.

Ellis, Bret Easton. *American Psycho*. New York: Vintage, 1991.

Emmett, B. P. Forward to *Violence on Television*. London: British Broadcasting Corporation, 1972. v–viii.

Encinar, Ángeles, and Kathleen M. Glenn, eds. *La pluralidad narrativa: Escritores españoles contemporáneos (1984–2004)*. Madrid: Biblioteca nueva, 2005.

Epps, Brad, and Luis Fernández Cifuentes, eds. *Spain beyond Spain: Modernity, Literary History and National Identity*. Lewisburg: Bucknell UP, 2005.

"España: Ley de memoria histórica." *La Insignia* 1 Nov. 2007. 18 Aug. 2009. <http://www.lainsignia.org/2007/noviembre/cul_002.html>.

Estrada, Isabel. "Victimismo y violencia en la ficción de la Generación X: *Matando dinosaurios con tirachinas* de Pedro Maestre." *Ciberletras* 6 (Jan. 2002). 24 Sept. 2009. <http://www.lehman.cuny.edu/ciberletras/v06/estrada.html>.

Etxebarria, Lucía. *Amor, curiosidad, prozac y dudas*. Barcelona: Plaza y Janés, 1997.

———. *Beatriz y los cuerpos celestes*. Barcelona: Destino, 1998.

———. *De todo lo visible y lo invisible*. Madrid: Espasa, 2001.

———."Entrevista con Lucía Etxebarria, Aberdeen, 18 de noviembre de 2000." Interview. By Pilar Escabias Lloret. *Journal of Iberian and Latin American Studies* 8.2 (2002): 201–12.

———. *La letra futura. El dedo en la llaga: Cuestiones sobre arte, literatura, creación y crítica*. Barcelona: Destino, 2000.

———. *Yo no sufro por amor*. Madrid: Martínez Roca, 2005.

Everly, Kathryn A. *Catalan Women Writers and Artists: Revisionist Views from a Feminist Space*. Lewisburg: Bucknell UP, 2003.

Falcón, Lidia. "Violent Democracy." *Journal of Spanish Cultural Studies* 3.1 (2002):15–28.

"Fallece en Madrid a los 49 años la escritora Dulce Chacón." *El País.es*, Cultura sec. 4 Dec. 2003. 23 Feb. 2006. <http://www.elpais.es/articulo.html?xref=20031204elpepucul_1&type=Tes&anchor=elpporcul&d_date=20031204>.

Ferrari, Enrique. "¿Hubo una Generación X en España?" *Siglo XXI: Literatura y cultura españolas* 2 (2004): 259–63.

Folkart, Jessica. "Body Talk: Space, Communication, and Corporeality in Lucía Etxebarria's *Beatriz y los cuerpos celestes*." *Hispanic Review* 72 (2004): 43–63.

Fortes, José Antonio. "Del 'realismo sucio' y otras imposturas de la novela española última." *Ínsula* 589–90 (1996): 21, 27.

Foucault, Michel. *The History of Sexuality*. Trans. Robert Hurley. New York: Vintage, 1990.

Fouz-Hernández, Santiago. "¿Generación X? Spanish Urban Youth Culture at the End of the Century in Mañas's/Armendáriz's *Historias del Kronen*." *Romance Studies* 18.1 (June 2000): 83–98.

Galerstein, Carolyn. "The Spanish Civil War: The View of Women Novelists." *Letras Femeninas* 10.2 (1984): 12–18.

Gil Casado, Pablo. "*Tetralogía Kronen*: Realismo, dimensión criticosocial y posmodernidad (I)." *Ojácano* 26.10 (2004): 77–102.

Girard, René. *Violence and the Sacred*. 1972. Trans. Patrick Gregory. Baltimore: Johns Hopkins UP, 1989.

Glenn, Kathleen M., and Kathleen McNerney, eds. *Visions and Revisions: Women's Narrative in Twentieth-Century Spain*. Foro Hispánico 31. New York: Rodopi, 2008.

Glenn, Kathleen M., Mirella Servodidio, and Mary S. Vásquez. *Moveable Margins: The Narrative Art of Carme Riera*. Lewisburg: Bucknell UP, 1999.

Goicoechea, Alicia Redonda. "Los modelos de mujer de Lucía Etxebarria." *Mujeres novelistas: Jóvenes narradoras de los noventa*. Madrid: Narcea, 2003. 109–21.

Works Cited

Gómez López Quiñones, Antonio. "La Guerra Civil española: *Soldados de Salamina* de Javier Cercas." *La palabra y el hombre* 127 (2003): 115–29.

Gracia, Jordi. "Nuevas fricciones entre historia y novela." *Hijos de la razón: Contraluces de la libertad en las letras españolas de la democracia.* Barcelona: Edhasa, 2001.

Graham, Helen, and Jo Labanyi, eds. *Spanish Cultural Studies: An Introduction.* New York: Oxford UP, 1995.

Grohmann, Alexis. "La configuración de *Soldados de Salamina* o la negra espalda de Javier Cercas." *Letras Peninsulares* 17.1–2 (2004–05): 297–320.

Gullón, Germán. "La novela neorrealista de José Ángel Mañas en el panorama novelístico español." Introduction. *Historias del Kronen.* By José Ángel Mañas. Barcelona: Destino, 1998. v–xxxix.

Rev. of *Henry: Portrait of a Serial Killer*, dir. John McNaughton. *Reel.com.* 1986. n.pag. 9 Oct. 2009. <http://www.reel.com/movie.asp?MID=2149>.

Henseler, Christine. "Acerca del 'fenómeno' Lucía Etxebarria." *Revista de Literatura* 67.134 (2005): 501–21.

———. *Contemporary Spanish Women's Narrative and the Publishing Industry.* Urbana and Chicago: U of Illinois P, 2003.

———. "Etxebarria Ecstacy: The Publishing Industry Exposed." Henseler, *Contemporary* 109–26.

———. " Pop, Punk, and Rock and Roll Writers: José Ángel Mañas, Ray Loriga, and Lucía Etxebarria Redefine the Literary Canon." *Hispania* 87.4 (2004): 692–702.

Herzberger, David K. *Narrating the Past: Fiction and Historiography in Postwar Spain.* Durham and London: Duke UP, 1995.

Iser, Wolfgang. "Interaction between Text and Reader." *The Reader in the Text: Essays on Audience and Interpretation.* Ed. Susan Suleiman and Inge Crosman. Princeton: Princeton UP, 1980. 106–19.

Jordan, Barry. "Redefining the Public Interest: Television in Spain Today." Graham and Labanyi 361–69.

Jordan, Barry, and Rikki Morgan-Tamosunas, eds. *Contemporary Spanish Cultural Studies.* London: Arnold; New York: Oxford UP, 2000.

Kinder, Marsha, ed. *Refiguring Spain: Cinema/Media/Representation.* Durham: Duke UP, 1997.

Klodt, Jason E. "'Nada de nada de nada de nada': Ray Loriga and the Paradox of Spain's Generation X." *Tropos* 27 (2001): 42–54.

Works Cited

Kofman, Sarah. "The Narcissistic Woman: Freud and Girard." *Diacritics* 10.3 (1980): 36–45.

Kristeva, Julia. *Revolution in Poetic Language*. Trans. Margaret Waller. New York: Columbia UP, 1984.

Labanyi, Jo. "Introduction: Engaging with Ghosts; or, Theorizing Culture in Modern Spain." *Constructing Identity in Contemporary Spain: Theoretical Debates and Cultural Practice*. Oxford: Oxford UP, 2002. 1–14.

Loriga, Ray. *Caídos del cielo*. Barcelona: Plaza y Janés, 1995.

———. "Entrevista: Ray Loriga. La literatura le da a la vida una lógica que no tiene." Interview. By Javier Rodríguez Marcos. *El País.es*. 31 Jan. 2004. 6 July 2004. <http://www.elpais.es/articuloCompleto.html?xref=20040131elpbabese>.

———. *El hombre que inventó Manhattan*. Barcelona: el Aleph, 2004.

———. "El hombre que inventó Manhattan." Interview. *Clubcultura*. Clubliteratura sec. n.d. 24 Sept. 2009. <http://www.clubcultura.com/clubliteratura/rayloriga/>.

———, screenplay. *La pistola de mi hermano*. Dir. Loriga. Perf. Daniel Gonzáles, Nico Bidásolo, Karra Elejalde. Enrique Cerezo Producciones, 1997.

———. "Retrato de un exilio: Nueva York soñado." Interview. By David Trueba. *El mundo*. Suplemento de *La Luna* 259. 5 Mar. 2004. 22 June 2004. <http://www.elmundo.es/Laluna/2004/259/1078336145.html>.

Luengo, Ana. "Soldados de Salamina (2001): La reconstrucción del héroe republicano—a su pesar." *La encrucijada de la memoria. La memoria colectiva de la Guerra Civil Española en la novela contemporánea*. Berlin: Walter Frey, 2004. 233–56.

Lunati, Montserrat. "Travelling by the Book: Perpetuating a Masculine Tradition in Ray Loriga's *Caídos del cielo* (1995)." *Letras Peninsulares* 17. 2–3 (Fall/Winter 2004–05): 427–47.

Mangini, Shirley. *Memories of Resistance: Women's Voices from the Spanish Civil War*. New Haven: Yale UP, 1995.

Mañas, José Ángel. *Caso Karen*. Barcelona: Destino, 2005.

———. *Ciudad rayada*. Madrid: Espasa Calpe, 1998.

———. *Historias del Kronen*. Barcelona: Destino, 1994.

———. *Mensaka*. Barcelona: Destino, 1995.

———. *La pella*. Madrid: Lengua de trapo, 2008.

———. *Sonko 95*. Barcelona: Destino, 1999.

———. *Soy un escritor frustrado*. Madrid: Espasa Calpe, 1996.

Works Cited

Martínez-Gutiérrez, Josebe. "Margarita Nelken: Feminist and Political Praxis during the Spanish Civil War." Trans. H. Patsy Boyer. *Recovering Spain's Feminist Tradition*. Ed. Lisa Vollendorf. New York: MLA, 2001. 278–92.

Maxwell, Richard. "Spatial Eruption, Global Grids: Regionalist TV in Spain and Dialects of Identity Politics." Kinder 260–83.

Medio, Dolores. *Atrapados en la ratonera*. Madrid: Alce, 1980.

Moi, Toril. "The Missing Mother: The Oedipal Rivalries of René Girard." *Diacritics* 12.2 (1982): 21–31.

Moix, Llàtzer. "Veinteañeros, audiovisuales y psicópatas." *La vanguardia* 8 Jan. 1994.

Molinaro, Nina L. "The 'Real' Story of Drugs, *Dasein* and José Ángel Mañas's *Historias del Kronen*." *Revista Canadiense de Estudios Hispánicos* 27.2 (2003): 291–306.

Moreiras Menor, Cristina. *Cultura herida: Literatura y cine en la España democrática*. Madrid: Libertarias, 2002.

Nash, Mary. *Defying Male Civilization: Women in the Spanish Civil War*. Denver: Arden, 1995.

Navarro Martínez, Eva. "Una realidad a la carta: La televisión en algunas novelas de la última década del siglo XX." *Espéculo: Revista de Estudios Literarios* 25 (2003–04). 6 July 2004. <http://www.ucm.es/info/especulo/numero25/alacarta.html>.

Nichols, Geraldine C. "'Tras su hache mayúscula': Carme Riera and the Exploration of History in *Dins el darrer blau*." Glenn, Servodidio, and Vásquez 200–17.

Nietzsche, Friedrich. *Untimely Meditations*. Cambridge: Cambridge UP, 1997.

Nowak, Susan. "The Girardian Theory and Feminism: Critique and Appropriation." *Contagion* 1 (Spring 1994): 19–29.

Núñez, Mercedes. *Cárcel de ventas*. Paris: Editions de la Librairie de Globe, 1967.

Odartey-Wellington, Dorothy. *Contemporary Spanish Fiction: Generation X*. Newark: U of Delaware P, 2008.

Owen, Rob. *Gen X TV: The Brady Bunch to Melrose Place*. Syracuse: Syracuse UP, 1997.

Pao, María T. "Sex, Drugs, and Rock&Roll: *Historias del Kronen* as Blank Fiction." *Anales de la Literatura Española Contemporánea* 27.2 (2002): 245–60.

Pérez, Janet. "Text and Context in Carme Riera's *Dins el darrer blau*." *Letras Peninsulares* 12.2–3 (1999–2000): 239–54.

Works Cited

Pérez, Jorge. "Suspiros de España: El inconsciente político nacional en la narrativa de José Ángel Mañas." *España Contemporánea* 18.1 (2005): 33–51.

Pérez Miguel, Leandro. "Ascendí de Tercera a Primera División sin pasar por categorias intermedias." *El Mundo,* Cultura sec. 7 Dec. 2001.

Pope, Randolph. "Between Rock and the Rocking Chair: The Epilogue's Resistance in *Historias del Kronen*." *Generation X Rocks: Contemporary Peninsular Fiction, Film, and Rock Culture*. Ed. Christine Henseler and Randolph Pope. Nashville, TN: Vanderbilt UP, 2007. 115–25.

Prat, Joaquín. "*La voz dormida*: Entrevista con Dulce Chacón." *Puerta del sol* 12.1 (2004): 8–11.

Riera, Carme. "An Ambition without Limits." Glenn, Servodidio, and Vásquez 30–38.

———. *Dins el darrer blau*. Barcelona: Destino, 1994.

———. *La meitat de l'ànima*. Barcelona: Proa, 2004.

Richter, David F. "Memory and Metafiction: Re-membering Stories and Histories in *Soldados de Salamina*." *Letras Peninsulares* 17.2–3 (Fall/Winter 2004–05): 285–96.

Rodríguez, María Pilar. "Disidencias históricas: Rescates y revisiones en la narrativa femenina española actual." *Arizona Journal of Hispanic Cultural Studies* 4 (2000): 77–90.

———. "Exclusión y pertenencia: Nación y responsabilidad histórica en *En el último azul*." *El espejo y la máscara*. Ed. Luisa Cotoner. Barcelona: Destino, 2000. 241–63.

Rodríguez Martorell, Carlos. "Javier Cercas: The Perils of War and Fame." Interview. *Críticas*. 1 Aug. 2005. 6 Jan. 2009. <http://www.criticasmagazine.com/article/CA631486.html>.

Rogers, Pat. "The Parthian Dart: Endings and Epilogues in Fiction." *Essays in Criticism* 42.2 (Apr. 1992): 85–106.

Rojas, Rafael. "¿Qué fue de la Generación Kronen?" 10 Apr. 2007. <http://www.ociototal.com/recopila2/r_news/kronen.html>.

Romeu Alfaro, Fernanda. *El silencio roto*. Oviedo?: J.C. Producción, 1994.

Ross, Catherine. "Sex, Drugs and Violence in Lucía Etxebarria's *Amor, curiosidad, Prozac y dudas*." Durand and Mandel 153–62.

Sanz Villanueva, Santos. "Archipiélago de la ficción." *Ínsula* 589–90 (1996): 3–4.

Sarto, Ana, Alicia Ríos, and Abril Trigo, eds. *The Latin American Cultural Studies Reader*. Durham: Duke UP, 2004.

Works Cited

Saval, José. V. "Simetría y paralelismo en la construcción de *Soldados de Salamina* de Javier Cercas." *Letras Hispanas* 4.1 (Spring 2007): 62–70.

Sieburth, Stephanie. *Inventing High and Low: Literature, Mass Culture, and Uneven Modernity in Spain*. Durham: Duke UP, 1994.

Smith, Paul Julian. "Quality TV? The *Periodistas* Notebook." *Contemporary Spanish Culture: TV, Fashion, Art and Film*. Cambridge: Polity, 2003. 9–33.

Sontag, Susan. *Regarding the Pain of Others*. New York: Farrar, Straus and Giroux, 2003.

Sperry, Sharon Lynn. "Television News as Narrative." *Television as a Cultural Force*. Ed. Richard Adler and Douglass Cater. New York: Praeger, 1976. 129–46.

Spigel, Lynn. Introduction. *Television after TV*. Ed. Lynn Spigel and Jan Olsson. Durham: Duke UP, 2004. 1–34.

Spires, Robert C. "Depolarization and the New Spanish Fiction at the Millennium." *ALEC* 30.1–2 (2005): 485–512.

———. "Una historia fantasmal: *Soldados de Salamina* de Javier Cercas." Encinar and Glenn 75–88.

Stewart, Melissa. "Shifts in Textual Author(ity): Grappling with Unstable Identities in Carme Riera's *La meitat de l'ànima*." *Letras Peninsulares* 19.2–3 (Fall/Winter 2006–07): 235–42.

Subirats, Eduardo. *El final de las vanguardias*. Barcelona: Anthropos, 1989.

"Tres expertos confirman que Lucía Etxebarria 'no plagió' a Antonio Colinas." *Clubcultura*. 19 Feb. 2003. 27 Sept. 2006. <http://www.clubcultura.com/noticias/leer.php?not_id=2642>.

Trueba Mira, Virginia. "Arañas y algas: Imágenes de la opresión y la resistencia (sobre *La voz dormida* de Dulce Chacón)." *Nueva Literatura Hispánica* 8–9 (2004–05): 313–38.

Tsuchiya, Akiko. "Discourse and the Strategies of Power in Carme Riera's *En el último azul*: A Cultural Analysis of the Inquisition." *Tesserae: Journal of Iberian and Latin American Studies* 7.1 (2001): 77–84.

———. "The 'New' Female Subject and the Commodification of Gender in the Works of Lucía Etxebarria." *Romance Studies* 20.1 (June 2002): 77–87.

Urioste, Carmen de. "La narrativa española de los noventa: ¿Existe una "generación X?" *Letras Peninsulares* 10.3 (Winter 1997–98): 455–76.

———. "Punk y ruido en la "Tetralogía Kronen" de José Ángel Mañas." *España Contemporánea* 16.2 (2003): 29–52.

Velázquez Jordán, Santiago. "Dulce Chacón: La reconciliación real de la guerra civil aún no ha llegado." *Espéculo: Revista de Estudios Literarios* 22 (2002). 26 Sept. 2005. <http://www.ucm.es/info/especulo/numero22/dChacón.html>.

Vollendorf, Lisa. "Owning Up to History: Ethics and Aesthetics in Carme Riera's *Dins el darrer blau*. Glenn and McNerney 147–67.

White, Hayden. *The Content of the Form*. Baltimore: Johns Hopkins UP, 1987.

———. *Tropics of Discourse*. Baltimore: Johns Hopkins UP, 1978.

———. "The Value of Narrativity in the Representation of Reality." *On Narrative*. Ed. W.J.T. Mitchel. Chicago: U of Chicago P, 1980. 1–23.

Williams, Raymond. *Culture and Society 1780–1950* London: Chatto and Windus, 1958.

———. *Television: Technology and Cultural Form*. London: Fontana, 1974.

Yushimito del Valle, Carlos. "Soldados de Salamina: Indagaciones sobre un héroe moderno." *Espéculo: Revista de Estudios Literarios* 23 (2003). 11 June 2006. <http://www.ucm.es/info/especulo/numero23/Salamina.html>.

Index

audiovisual. *See* media
author
  implied author, 23, 60–61, 136, 141–42, 147, 171, 177
  and model reader, 26, 48, 52, 54–57, 61. *See also* novel
  relationship to reader, 5, 22–24, 55, 146–47, 192n6

Bakhtin, Mikhail, 23–24
Barthes, Roland, 113–14, 184
Baudrillard, Jean, x, 18–19, 112, 187. *See also* hyperreality
  simulacra, 19–20, 127–32, 135, 137, 187–88
Benjamin, Walter, 22–23
body
  female eroticized, 148–52
  as site of violence, 135, 138. *See also* violence
Booth, Wayne, 23–24, 89, 141, 142, 147
Bourdieu, Pierre, 12–15, 120, 122–23, 184, 189n6

Caídos del cielo (Loriga), x, 8, 19, 23, 116, 119, 121–23
Cercas, Javier, ix, 48, 85–109, 193n1
  Relatos reales, 85
  Soldados de Salamina, ix, 7, 26, 54, 85–101, 171, 178
  La velocidad de la luz, ix, 7, 86, 101–09, 178
Chacón, Dulce, ix, 48, 63–67, 69–84, 109, 192n2
  La voz dormida, ix, 7, 22, 26, 63–84, 139
Cixous, Hélène, 45, 65, 66, 69–70

conversos. See Dins el darrer blau
criptojudíos. See Dins el darrer blau
culture
  definition of, vii, 6–8
  development of, 8–12
  high and low, 9–11
  and history, 15–18
  and the hyperreal, 18–21
  and the Internet, 3
  popular, 11–12
  violence in, 21–25

De todo lo visible y lo invisible (Etxebarria), xi, 8, 22, 134–48, 151–52, 156
  in relation to Mañas's works, 171, 178, 180
diary. *See* documents used in literature: diary
Dins el darrer blau (Riera), 6, 7, 31–46, 185
  auto de fe, viii, 28, 35, 42
  conversos, 31–32
  problematic representation of, 36–37
  women, 41–44
documents used in literature
  forms, 139–40, 195n3
  diary, 95–97
  letters, 53–54, 66–67, 71, 78–80, 192n6

Eco, Umberto, ix, 48, 54, 60–61, 155, 190n12, 191ch2n4
  model reader, 26. *See also* author: model reader
  open and closed texts, 50–52
epilogue, 157–58, 160, 165–69
Etxebarria, Lucía, xi, 5, 112–13, 117, 187–88, 195n1
  Amor, curiosidad, prozac y dudas, 150

211

Index

Etxebarria, Lucía (*continued*)
   Beatriz y los cuerpos celestes, 5, 135
   De todo lo visible y lo invisible, xi, 8, 22, 134–48, 151–52, 156
   in relation to Mañas's works, 171, 178, 180
   and the Internet, 134, 148–52
   La letra futura, 133
   Yo no sufro por amor, 189n5

female solidarity, 38–39
feminism. *See* women
film, x, 119–20, 123–27, 144, 161–63, 195ch5nn5–6
Franco, Francisco, 17, 69, 118. *See also* Spanish Civil War

Generation X, viii, 111–14, 115, 181, 193n3, 194n1
   criticism of, 116–17, 133
   as defined in Spain, 4–6
   Generation X: Tales of an Accelerated Culture, 117
   and violence, 21, 113
Gerard, René, ix, 22, 33, 38, 40, 44, 191nn5–7
   feminist criticism of, 35–37
globalization, 3, 5, 7–8, 24, 112–14, 117–18, 156

hero, 88, 98–100, 103–08
Historias del Kronen (Mañas), xi, 8, 23, 155–70
   American Psycho in, 163, 168–69, 196n7, 197n8, 197n12
   A Clockwork Orange in, 161–63, 196n7
history. *See also* Nietzsche, Friedrich
   fictionalization of, 89, 98–100, 103–05
   and "reality," 27–29
   as represented in the present, 45–46, 64–65
   writing women into, 69–70. *See also* Cixous, Hélène
   and violence, 31–32
hombre que inventó Manhattan, El (Loriga), x, 8, 116, 127–32
hyperreality, xi, 15, 111–14, 187, 189n1, 189n8. *See also* Baudrillard, Jean
   in Etxebarria's works, 135, 137, 140, 145, 147, 152
   in Loriga's works, 127, 131–32
   in Mañas's works, 178

identity
   crisis, 158
   and memory, 57–59
   Spanish national, vii, 16–17
Internet. *See* media
intertextuality, xi, 156, 165, 172

Jews in Spain. See *Dins el darrer blau*

Kristeva, Julia, 58, 192n5, 197n14

language
   appropriation of English, 178–80
   gendered, 74–75
   literary, vii, 3, 11, 65, 116
   visual and verbal, xi, 115, 165. *See also* film
letters. *See* documents used in literature: letters
Loriga, Ray, x, 4, 112–13, 115, 135–36, 187, 194ch5n2, 195n8
   Caídos del cielo, x, 8, 19, 23, 116, 119, 121–23
   criticism of Gen X movement, 116–17, 133

Héroes, 116
El hombre que inventó Manhattan, x, 8, 116, 127–32
Lo peor de todo, 115
La pistola de mi hermano, x, 116, 119–20, 123–27

Mañas, José Ángel, xi, 4, 112–13, 116–17, 196n1
Caso Karen, 171
Ciudad rayada, 172, 178
Historias del Kronen, xi, 8, 23, 155–70
  American Psycho in, 163, 168–69, 196n7, 197n8, 197n12
  A Clockwork Orange in, 161–63, 196n7
Mensaka, 172
La pella, xii, 8, 170–82
  economic class in, 172–77
  language in, 178–80
El secreto del oráculo, 170
Sonoko 95, 172
Soy un escritor frustrado, 171
media, viii, xi, 5–6, 26, 112–14
  and culture, 6–7, 164
  e-mail, 145–46
  Internet, 3, 5, 112–13, 133–34, 148–51
  television, 19, 26, 115–16, 118–27
  in Spain, 118–19, 194n4, 195n7
meitat de l'ànima, La (Riera), ix, 7, 47–62, 87, 156

narrative. *See also* novel
  historical, 3, 98, 111–12
narrator
  identity, 103
  relation to reader, 56–57
  self-reflexive, 47–48, 54–55, 60
  unreliable, 90–91

Nietzsche, Friedrich, 17–18, 185, 193n2. *See also* history
history as progress, 32, 86–87, 98, 101–02, 109
monumental history, 64–65, 103, 106
novel. *See also* narrative
  as genre, xi, 20, 23
  historical, 27–29
  innovations in form, x, 2, 7, 23–25
  role of reader, 25, 26, 50–52, 146, 159, 190n12. *See also* author
  trends in contemporary, vii, 1, 6

La pella (Mañas), xii, 8, 170–82
  economic class in, 172–77
  language in, 178–80
photography, 73, 75, 77, 193n9
pistola de mi hermano, La (Loriga), x, 116, 119–20, 123–27
postmodernism, 18, 21, 56, 112, 164, 189n2

reality, x, 2–3, 113, 127, 140. *See also* hyperreality
  historical, 28, 64
  problematic representation of, 15, 19, 22, 108–09
  and television, 19
Riera, Carme, viii, ix, 5–6, 53–62, 109, 190n3
  "An Ambition without Limits," 61
  Dins el darrer blau, viii, 6, 7, 31–46, 185
  La meitat de l'ànima, ix, 7, 47–62, 87, 156
  and revisionist history, 31–35
  self-conscious narrative, 47–48, 60

213

Index

Second Republic, Spanish, 67–69
self-reflexivity. *See* narrator
sexuality. *See* women: and sexuality
Shangay Lily, 143–44, 195ch6n5
simulacra. *See* Baudrillard, Jean: simulacra
Soldados de Salamina (Cercas), ix, 7, 26, 54, 85–101, 171, 178
Spanish Civil War, ix, 17, 48, 66, 88–89
    Ley de la Memoria Histórica, 183–84, 198n1
    Las Trece Rosas, 70–72
    Ventas jail, 72, 192n1
    and women, 63–64, 67–69, 83–84, 192nn3–4, 193nn5–7
Spanish Inquisition. See *Dins el darrer blau*

technology. *See* media
television. *See* media
Trece Rosas, las, 70–72
truth
    and individual memory, 56, 105

and reality, 3, 15, 22, 108
historical, 3, 20, 37, 49–50. *See also* Spanish Civil War

velocidad de la luz, La (Cercas), ix, 7, 86, 101–09, 178
violence, 33–34, 107, 161–70, 136–37. *See also* Generation X
    against women, 21, 33–35, 43–44, 148–52
voz dormida, La (Chacón), ix, 7, 22, 26, 63–84, 139

White, Hayden, 28–29, 46, 111–12, 185
women. *See also* violence
    during Spanish Civil War, 63–64, 67–69, 83–84, 192nn3–4, 193nn5–7
    feminism, 21, 34–35, 69–70
    and Inquisition, 41–44
    sacrifice of, 33, 35, 39
    and sexuality, 39, 40–41, 149
    repression as discourse, 150

About the Author

Kathryn Everly is an associate professor of Spanish at Syracuse University. She is the author of *Catalan Women Writers and Artists: Feminist Views from a Revisionist Space* (2003). She has published articles and chapters in *Hispanic Journal, Catalan Review, Monographic Review, Letras Peninsulares*, and in various anthologies. Her current research focuses on aspects of surrealism in the works of Mercè Rodoreda.